Building a Global Bank

MAURO F. GUILLÉN
ADRIAN TSCHOEGL

Building a Global Bank
The Transformation of Banco Santander

PRINCETON UNIVERSITY PRESS

PRINCETON AND OXFORD

Copyright © 2008 by Princeton University Press

Published by Princeton University Press, 41 William Street, Princeton, New Jersey 08540

In the United Kingdom: Princeton University Press, 6 Oxford Street, Woodstock, Oxfordshire OX20 1TW

All Rights Reserved

Library of Congress Cataloging-in-Publication Data

Guillén, Mauro F.

Building a global bank : the transformation of Banco Santander / Mauro F. Guillen, Adrian Tschoegl.

p.   cm.

Includes bibliographical references and index.

ISBN 978-0-691-13125-2 (cloth : alk. paper)

1. Banco Santander Central Hispano—History.   2. Family corporations—Spain—Case studies.   I. Tschoegl, Adrian E.   II. Title.

HG3188.S37G85 2008

332.1'50946—dc22   2007045932

British Library Cataloging-in-Publication Data is available

This book has been composed in Palatino

Printed on acid-free paper. ∞

press.princeton.edu

Printed in the United States of America

10   9   8   7   6   5   4   3   2   1

For Sandra and Naomi

CONTENTS

Appendix

PREFACE

Although many people consider finance to be a purely global activity, commercial banking does not naturally lend itself to cross-border expansion, for reasons having to do with the many economic, regulatory, political, and cultural barriers that continue to fragment markets along national lines. Perhaps this is the best reason to write a book about Banco Santander, one of the few banks that has managed to overcome such daunting obstacles. Moreover, Banco Santander has done so within a strikingly short period of time and while working from its headquarters in Spain, a country that does not normally come to mind as a financial powerhouse.

Santander stands as a stark reminder that, in the global economy, structural disadvantages can be circumvented in creative ways. Its rapid rise to global prominence as one of the world's top ten banks also indicates that bold, decisive action and a willingness to take calculated risks in an industry undergoing rapid transformations are what distinguishes the leaders from the followers.

Writing this book has taken us to different parts of the world and forced us to familiarize ourselves with developments not only in banking but also in politics and the economy more generally. Our foremost gratitude is to the bankers, executives, policymakers, regulators, and scholars who agreed to be interviewed. We are also indebted to the colleagues who saved us from failures of reasoning and factual inaccuracies, including José Manuel Campa of IESE Business School, Julio García-Cobos of Universidad Carlos III de Madrid and PQ Axis, and Esteban García-Canal of Universidad de Oviedo. The two anonymous reviewers for Princeton University Press provided us with an embarrassment of riches in terms of suggestions for improvement, as did our editor, Tim Sullivan.

We would not have been able to complete the research and analysis for this book without the able assistance of our Wharton and Penn students, including Kwame Abrah, Carlos Colomer, Erangi Dias, Arun Hendi, Misun Jun, and Sameer Khetan. Irene Corominas and Tammy Nakandakare helped us coordinate interview schedules in Latin America. In Spain, Esteban García-Canal gave us innumerable insights and also assisted in the calculation of abnormal stock returns. Julio García-Cobos and his assistant Antón Hierro helped us navigate the complexities of bank-industry relationships. Paloma Martínez Almodóvar provided us with an analysis of equity analysts' reports, and Purificación Flórez helped organize information from newspapers and magazines as well as prepare the Spanish edition of the book. We would also like to thank the scholars and librarians who provided us with data and historical materials. The libraries at the University of Pennsylvania and at the Banco de España in Madrid were especially useful.

We are particularly grateful to Raphael Amit of Wharton, who single-handedly created the Wharton Global Family Alliance, the research initiative that generously funded this book. We are indebted to him for both his encouragement and his own scholarly work on family corporations, which provided invaluable guidance when we were drawing conclusions from our analysis.

Our respective wives—Sandra and Naomi—encouraged us to persist, especially in moments we felt discouraged and disoriented. They also tolerated our forsaking family to take relatively long research trips to Latin America and Europe. This book is dedicated to them.

Philadelphia, Pennsylvania, Fall 2007

Building a Global Bank

1

Family-Led Banks in the Global Economy

> Twenty years ago I would never have dreamt that we would be the ninth-largest bank in the world.
>
> —Emilio Botín III, in *Euromoney*, 1 July 2005

> Santander is one of the most remarkable stories in modern banking.
>
> —*Euromoney*, 1 July 2005

Banco Santander is an oddity in the big leagues of global banking. Barely two decades ago, this proud financial institution was no more than a second-tier player in Spain, a country rarely if ever regarded as being on the cutting edge of banking. Nowadays, Santander is not only one of the world's ten largest banks but also the pioneer in European cross-border banking acquisitions with its 2004 takeover of Abbey National in the United Kingdom, a deal worth US$15 billion. This book tells the story of Santander's striking transformation from being a medium-sized Spanish bank to becoming the largest financial institution in Latin America, the largest bank in the Euro Zone with a market capitalization of nearly US$115 billion, and a major competitor in consumer finance in Northern and Eastern Europe. The bank has also made headlines around the world through alliances and equity stakes in MetLife, First Union, Royal Bank of Scotland, Société Générale, Vodafone, Shinsei Bank, and a number of other companies, from which it eventually divested and obtained more than US$7 billion in capital gains.

Santander stands out as an example of a modern corporation blending family guidance at the top with professional management throughout the organization. It is the only large bank in the world in which three successive generations of the same family have held the top executive position, despite owning a mere 2.5 percent of the equity. After taking the helm in 1986, Emilio Botín III embraced deregulation of the domestic banking sector and initiated a series of bold competitive moves, first in Latin America and later in Europe and the United States, that eventually catapulted the bank from 152nd in the world to the number 10 spot. When he retires sometime in the next few years, his daughter Ana Patricia, a seasoned executive, could well become the first woman to run one of the world's largest and most influential financial institutions.

Santander is neither as global in geographic reach nor as diversified in terms of the services it offers as Citibank or HSBC, the world's two largest banks. Most of its operations are focused on commercial (e.g., retail) banking, an activity in which operational efficiency, information technology, and marketing are fundamental tools when it comes to increasing market share or boosting profitability. Higher-margin activities such as wholesale, private, and investment banking represent very small shares of revenues or profits at Santander. Still, in 2006 the bank reported the seventh-largest banking profits in the world, €7.6 billion (about US$10.3 billion). After years of depressed profitability due to financial crises in Latin America and acquisitions in Europe, the bank's 2.3 million individual shareholders are now enjoying annual returns in excess of 30 percent, above those for most other comparable banks.

The rapid rise to global prominence of a family-led bank originating 150 years ago from a rather marginal provincial town in northern Spain raises a key question. In a recent article, the *Economist* (16 February 2006) asked, "Why are Spanish companies—hailing from a middle-sized country with little entrepreneurial tradition, income levels that are still below the European Union average, weak language skills and few natural resources—becoming the hunters, and not the hunted?" Much of the evidence in this book focuses on the two main answers to that tantalizing question, as reported by the same magazine: "First, many used expansion in Latin America as a training ground, gaining size and management skills, and hoarding cash. Second, Spain has opened its domestic markets to competition more quickly and more thoroughly than many other European countries. That has taught Spanish firms to sink or swim."

Besides the more general question of what has made a number of Spanish companies successful in the global economy, Santander itself raises intriguing questions specific to its own experience. What capabilities have made it possible for a firm in a mature industry to better its rivals in so many different countries around the world? What aspects of family-led management have made it possible to grow so fast via acquisition? How has the family managed to exercise influence over corporate governance and strategic decision making while owning just 2.5 percent of the shares? What are the issues surrounding managerial succession? This book seeks to answer these questions by analyzing Santander in the context of a banking industry undergoing rapid technological and competitive changes since the mid 1980s and by providing information and insights into not just Santander but also its global competitors in Europe and the Americas.

We begin our journey in this chapter by reviewing the characteristics of banking as an economic activity and examining the prevalence of family banks in the world in general and Spain in particular. In chapters 2 and 3, we tell the story of the humble origins of Banco Santander in the mid-nineteenth century; its growth via acquisition starting in the 1940s to become a national bank, with the Botín family already leading the bank; and its daring diversification into a wide variety of businesses during the 1960s and 1970s, albeit to a lesser degree than its competitors, which helped it weather the industrial crisis of the 1970s and 1980s. Chapter 4 delves into the complex and intrigue-filled process that led to the combination of three of Spain's largest banks (Banesto, Central, and Hispano Americano) with Santander to create SCH (Santander Central Hispano). In this chapter we will also point out that Santander's family character enabled it to take the initiative while its rivals were enmeshed in difficult mergers and managerial struggles. Chapters 5, 6, and 7 focus on Santander's internationalization, first in Latin America through acquisitions and in the United States through minority positions in the Mid-Atlantic region, then in Europe in the form of alliances with other banks, and lastly with acquisitions in Europe. In those chapters, we also deal with the bank's increasing sophistication in the areas of information technology and marketing. Chapter 8 deals with the impact that family leadership has had on Santander over the years, highlighting the issues of decision-making style, corporate governance, and managerial succession. Finally, Chapter 9 looks at Santander's performance and at the future, analyzing the bank's strengths and weaknesses, its growth options, and its potentially pivotal role in markets as disparate as Europe, Latin America, the United States, and China.

The evidence presented in this book comes from a variety of sources, including interviews with more than fifty executives, policymakers, equity analysts, and journalists; legal filings; internal documents given to us during interviews; financial data on the performance of Santander in comparison to other banks; equity analyst reports; and newspaper articles. We attribute information or points of view to specific individuals or organizations whenever possible, unless an interviewee specifically asked us to keep the source confidential. The book thus rests on various kinds of information, both quantitative and qualitative, which we present descriptively and analytically using statistical methods of analysis. The narrative is largely chronological, given that the temporal ordering of decisions and events was material to the emergence of Santander as one of the world's largest banks. However, we have structured the various chapters on a chronological sequence by topic: the origins of the bank (1857–1950), the creation of an industrial group (1950–86), growth through domestic mergers and acquisitions (1986–99), international expansion in Latin America and Europe (1982 to the present), corporate governance (1980 to the present), and performance (1986 to the present).

Bankers and Banks Worldwide

In the course of history, bankers have engaged in many different types of financial activities, ranging from issuing currency, taking deposits, and extending loans, to discounting paper, providing capital to manufacturing firms, brokering all sorts of transactions, making markets, and managing assets.[1] Historians, clerics, economists, princes, and potentates have variously depicted the bankers and their banks as the heroes and the villains of the market economy. Bankers have occupied the spotlight because of both their rise to prominence during boom times and their fall from grace during financial panics. The popular imagination has always portrayed banks as powerful actors. Thomas Jefferson thought that "banking establishments are more dangerous to our liberties than standing armies." Mark Twain was no less critical: "A banker is a fellow who lends you his umbrella when the sun is shining, but wants it back the minute it begins to rain." Fully cognizant of the role of banks during the nineteenth century, before governments around the world asserted their authority over monetary matters, Mayer Anselm Rothschild used to say: "Permit me to issue and control the money of a nation, and I care not who makes its laws." And industrialists the world over have tended to fear and loath their power. As a representative of many similar statements, Henry Ford's declaration captures the sentiment: "It is well enough that people of the nation do not understand our banking and monetary system, for if they did, I believe there would be a revolution before tomorrow morning."[2]

Banking, Industrialization, and the State

Banking is a prominent and symbolic activity because banks tend to play a crucial role in economic development. Manufacturing growth requires the transfer of massive amounts of resources from backward to dynamic economic sectors and often from foreign lenders to targeted domestic recipients. Beginning with Gerschenkron's landmark book, *Economic Backwardness in Historical Perspective* (1962), the literature has studied banks in the abstract, focusing mainly on their contribution to the development of manufacturing industry and placing a strong emphasis on state-bank and bank-industry relations. Despite decades of research, there is no agreement in the literature as to whether the banking sector—and financial markets in general—should be organized according to market- or state-centered principles in order to accelerate economic development (Cameron 1972; Cameron et al. 1967; Fry 1995; Haggard and Lee 1993; Loriaux 1991, 1997a, 1997b; Zysman 1983), though some recent research shows that government ownership of banks during the 1970s was associated with slower subsequent financial development and lower growth of per capita income and productivity (La Porta et al., 2002).

Due to historical legacies, power struggles, and political compromises, countries have adopted different systems of banking regulation. In some countries, such as the United States, legislation in the early twentieth century restricted the power and range of activity of banks, resulting in a system in which retail banks are not as prominent as in other countries, such as Germany, which allowed them to operate as universal financial institutions engaging in both commercial and investment banking (Deeg 1999; O'Sullivan 2000). In other countries, banks have operated under strong state controls, as in South Korea until the mid-1980s (Fields 1995; Woo 1991); in still other countries, such as India, the state owns much of the banking sector.

Previous scholarship on economic development has largely focused on the determinants of *industrial* growth, under the assumption that services merely "support" industrialization (Amsden 1989; Guillén 2001; Haggard and Maxfield 1993). However, banks are part of the financial system. In theory, effective financial systems allocate capital to the "best," or highest return-for-risk, projects. In doing this, they maximize value added for a given capital cost by identifying and funding those firms and entrepreneurs with good projects but insufficient resources. (What is perhaps less appreciated is that they also deny funding to poor projects. Furthermore, the better the financial system, including the banks, the less funding there is of bad projects, and the less rejection of good ones.) Effective financial systems equalize the cost of capital across similar projects and lower it by borrowing from the most patient, allocating risk to the least risk-averse, and by transforming risk and liquidity through credit contracts and risk pooling. They do this by developing new products, distribution channels, and services. The lower cost of capital then increases potential output. These tasks are not trivial, and it is clear that finance matters to development (de Gregorio and Guidotti 1995; King and Levine 1993; Lewis 1978).

A vibrant banking sector can potentially offer many other benefits in addition to effective and efficient resource mobilization and allocation to investors. First, it has the potential of creating large numbers of jobs, ranging from low-skilled bank tellers to highly educated financial analysts and managers. Second, it can generate multiple linkages to other activities, such as insurance, tourism, education, information services, software, and telecommunications. Third, if banks become internationally competitive and start expanding abroad, they may create new market opportunities for other domestic firms, manufacturing or otherwise.

The Rules of Competition in Retail Banking

Given our focus on banking as a service activity in its own right and the fact that Santander has over the years come to concentrate its competitive efforts in retail banking, it is important to review the basic rules of competition in this industry. Banks attempt to borrow cheap and lend dear; the resulting interest rate spread is a primary source of income, one that observers commonly label "asset-based income." Banks also obtain income from the fees and commissions they charge for services, such as funds transfers and brokerage. The common label here is "fee-based income." Not surprisingly, the saying in the industry is that "retail banking is boring, and if it is not boring, then it isn't retail banking." Lastly, banks may earn capital gains on more speculative activities, such as trading in the foreign exchange or interest rate markets, or holding securities in countries where they may invest in nonfinancial enterprises. This abstract characterization, however, omits the creativity involved in improving processes to cut costs and in marketing efforts to develop innovative products that offer convenience, reward customer loyalty, or solve customers' problems. In all of these activities, there is money to be made. As a result, successful, large retail banks command a great deal of power and influence in many countries around the world.

One may think of a bank's strategy from two, complementary perspectives. First, there are Porter's (1980) three generic strategies. Overall cost leadership involves establishing efficient operations and taking advantage of economies of scale. Product differentiation, by contrast, is all about quality and service. Finally, a niche strategy entails segmenting the market in order to identify profitable groups of customers. These three strategies are not mutually exclusive and banks typically pursue all, though with differing priorities depending on the market, and especially on the behavior of competitors.

The second perspective is a spatial one. Walter (1988) coined the acronym CAP—for client, arena, and product—to describe the three-dimensional matrix or space that a financial institution occupies. The description of a cell in this matrix requires that one specify which type of customer the bank is serving, where in physical space the customers are, and what product the institution is delivering to these clients. Clients may be governments, nonfinancial corporations, financial corporations, high-net-worth (wealthy) individuals, and retail customers. A bank's strategy then consists of enumerating where the bank chooses to locate itself in this three-dimensional space. To these three dimensions, one may add a fourth reflecting the value-added chain of linked activities, including where the various parts of the production process for a particular product take place (Tschoegl 2000). The full strategy then consists of which cells in the matrix the bank occupies, and how it competes in each space.

The banking sector is undergoing some important changes worldwide. A key trend has to do with deregulation of financial markets, which has facilitated the international expansion of some banks. This change has taken place during different periods of time and at varying rates of speed depending on the country. As a result of these differences, distinct patterns of international expansion of banks (including Santander) have taken place. Another important trend is disintermediation, or the arrival of competition for banks from nonbanks such as retailers (e.g., Wal-Mart or Carrefour), the financial arms of industrial firms (GE Capital, Honda Financial, Ford Financial Services), hotel chains (Hilton), or Internet-based intermediaries (PayPal). Technological change also has profound implications for back-office operations, customer interface, data interchange, fund transfers, and the enhanced potential for the offshoring of back-office and customer service operations. Finally, the financial and technological culture of the population in various parts of the world has also shifted.

One area in which these changes are readily visible is the choice of distribution channel. Nowadays, about 40 percent of banking transactions in the United States takes place inside a bank branch, 30 percent through an automatic teller machine (ATM), nearly 20 percent over the Internet, and 10 percent over the phone. The trend is toward a greater proportional importance of the Internet channel, whose cost per transaction is only one-hundredth the one at a traditional bank branch. Still, research indicates that banks find it much easier to sell new products at a branch or over the telephone than over the Web, indicating that customers very much desire interaction with human beings when it comes to making important financial decisions (Capgemini 2006). Automated delivery of services, whether via ATMs or the Internet, is most suitable for routine transactions. First-time or one-time transactions appear to require human interaction.

The successful incorporation and exploitation of technology in banking is not straightforward because many applications entail the development of two-sided networks in which the value of the network to an existing participant on one side increases with each additional participant on the other side (Eisenmann et al. 2006). For instance, an ATM network becomes more valuable to a customer if the service is available through more banks and at a greater number of locations. Conversely, a bank will find the ATM network more attractive to the extent that it has customers using it. Similarly, credit cards are more valuable the greater the number of merchants that accept them, and merchants will be more eager to join if more customers use them as a means of payment. Two-sided network dynamics generate winner-take-all races, enhance the value of loyalty, and invite pricing structures in which the provider uses one side of the network to subsidize the other in order to gain scale. Thus, banks have pursued alliances and other arrangements to roll out technological platforms successfully.

In spite of deregulation, disintermediation, and technological change, retail banking continues to be a business driven by the classic forces of competition (Porter 1980). Like companies in other industries, retail banks seek to erect barriers to entry, reduce rivalry, preempt the threat of substitute products, and reduce the bargaining power of customers and suppliers. Let us analyze each in turn.

To keep competitors at bay, retail banks use several techniques. The most important historically has involved establishing extensive branch networks and fostering customer loyalty. While telephone and Internet banking are eroding the effectiveness of this barrier to entry, bankers reckon that it is not easy to use those channels to enter a new market or dislodge an incumbent bank with many physical branches. Moreover, people trust their bank and are reluctant to switch to a new entrant. This is the main reason why banks prefer to use acquisitions as their preferred mode of entry, especially in foreign markets, as the Santander story illustrates. In some industries, economies of scale too can be a barrier to entry, although in banking increasing size beyond a certain minimum threshold seems to offer little advantage (for a review of the evidence, see Tortella 2001; Walter 2004), except for a few activities such as global custody, asset management, back-office operations, and information systems. Another key barrier to entry, capital requirements, has diminished with the globalization of financial markets. Finally, technology can be a barrier to entry because purchasing it is easy but blending it with existing operations and using it effectively is not. In general, deregulation of banking around the world has tended to lower barriers to entry.

Like companies in other industries, retail banks seek to reduce rivalry as a way to enhance profits. Rivalry in retail banking markets is higher in developed than in developing countries, a fact that has prompted many banks, including Santander, to pursue growth in emerging economies. In developed markets, the best option to reduce rivalry is to engage in product and service differentiation, a strategy that most banks have followed through marketing and technological innovation. Looking for attractive market niches in which to launch highly specialized products is another way in which banks have sought to enhance profitability. The case of private banking's catering to the needs of high-income customers is perhaps the best illustration.

Retail banks are on safer ground when it comes to substitute products. For instance, consumer finance has recently risen as a major alternative to traditional lending products. Credit cards have also revolutionized consumer borrowing in many markets around the world. Banks, however, have moved swiftly into these new areas, frequently in competition with nonbank financial intermediaries. Retail banks have been strikingly effective at preempting the competitive threats stemming from substitute products, as the story of Santander also illustrates.

Finally, retail banks can be quite effective at reducing the bargaining power of customers and suppliers alike. Because retail banks deal with millions of customers, it is relatively easy and cost-efficient for them to generate customer loyalty for some products, particularly the basic bank account. The challenge is to sell the customer other products, a skill that large banks such as Santander have come to master in their home markets. Moreover, the globalization of financial markets and the increasing sophistication of financial products make it hard for customers to do without banks when it comes to satisfying their financial needs, except for the very powerful customers, who can bypass the bank. On the supplier side, retail banks are blessed by the growing importance of global financial markets and the evolution of the information technology (IT) industry toward fierce competition. Hence, banks can secure their most important inputs at low cost, although it is true that IT applications need to be customized to the bank's specific needs and that personnel needs to be trained. In general, retail banks can exert a reasonable degree of bargaining power over both customers and suppliers.

In sum, retail banks have two basic competitive tools at their disposal. First, they may use marketing to enhance brand reputation and awareness, segment the market, cross-sell products, and generate customer loyalty. Second, they may leverage technology to cut costs as well as support marketing. As the next chapters show, Santander has over the years sought to develop these marketing and technological capabilities in the home country and to exploit them in foreign countries.

The Global Potential of Retail Banking

While retail banking continues to be a relatively profitable activity thanks to the possibility of erecting barriers to entry, reducing rivalry, preempting the threat of substitute products, and reducing the bargaining power of customers and suppliers, retail banks have historically had a very hard time expanding beyond their domestic market. The rise of multinational retail banks such as Citibank, HSBC, BNP Paribas, Santander, BBVA, ABN AMRO, or Royal Bank of Scotland has taken place in an industry that does not naturally lend itself to global expansion (Claessens et al. 2001; Demirgüç-Kunt and Huizinga 1999; Dopico and Wilcox 2002; Grubel 1977; Jones 1993; Tschoegl 1987). The reasons are diverse and have to do with market, cost, regulatory, and competitive factors (Yip 1989).

Retail banking markets differ massively from country to country, making it harder for foreign banks to compete against local banks. A first important dimension is customer preferences and tastes. For instance, in markets such as the United States, customers prefer fixed-rate mortgages, whereas in most of Continental Europe the norm is variable-rate mortgages. Differences in preferences also extend into the way in which the service is delivered. In most of Europe and in Latin America, for example, face-to-face interaction is preferred. As a result, in some countries banks maintain extensive branch networks. Spain is one such country, with about ninety-six branches per 100,000 inhabitants. By contrast, Germany has forty-nine; Canada, forty-six; and France, forty-three. In the United States and the United Kingdom, the numbers are thirty-one and eighteen, respectively. Banks themselves have contributed to the differences by adapting marketing strategies to the specific characteristics of local markets and even having different brands for different markets.

Another major source of cross-national fragmentation in retail banking has to do with government regulation. Although cross-border capital flows are relatively free and technical standards have converged, thanks to arrangements such as the Basle Accords, regulations concerning licenses, minimal capital requirements, deposit coefficients (required reserves), legal acceptability of diversification into other financial services, and specific product regulations differ greatly from market to market. As noted previously, in some countries regulations restrict banks in the extent to which they can deal in securities, offer insurance products, engage in real-estate activities, or hold stakes in nonfinancial firms. For example, in terms of product regulations, Chile forbids lottery-linked savings accounts, whereas neighboring Argentina permits them (Guillén and Tschoegl 2002).

The degree of market concentration too differs from country to country, both reflecting and affecting the competitive situation. The only developed banking markets that are very highly concentrated are those of relatively small countries. For instance, in Canada, Belgium, Sweden, or the Netherlands, the top four banks account for upward of 75 percent of total deposits or loans. In midsized countries such as Italy, Spain, or France, the top four banks represent between 30 and 60 percent, a moderate degree of concentration. In large economies such as Germany or the United States, the top four banks account for less than 25 percent. In these markets, savings and loans or other types of regional and local financial institutions have proliferated over the years. Among emerging economies, Chile, Mexico, and Brazil have very high concentration, while South Korea or Argentina do not. Differences in concentration from market to market make it harder for any bank to pursue uniform, global strategies.

Lastly, from the point of view of cost, the retail banking industry is more global and less fragmented than market, regulatory, and competitive factors suggest. The opportunities for outsourcing back-office and customer service operations ("call centers") are growing very quickly thanks to improvements in telecommunications technology (UNCTAD 2004). Economies of scale may not be very steep beyond a certain minimum threshold, but the globalization of financial markets has made wholesale and corporate banking more subject to them (Walter 2004). Finally, economies of scope are becoming ever more important as restrictions on universal banking are disappearing and banks seek to cross-sell products in order to enhance customer loyalty and boost profitability.

The relatively high level of fragmentation of retail banking markets around the world has several implications, which one must keep in mind when analyzing Santander's pattern of growth over the past two decades. Foreign entrants tend to acquire local banks instead of building their operations from scratch. This accomplishes two goals. First, in moderately to highly concentrated markets, acquisitions help overcome competitive barriers to entry. Second, the acquisition of local assets offers the foreign entrant knowledge about the peculiarities of the local market. Fragmentation also leads foreign entrants to organize their operations on a country-by-country basis, with cross-border coordination oftentimes limited at best to some back-office operations.

Santander as a Family-Led Bank and a Professional Bank

The complexity, sophistication, and fragmentation of competition in retail banking cumulate to create what many regard as too daunting a challenge for any bank to overcome on an international basis. In the past, few banks were strong players in the retail segment in more than one country, as the literature has pointed out (Tschoegl 1987). Santander not only is one of those rare multinational retail banks but is also the only bank among the world's top ten in which three generations of a family have exerted a key influence over decisions concerning corporate governance and overall strategy. Because of this combination of features, Santander is an almost irresistible case study in which to explore the advantages and disadvantages of family control and management. The fact that members of the family own only 2.5 percent of the equity makes their influence even more intriguing to study.

Family dynasties are part of the folklore of the banking industry. The stories of the Medicis and the Fuggers in early modern Europe, the Rothschilds, Bleichröders, and Peréires during the nineteenth century, the Morgans, Warburgs, Mellons, and Rockefellers during the Gilded Age, and the Wallenbergs and Botíns during the second half of the twentieth and into the twenty-first century show that banking has often been a family affair. Many of today's large banks have a family origin, including Barclays, Mitsubishi-Tokyo, Paribas, or JP Morgan Chase. In a study of the international growth of Singapore's largest banks, several of which are or were owned, controlled, and managed by families, Tschoegl (2002b) argued that although family management could provide higher growth through the lessening of principal-agent problems, it might do so at the cost of higher risk due to less effective governance. As Landes (1993) demonstrates in his paper on two of the great nineteenth-century German private banks, Bleichröders and Rothschilds, succession is a problem with idiosyncratic elements that can contribute to deteriorating performance (Bleichröders) or continuing success (Rothschilds). Many family banks have successfully made the transition from family to professional management, without the family losing control, as in the cases of Singapore's Oversea-Chinese Banking Corporation (Tsui-Auch 2004), Sweden's Skandinaviska Enskilda Banken (Lindgren 2007; Sjögren 2006), or Santander itself (for these and other family banks, see table 1.1).

In this book, we seek to understand how a bank led by the third, and perhaps one day the fourth, generation of a family manages to outgrow not only its domestic counterparts but also most of its international competitors. One may argue that family leadership can be a source of competitive advantage in an oligopolistic industry characterized by entrenched incumbents and high barriers to entry because decisive action is necessary to counter competitors' moves and to pursue acquisitions aggressively whenever the opportunity arises to enter a new market. In fact, our previous research suggests that Emilio Botín III has been central to the identification and pursuit of specific merger and acquisition opportunities over the past fifteen years (Guillén 2001, 2005; Guillén and Tschoegl 2000). Many observers attribute Santander's rapid growth to his charismatic and decisive management style, which has enabled the bank to seize unique opportunities and to deliver good returns to shareholders.

We seek to use the case study of Santander to better assess the transformation of family firms over time. Santander underwent four transitions. It began as a provincial bank back in 1857, only becoming a national bank a century later, that is, during the 1950s and 1960s. Then it went from being a focused retail bank to an emerging diversified financial and industrial business group during the 1970s and early 1980s. Next, it transformed itself from being a mostly

TABLE 1.1

Large Banks with a Family Connection, Ranked by Tier-One Capital, End of 2005

Global Rank in The Banker	Tier-One Capital (billion US $)	Bank	Country	Family	Family Officers	Family Equity Stake (%)
10	38.4	Santander	Spain	Botín	President and directors	2.16[a]
42	13.8	MBNA Corporation[b]	United States	Lerner	Chair and directors	6.74
64	9.1	Golden West Financial Corporation	United States	Sandler	Chair, CEO, and directors	13.88
69	8.3	Banco Bradesco	Brazil	Aguiar	Directors	10.99
90	7.0	Banco Itaú	Brazil	Egydio de Souza Aranha (Setubal and Villela)	CEO, chair, and directors	53.93
93	6.7	Skandinaviska Enskilda Banken (SEB)	Sweden	Wallenberg	Chair and directors	19.40
99	6.3	United Overseas Bank	Singapore	Wee	Chair, CEO, and directors	17.10
112	5.6	OCBC (Oversea-Chinese Banking Corporation)	Singapore	Lee	Director	24.00
113	5.5	EFG Bank	Switzerland	Latsis	Chair and directors	60.00
124	4.9	Fubon Financial	Taiwan	Tsai	Chair, CEO, and directors	27.40

(continued)

TABLE 1.1 *(continued)*

Global Rank in The Banker	Tier-One Capital (billion US $)	Bank	Country	Family	Family Officers	Family Equity Stake (%)
141	4.0	Unibanco—União de Bancos Brasileiros	Brazil	Moreira Salles	Vice-chair, directors, and CEO	18.30
148	3.7	Bank Hapoalim	Israel	Arison	Directors	22.00
149	3.7	Franklin Resources	United States	Johnson	Chair, directors, and CEO	33.00

Sources: The Banker (July 2006); Factiva.

[a] By the end of 2006 the percentage had climbed to 2.5 percent.

[b] Acquired by Bank of America in 2005.

domestic financial institution into one with a strong presence in Latin America during the 1990s, at a time when it also decided to refocus on retail banking. In the first five years of the new century, it has shifted from being a Spanish-speaking bank to a European financial powerhouse with global ambitions. In each of these shifts, successive generations of the Botín family have played a crucial role. How exactly did Banco Santander manage to outsmart its Spanish and European competitors to reach its present position? What have been the risks associated with Santander's expansion strategy, and what role did its family-led character play in assuming or mitigating those risks? Did family influence interact in any significant way with the external environment of liberalization and deregulation to produce better performance? How can control be exercised in excess of ownership without dual-class shares or ownership pyramids? These are the key questions pursued in the chapters that follow.

2

A Family Bank's Origins

The one who strikes first, strikes twice.[1]

—Emilio Botín I, in *El País,* 3 February 2002

There is no family privilege, no inheritance, which is not subject to the merciless law of the free market.[2]

—Emilio Botín II, in *El País,* 1 August 1976

Mr. Botín [III] ... differs from his forebears in the scope of his ambitions.

—Leslie Crawford, *Financial Times,* 22 February 2002

The origins of Banco Santander have deep roots in the vicissitudes of the Spanish political economy of the nineteenth century, as the country struggled to adopt a political and economic model that would enable it to catch up with the more developed parts of Europe. During its first half century, the bank merely grew with the rest of the economy without differentiating itself from its rivals, its operations confined to a relatively small part of northern Spain in which it competed with other local banks. It was not until the early twentieth century that Santander's executives made some crucial decisions concerning the focus on retail banking, and not until the middle of the century that members of the Botín family adopted a decisively leading role. Although Santander's present global prominence has its roots in events and decisions going back to no earlier than the 1950s, it is instructive to review its relatively humble origins in the nineteenth century, its early reluctance to get involved in risky industrial or infrastructure investments, and its preference for the retail banking business.

A Bank for Santander's Business Community

In 1857 six businessmen founded Banco de Santander in their provincial town located on the periphery of a declining European power with a waning overseas empire, which at the time included Cuba, Puerto Rico, the Philippines, and a few isolated enclaves in North and West Africa. The country had fallen badly behind England, France, and other European economies in terms of industrial development. In 1860 the Spanish economy was about one-fourth the size of Britain's, France's, or the United States', and one-third the size of Germany's. Per capita income was only about 40 percent that of the Britain or the United States, and about 65 percent the level of France or Germany, and the population had a literacy rate of only 24 percent. Between 1860 and 1914 the standard of living grew by about 60 percent, keeping pace with the most dynamic European countries, though not with the United States. Thus, Spain failed to close the gap that separated it from the most advanced countries in the world (Maddison 2001).

The 1850s and 1860s were years of economic change. The government favored foreign investments in railways, a move that created a speculative bubble in track construction but fell short of articulating a unified national market for goods, a goal that had historically proved elusive given the country's rugged geography. In 1868 Spain adopted the peseta as the national currency, and a year later a tariff reform lowered barriers to imports. In 1873 the monarchy collapsed and the First Spanish Republic was proclaimed, which lasted less than two years before Alfonso XII—the great grandfather of today's King Juan Carlos I—ascended to the throne. The year 1876 marked the end of the series of civil wars between conservative and the liberal forces over the succession to the Spanish throne, conflicts that had torn the country apart for two generations. The peace ushered in a new era of oligarchic rule and economic growth, one that would last, albeit with several ups and downs, until the 1920s.

The town of Santander was the capital of La Montaña (nowadays known as Cantabria, one of Spain's nineteen autonomous commonwealths), a small province sandwiched in between the sea (Mar Cantábrico) and the snow-covered peaks of the Cordillera Cantábrica, which separates the coastal seaboard from the Castilian plateau. The population census of 1857 identified 28,907 people as living in the city of Santander, and 214,441 in the province as a whole—barely 1.4 percent of Spain's total population of 15.5 million. Though relatively isolated by land, Santander, known to the Romans as Portus Victoriae, was an important short- and long-distance harbor, with an emerging commercial bourgeoisie. More than three peasants in four were landowners, which engendered a thriving commercial economy and a cohesive social structure. In 1865 Santander was home to 561 businessmen (roughly 2 percent of the population), 184 professionals (lawyers, physicians, etc.), and 132 "owners" (Hoyo Aparicio 1993, 19–20).

Santander had experienced rapid commercial growth since the 1820s, and especially during the 1830s, as the Basque ports to the east suffered from the first civil war between the liberals and the conservatives. Santander's harbor specialized in the transportation of Castilian wheat and flour destined for the biggest Spanish population centers (especially Catalonia) and, prior to 1898, the protected market of Cuba. The ships returned from across the Atlantic loaded with sugar, cocoa, and other colonial products. Starting in the late 1850s and during the 1860s, the traditional origins and destinations of maritime trade shifted as the United States became a more important trading partner for the Caribbean islands, and the railroad boom in Spain made it easier to move agricultural produce over land. In response, Santander's shipping activity started to focus more on the transportation of the zinc, iron, copper, and lead mined in the local area and largely destined for Belgium and Britain. Local manufacturing, though modest in scale, also rose in importance, especially in metalworking, textiles, and chemicals. Still, Santander and its surrounding region continued to be a predominantly agricultural and commercial economy until well into the twentieth century (Hoyo Aparicio 1993).

The Political and Economic Backdrop

The nineteenth century was not kind to Spain. The convulsions started with the Napoleonic invasion of 1808 and the absolutist restoration of 1814 and continued with the independence of the colonies in the Americas, three civil wars that debilitated the state, several army-led takeovers of power, a short-lived republic, and the loss of Cuba, Puerto Rico, and the Philippines in the wake of the Spanish-American War of 1898. Although a measure of political stability obtained between 1876 and the late 1920s, fundamental social and political issues such as illiteracy, poverty, and election fraud went unresolved. The rise of centrifugal nationalist movements in the two most advanced industrial areas—the Basque Country and Catalonia—and an incipient labor movement put even more stress on the already overwhelmed Spanish state. Not surprisingly, Spain faced an acute identity crisis (Alvarez Junco 2001).

The economy was subject to sharp ups and downs, and economic policy also fluctuated between the extremes of free trade and protectionism (Tortella 1994). One of the most prominent economic historians chose a revealing title for his most influential book, *The Failure of the Industrial Revolution in Spain, 1814–1913* (Nadal 1975). Despite the efforts to pursue an English-style model of industrialization during the nineteenth century, in 1900 roughly two-thirds of Spain's labor force worked in agriculture. Nevertheless, industry developed in a few enclaves: large iron and steel plants in the northern regions of Asturias and the Basque Country (Santander being located in between those two areas), metalworking industries in the same two areas and in Catalonia, coal mining in Asturias, and a relatively highly mechanized textile industry in Catalonia. Domestic industrial prices remained well above international levels, even after accounting for transportation and other distribution costs due to the isolation of the country from foreign competition. Spanish industry fell victim to the everlasting problems with the state budget deficit, the failed waves of Prussian-style agrarian reform, the speculative nature of many investments (both national and foreign), a stubborn exploitation of relatively uneconomical coal deposits, the building of an inadequate and expensive railway infrastructure, the high illiteracy rate among the working class and the peasantry, the scarcity of entrepreneurial initiatives, and the lack of technical knowledge. Given the incapacity of industrial producers to compete internationally, the limited size of the Spanish market only exacerbated its problems. Spain's agriculture (except in the export-oriented Levant) remained subsistence- rather than market-oriented and was subject to recurrent crises that, in turn, affected industry severely (Nadal 1975; Tamames 1986; Tuñón de Lara 1984).

The volatile political situation, in which the central state was challenged by the working class in the industrial enclaves and by the conservative nationalist movements in the Basque Country and Catalonia compounded the problems. As sociologist Juan Linz observed, there is a "recurrent pattern" in contemporary Spanish history of

> short periods of high revolutionary enthusiasm carried by
> the hopes of broad segments of the citizenry, activation
> of radical masses pushed by poverty, withdrawal of the
> moderate reformist element, defeat of the forces of change
> by the intervention of the army, establishment of a con-
> servative government, and a relatively prolonged period
> of peace and prosperity—without, however, arriving at
> a solution of basic underlying problems or creating fully
> legitimate institutions. (Linz 1973, 56)

The Restoration of 1876–1923, a liberal-oligarchic constitutional monarchy, represented one such long period of peace and relative prosperity, except for important crises during the early 1900s and after 1918. The loss of Cuba, Puerto Rico, and the Philippines in 1898 had ambiguous effects. The repatriation of capital from the colonies helped create powerful banks linked to industrial interests (see chapter 3). But with the colonies went the protected overseas markets so lucrative to certain industrial sectors, such as the Catalan textile manufacturers (Nadal 1975).

Much of the problem of Spain's economic decline had to do with the chronic lack of fiscal discipline and the misguided policies implemented to tackle the problem. According to economist Juan Velarde Fuertes, from the mid-nineteenth to the mid-twentieth century, Spain

> organized its economy on six bases: a fiscal policy based
> on the 1845 tax system with rather petrified direct taxes; a

monetary policy that avoided the discipline of international monetary schemes; a banking system with a private issuing bank at its core which in 1900 turned itself into a central bank supporting the growth of a mixed system of private banks along continental lines; a growing isolation from the outside world, especially after the protectionist turn of 1876 and the economic nationalism announced by the minister of finance, Cambó, in 1918, on the 1200th anniversary of the battle of Covadonga [against the invading Moorish armies]; state interventionism which takes the Spanish economy away from the principles of the market, starting with the cartelization of Unión Española de Explosivos in 1896 and reaching a climax in the 1940s with the nationalization of Renfe (railways), Telefónica and INI (the state holding company); and, finally, a populist social policy ... designed to tackle the utopian radicalism of organized labor. (quoted in Pablo Torrente 2003, 14–15)

The Founding and Early Growth of Banco de Santander

At the time that the small group of businessmen founded Banco de Santander, the financial system was rudimentary and dominated by the perennial difficulties of the state treasury. The first bank of issuance, the Banco Nacional de San Carlos, had been founded in 1782; this was renamed Banco Español de San Fernando in 1829. In 1844 a group of financiers including José de Salamanca founded Banco de Isabel II, which was also authorized to issue notes and which, in 1847, merged with San Fernando. The creation of Banco de Barcelona, established in 1844 as the first nonofficial bank in Spain, and Banco Español de Cádiz, established in 1846 as a branch of Banco de Isabel II, followed. These banks competed with each other in discounting bills, lending, and offering deposit accounts (García López 1994; Tedde de Lorca 1994).

The very first comprehensive banking legislation did not come into effect until early 1856. The new law authorized the Council of Ministers to evaluate applications for a banking license and approve them by royal decree. Banks were seen as issuing institutions, not necessarily as commercial or industrial ones. The law changed the name of the Nuevo Banco Español de San Fernando to the Banco de España but left it burdened with bad loans given by the governments of Queen Isabel II to certain companies (Tortella 1994, 139–41). The law contemplated two types of institutions: banks of issuance and credit societies. On the same day that the law was passed, the government extended licenses to Isaac and Émile Peréire, Prost, and the Rothschilds, who were to operate credit societies. While the latter two operations were short-lived, the first—the famous Crédito Mobiliario Español, set up by the Peréire brothers' Crédit Mobilier—grew rapidly by financing railway, gas, and mining companies (Tedde de Lorca 1994). As of 1864, its paid-in capital amounted to almost one-third of the total for the approximately sixty banks by then operating in Spain (Alvarez Llano and Andreu García 1986, 1:52–54).

The first important bank of issuance that the government authorized under the new law was Banco de Bilbao, on 19 March 1857. Banco de Santander received its license on 15 May 1857, but it actually started to operate some four days earlier than Bilbao, on 20 August 1857. The bank initially had seventy-two members or shareholders, roughly one in seven of all businessmen in town (Hoyo Aparicio 1993, 224–36: Jado Canales 1957; Rivases 1988, 113, 207–9). Banco de Santander was relatively tiny. In 1864 its paid-in capital amounted to just about 0.5 percent of the total for all banks operating in Spain. Bilbao was equally small, its paid in capital accounting for 0.7 percent (Alvarez Llano and Andreu García 1986, 1:52–54). It is intriguing to note that today these two rivals since birth form the core of Spain's two largest banks, and rank among the top thirty banks in the world.

Before the panic of 1866 brought financial activity to a standstill, the government approved as many as seventeen new banks of issuance (in addition to Banco de España, Banco de Barcelona, and Banco de Cádiz, already in existence by 1856) and thirty-five credit societies. The financial misfortunes of the railway companies as well as of the government itself precipitated the crisis (Nadal 1975, 37–50; Tedde de Lorca 1994), which affected several credit institutions and led to the adoption of fairly liberal trade and foreign investment policies. The crisis also led to the establishment in 1874 of a monopoly of issuance for the Banco de España, a monopoly that persisted until Spain's adoption of the euro in 1999. Although most of the private banks of issuance merged with the Banco de España,

Santander and Bilbao were among the very few that did not, and instead transformed themselves into credit societies (Tedde de Lorca 1974; Tortella 1994, 141–48). The rotating president of Santander at the time, Agustín González Gordón, displayed his indignation in the 1873 annual report to shareholders: "Our promising state of affairs was deeply disrupted by the Decree of 19 March [1874], which requires the merger of regional banks into the Banco de España. This decree has proved impossible to derogate, even with the protests and complaints that, following its duty, our governing board has made, supporting its case on the law and even on the manifestations of public opinion."

Unlike Santander, which merely protested, Bilbao actually challenged the government's decree, refusing to take its issued notes out of circulation. At the time the decree came into effect, the city of Bilbao was actually isolated from the rest of the country by the army that challenged the legitimacy of the queen during the civil wars. The government had no option but to sue Banco de Bilbao. The dispute lasted until 1878, when the bank finally caved in.

The competition among the banks was intense. Between 1874 and 1892 as many as fifty-eight banks came and went. By 1890 only four banks survived in relatively good shape: Barcelona, Bilbao, Santander, and Crédito Mobiliario Español, which by this time had so declined in size and prestige that it was liquidated in 1902. Santander grew in size but only reached 0.9 percent of total paid-in capital in the system as of 1892. At this time, Bilbao was about five times larger (Alvarez Llano and Andreu García 1986, 1:86).

The activity of banks and other credit institutions proceeded rather smoothly until the colonial crisis of 1898. The repatriation of capital after the loss of Cuba, Puerto Rico, and the Philippines resulted, directly or indirectly, in the foundation of some of the banks that would become large players during the next decades: Banco Guipuzcoano, Banco Hispano-Americano, Banco de Vizcaya, and Banco Español de Crédito (Banesto). The other big Spanish banks of the twentieth century date from the late 1910s and 1920s: Urquijo in 1918, Central in 1919 (in whose founding Santander played a part together with seven other small banks), Popular in 1926, and Exterior in 1929 (Tedde de Lorca 1974). These banks would spearhead the country's industrial development during the 1910s and 1920s, especially in electricity, oil, steel, and chemicals. In the wake of the repatriation of capital from the colonies and the founding of several large banks, Santander's relative importance again declined. In 1922 the bank was not even among the top fifty in the country. Its paid-in capital amounted to a mere 0.3 percent of the total for all banks, its reserves to 1.5 percent, and its deposits and other liabilities to about 0.8 percent. At this time Banco Santander's fiercest local competitor was Banco Mercantil. Founded in the same period as the other big banks, it was about three times as big (Alvarez Llano and Andreu García 1986, 1:106–9).

During the 1930s Spanish banks saw their profits decline amid an economic slowdown and the political instability that led to the Civil War of 1936–39. As was the case for many other banks, Santander's branches happened to be located on both sides of the initial line dividing the two belligerents, though most of the branches were in territory loyal to the government of the Republic. The north central region of Spain, including the city of Santander, was isolated from the rest of the loyal area. Banco de Santander participated together with the other local banks in a government-sponsored issuance of notes in order to avoid the exchange problems brought about by the isolation of the city. These notes circulated until the nationalist army of General Franco entered the city of Santander in August 1937, slightly more than a year after the war had begun. The top officers of Banco de Santander resumed their positions.[3] The late 1930s and early 1940s were years of hardship, economic blockade, autarky, and economic stagnation, reflected in the meager growth of the banking sector in Spain (Alvarez Llano and Andreu García, 1986, vol. 2). Banco de Santander did not experience growth until the late 1940s and the 1950s, when it became unequivocally linked to the Botín family.

The Botín Family Saga

The involvement of members of the Botín family in banking and other commercial activities dates back to the mid-nineteenth century.[4] A surgeon by the name of José María Botín, born in 1795 in the southern Spanish city of Cádiz, fell ill with tuberculosis while serving in the Spanish navy. In 1828 he decided to settle in Santander for his health. His knowledge of infectious diseases helped him gain local prominence when cholera struck the town in 1834. He married María Petra Aguirre Laurencin, widow of the noted local businessman José Ramón López-Dóriga y Vial, the representative of the Rothschilds in Santander, whose son Antonio López-Dóriga Aguirre was one of the six founders of Banco de Santander. The López-Dórigas were in fact central to the dense network of family-based commercial interests in town and were related by marriage to several other local commercial families. It should be noted that in Spain one adopts two last names, the first from the father and second from the mother, a practice that helps in tracking the patterns of intermarriage between prominent business families. The names Aguirre and Vial were also prominent in Santander's commercial circles in their own right (Hoyo Aparicio 1993, 108–39).

The López-Dórigas participated in the founding not only of Banco de Santander but also of Unión Mercantil, a financial company with a heavy involvement in the railway business, which went bankrupt in the wake of the 1866 crisis. Banco de Santander, however, followed a less risky investment strategy, weathering the financial meltdown with relative ease, and without suspending dividend payments. The bank witnessed a renewed period of expansion during the 1870s (Hoyo Aparicio 1993, 224–36). Thus, there is some early evidence of Banco de Santander's reluctance to participate in the development of industry and of its inclination to focus on the retail banking business. From the 1920s to the 1960s, this lack of appetite for universal banking limited the bank's domestic growth but laid the foundations for its international expansion during the 1980s and 1990s.

José María Botín participated in the booming export-import business (Hoyo Aparicio 1993, 221). His eldest son, Rafael Botín Aguirre, was active in the family's flour trading business and became first a member of the board of directors of the Banco de Santander credit society and then, in 1895, the bank's managing director, a position he held until his death in 1903. He was the first Botín to hold a key executive position at the bank. The board of directors appointed Rafael's nephew, José María Gómez de la Torre y Botín, as José María Botín's successor, who served until his retirement in 1923. José María Botín's other son, Emilio Botín Aguirre, became involved in the incipient electricity business. He went to Germany to pursue a business education and then onto London to work in banking. Upon his return, he invested money in several small mining, dairy, beer, and railway companies. In 1901 he was elected to the board of directors of Banco de Santander.

More important for the future, he was the father of Emilio Botín López (hereafter, Emilio Botín I), who became the first Botín to be appointed president of the bank in 1909. At this time, according to the bank's annual reports, the Botín family members owned about 1 percent of the total number of shares and were among some two hundred shareholders. Santander's bylaws specified that the Presidency was an annual, rotating position. Emilio Botín I returned to the presidency in 1911, 1913, 1917, and 1919. In 1920 the bank's bylaws were changed to make the presidency a fixed position. Emilio Botín I was the first to be appointed after the change, and he held the post until his death in 1923. He was also a director of Banco Central, the bank that Santander merged with in 1999 (see chapter 4).

Emilio Botín I married María Sanz de Sautuola y Escalante, a national celebrity who in 1879 had discovered, with her father, the Altamira cave, replete with stunning rock paintings dating back some 14,000 years. They had two daughters and two sons. One of them, Marcelino Botín-Sanz de Sautuola y López (1907–71; the composition of the name departs from the usual rule), was appointed to the board of Banco de Santander in 1946. His more lasting contribution was the creation of the Fundación Marcelino Botín in 1964, dedicated to the promotion of art and intellectual debate, which presently holds a 1.45 percent equity stake in Santander.

Upon the death of Emilio Botín I in 1923, the shareholders selected Saturnino Briz Larín as president, and he held the position until his retirement in 1949. He was well liked for his business acumen and for having bailed out the bank from some serious trouble, in part using his sizable fortune of some half million dollars in gold as collateral, a sum he had amassed in Cuba, where he had migrated as a child. Not until the mid-1920s did the bank make its first foray outside the province of Santander, crossing the mountains to open a branch in neighboring Palencia. Santander continued to be a small, provincial bank for the next two decades. Still, Briz Larín consolidated its presence in the Spanish financial system.

The bank grew organically and via acquisition during the 1940s (see the chronology in the appendix). A defining event took place in 1946 when Santander acquired its local archrival, Banco Mercantil. Of most significance for the future, Briz Larín came to admire and mentor his predecessor's son, Emilio Botín-Sanz de Sautuola y López (Emilio Botín II, 1903–93), whom he groomed as a manager and helped get elected to the board of directors in 1929. Emilio Botín II was appointed managing director in 1933, at a time when family members owned less than 2 per cent of the shares. In order to become the full-time manager, however, he had to resign from the board of directors, to which he returned in 1946. Even with the former president's support, it seems that he became the president of Banco de Santander only in 1950, after much negotiation. According to a well-informed account,

> It was not easy for him to persuade the board of directors of the modest, though influential, Banco de Santander of his intention to devote all of his time and energy to running the bank. They initially welcomed him as a director, but when they finally agreed to let him manage the bank they asked that he leave the board. Botín [II] managed Santander through the Civil War and the hardships of the first decade of Franco's rule. He also traveled and learned everything he could about banking in England and the United States, two countries for which he professes a profound admiration. He preserved his roots in Santander and Cantabria. His home was in Santander, and when in Madrid he would live at the bank's headquarters; it was much later that he established a residence in Madrid. (González Urbaneja 1993, 61)

Emilio Botín II guided Santander through the changing political waters and economic policies of the Franco regime. He was responsible for the bank's first few steps of internationalization, both in Latin America and in Europe, which started in the 1950s and continued throughout the 1960s and 1970s (see chapter 5). He consolidated Santander as a bank with further acquisitions during the 1950s. Still, Santander—like its rivals—did not grow much, especially because of the restrictions the government imposed on the opening of new branches. In fact, the bank's annual reports to shareholders contain veiled statements showing the frustration at not being able to expand more quickly. At the time of its 100th anniversary in 1957, Santander had 129 branches located in twenty-eight of Spain's fifty provinces and representative offices in London, Havana, Mexico City, and Caracas. In spite of acquisitions, one could not yet consider

Santander a bank of national scope. Its presence remained focused on northern Spain and on the biggest cities (Barcelona, Bilbao, and Madrid), with rather minimal operations in most rural areas (except around Santander and neighboring provinces), the South, and the Mediterranean periphery.

During the 1960s Emilio Botín II took advantage of the less restrictive regulatory environment by opening new branches. He also took a few more steps abroad, including stakes in banks in Brazil and Argentina. In 1965 he founded Bankinter, a much smaller bank, in a joint venture with Bank of America (see chapter 6). Various observers have noted that the actual reason behind this move was to safeguard part of the family's assets and presence in banking in the event of a nationalization, given that at the time both the far right and the left advocated a state takeover of the entire banking sector (González Urbaneja 1993, 65; Hernández Andreu 2000; Pérez 1997).[5] Its small-scale and conservative investments enabled Santander to weather the industrial crisis of the 1970s better than its rivals, as the next chapter documents.

Emilio Botín II consolidated the Botín family's position at the helm of Banco de Santander by appointing his son, Emilio Botín III, as second vice president in 1973 and as CEO in 1977, and then stepping down from his executive role in 1986. Thus, the story of the rise of the Botín family at Santander started slightly more than a century ago with Rafael Botín y Aguirre's term as managing director (1895–1903), continued through Emilio Botín I's intermittent years as president between 1909 and 1923, and then took hold with Emilio Botín II's tenure as managing director beginning in 1934, and later as president and CEO (1950–86), except for his last ten years as president, during which time his son served as CEO. Upon his retirement, Emilio Botín II passed on to his son a bank with nearly 1,500 branches throughout Spain, 150 abroad, and 10,000 employees. Though solid and domestically prestigious, the bank was relatively small by domestic, let alone international, standards.

Emilio Botín III stepped into his father's shoes with a clear vision in his mind: to turn Santander into a global financial powerhouse. While the father had succeeded at turning a sleepy provincial bank into one of Spain's big seven, the son would engage in a number of domestic and international mergers and acquisitions that would eventually catapult Santander to become one of the world's top ten banks. While the father had taken Santander to Europe and Latin

America, but was later forced to undo much of that expansion, the son managed to build Santander into one of only a few truly international retail banks, an exclusive club that includes ABN AMRO, Citibank, HSBC, ING, Royal Bank of Scotland, and BBVA, among a few others. As the next chapters document, the long road toward prominence in global retail banking started in the 1980s and 1990s with the skillful disposal of industrial holdings, domestic mergers, and international expansion, first into Latin America and then Western and Eastern Europe. Perhaps the most important foundation for the bank's subsequent stunning growth was its relative lack of involvement in the development of industry, the subject of the next chapter.

3

The Industrial Group

In business, you take either one percent or fifty-one percent.

—Attributed to Emilio Botín II

If Banco Santander has a distinctive characteristic that sets it apart
from its domestic competitors, it is its reluctance to get involved in
the development of industrial or infrastructural activities. The bank
has bought and sold stakes in nonfinancial companies, but has rarely
seen itself as a long-term shareholder. After becoming a national bank
during the 1940s and 1950s, Santander found itself at a crossroads
during the 1960s. Spain had just embarked on a set of liberal economic
reforms that, in due course, generated very rapid growth. The Franco
regime—after two decades of economic stagnation—switched from
autarky and import substitution to a policy of export-led growth. In
1964 the government approved the First Development Plan, modeled
after French "indicative planning" practices. The shift in economic
policy also provided more room for the private sector in the financing
and management of industrial firms. One after another, all of Spain's
major banks began to take stakes in industrial corporations (Muñoz
1967; Muñoz et al. 1978; Tamames 1977). Although Santander also participated in this trend, it chose not to become the center of a sprawling
industrial group. Consequently, the bank did not grow as much as its
domestic counterparts. Its reluctance to abandon its origins in commercial banking, however, helped it navigate the turbulent waters
of the industrial crisis of the 1970s much better than its rivals and
enabled it to enter the 1980s in much better shape financially.

As of the early 2000s, Santander had about 3.7 percent of its capital invested in other companies. These investments generated 7 percent of profits and represented 30 percent of unrealized capital gains (Echenique Gordillo and Grimà Térre 2001, 80). Most observers agree that during the late 1980s and 1990s Santander managed to outmaneuver its domestic competitors because it was a nimbler, more focused bank, and that a necessity of dealing with an extensive portfolio of industrial holdings would have delayed and limited its international expansion in commercial banking.

The Role of Banks in Industry

The financial system plays a critical role in economic development because laying the foundations for manufacturing growth, energy production, the transportation infrastructure, and the modernization of agriculture all require the transfer of massive amounts of resources from backward to dynamic economic sectors, and from foreign lenders to specific domestic recipients. The literature has mainly distinguished among three types of financial systems: market-centered, bank-centered, and state-centered (Cameron 1972; Cameron et al. 1967; Fry 1995; Guillén 2000; Loriaux 1991, 1997a; OECD 1995, 1998; Roe 1993; Zysman 1983).

In market-centered systems, the main sources of funding for firms are the equity and bond markets, with banks generally not owning stakes in nonfinancial firms. Scholars typically point to the United States during most of the twentieth century, though not before, as the quintessential example of a market-based system (e.g., O'Sullivan 2000). In the bank-centered system, nonfinancial companies mainly secure the necessary funds from banks in the forms of equity and loans. The exemplar of this type of system is usually Germany (Berglof 1988; Gerschenkron 1962; Zysman 1983). Finally, state-centered systems are those in which state-owned or state-controlled institutions dominate finance, as in the cases of France, South Korea and several Latin American countries during the 1950s, 1960s, and 1970s (Amsden 1989; Fields 1995; Haggard and Lee 1993; Haggard and Maxfield 1993; Loriaux 1997b; Woo 1991).

As this chapter documents, the Spanish financial system has historically evolved by varying combinations of elements from the bank-centered and state-centered models, with a preponderance of the former (Pérez 1997). In that context, most large banks grew even larger by taking part in the development of industry. Notably though, Santander did not. It focused on growing as a commercial bank while its main domestic competitors relied more on industrial holdings.

The Bank-Industry Link in Spain

The modern history of bank involvement in Spanish industrial enterprises begins during World War I, when the country's neutrality allowed its companies to become major suppliers to the warring European powers. In 1917 the Banco de España started to extend credit to the banks for up to 90 percent of their holdings of public debt, effectively freeing up funds that the banks could then channel to profitable opportunities in industry (Tortella and Palafox 1984). As Sofía Pérez (1997, 49) has wryly observed, however, the emerging Spanish model of bank-industry relations bore only superficial resemblance to the classic German model:

> Because industrial promotion was underwritten by inflationary public finance, it also stained the relationship between Spanish banks and the industrial sector with an "original sin": that of rendering industrial investment a source of extraordinary profits for the banks, not requiring them to develop the kind of internal capacity and culture necessary for the development of competitive, long-term industrial investment strategies. The banks' direct investment was heavily concentrated in those sectors that either were natural monopolies (energy) or benefited from heavy tariff protection. And, aside from their direct holdings, they financed industrial ventures predominantly through the rollover of short-term debt. There was never the "patient capital" link [of] the German case.

Most Spanish banks became "mixed" banks, in the sense of combining normal commercial business, such as taking deposits, extending short-term loans, and discounting paper, with investment activities, such as making long-term loans and holding shares and government debt (García Ruiz and Tortella 1994; Tortella 1994, 336). The largest banks (Hispano Americano, Bilbao, Urquijo, Central, Vizcaya, and Banesto) more than doubled their portfolios of industrial securities during the 1920s and early 1930s. They dispatched directors to the boards of the most prominent Spanish firms in mining, iron and steel, railways, and electricity (Tortella and Palafox 1984). They could even fix maximum interest rates on deposits and regulate conditions for entry into the banking sector, thanks to the corporatist Banking Law of 1921, which enshrined a banking cartel with a new, self-regulating institutional mechanism, the Higher Banking Council, composed of representatives from the private banking sector.

The rise of the mixed banks created a peculiar pattern of corporate development and control. According to the political economist Francisco Bernis, writing at the time, the business establishment at the turn of the century included bankers and industrialists of ancient Jewish origin, *indianos* (nouveaux riches returning from the colonies), competent managers working for foreign subsidiaries, some wealthy landowners, Jesuit priests (especially in hydroelectric power firms), and certain politicians sitting on the board of major oligopolistic firms (Roldán et al. 1973, 1:26–27). This financial and industrial oligarchy was quite effective at organizing powerful lobbies to obtain favorable tariff protection and labor legislation. The contemporary legislation reflected the oligarchy's ideology of economic nationalism and staunch resistance to granting workers or their organizations any concessions. It believed in their superior spirit, traditional authority, and legitimacy of their business successes, which justified their rule and control over both firms and workers (Montoya Melgar 1975, 73–77).

The 1930s initially represented a time of popular hope following the ousting of the monarchy and the proclamation of the Second Republic in 1931, but these changes soon gave rise to social and political convulsion, escalating violence, and civil war (1936–39). The Republic did little to change the banking status quo (Muñoz 1967, 167–73; Pérez 1997, 53–55; Tortella 1994, 334–35). The victory of General Franco's diverse amalgam of conservative, reactionary, and fascist political movements and interests gave way to a policy first of autarky and later of import substitution. The state started to intervene heavily in the economy, in part in response to the onset of World War II and the allied embargo during the late

1940s. Franco resisted the calls for nationalization of the banks by the fascist wing of his political movement (the Falange), largely because bankers and industrialists had supported him during the war (Tortella and García Ruiz 2003). In 1939 he signaled that the status quo was to remain in place. In 1940 banking secrecy received a legal foundation, and a 1941 decree imposed a limit on dividend payouts, something that over the next decades would contribute to the strengthening of the banks' balance sheets (Tortella and García Ruiz 2003). The 1946 Banking Law reinstituted the self-regulating banking cartel, which now included the big seven banks, namely, Banesto, Central, Hispano Americano, Bilbao, Vizcaya, Popular, and Santander. The cartel introduced maximum rates for deposits and minimum rates for loans and reviewed applications for new banking licenses (Muñoz 1967, 167–73). The Banco de España reestablished its practice of lending to the banks against their holdings of public debt. These practices enabled the large banks to grow even larger (Pérez 1997, 61), and the connections between the banks and the Franco regime proliferated. While between 1939 and 1945 only 11 directors of banks were also members of the executive or legislative branches of government, or of the regulatory agencies, by Franco's death in 1975 the Figure had grown almost twentyfold to 213 (Tortella and García Ruiz 2003).

As the model of inward-looking growth lost momentum and went into crisis in the mid- to late 1950s, the Franco regime managed to present itself as a useful bulwark against communism and successfully obtained the support of the United States and the International Monetary Fund. The new economic policy adopted in 1959 included currency convertibility, an attempt to compete in international product markets, and a new Banking Law (1962), which created French-style "privileged financial circuits" to channel funds to industry, following the blueprint of the state's "indicative" economic plan. The government established special credit lines at the Banco de España so that banks could rediscount their loans to companies. The banks benefited from the new framework and became important actors in the process that during the 1960s and early 1970s turned Spain into a fully industrialized country. Even the state's attempt to create specialized industrial banks had limited impact on the profitability and market share of the banking cartel, as nine of the newly created fifteen industrial banks were subsidiaries of the commercial banks. In spite of the opening of many sectors to foreign direct investment, the provision in the 1962 law to allow foreign entry into banking never took effect (Pérez 1997, 68–84).

Santander's Reluctant Role in Industry

Unlike most of its Spanish rivals, Santander is not a central Figure in the corporate network. Figure 3.1 shows a snapshot of the most significant equity ties between pairs of large Spanish firms as of the end of 2006. The central actors in the network are the savings banks La Caixa, Caja Madrid, and Caixa Galicia, construction firms ACS and FCC, automobile insurer Mutua Madrileña, and archrival BBVA—although in 2006 it announced that it would divest its holdings of Repsol-YPF and Telefónica. Santander's most significant investment is in the oil company CEPSA. During the fall of 2006, construction firms ACS, Acciona, and Sacyr-Vallehermoso became even more central to the network as leading shareholders of Iberdrola, Endesa, and Repsol-YPF, respectively. Santander provided both Acciona and Sacyr with the necessary financing.

Santander was historically a small and accidental player in the intercorporate network. As of the end of the 1960s—a decade during which the Spanish economy grew rapidly—Santander held stakes in about ten major beer, construction, electricity, steel, oil, automobile, and chemical companies (Muñoz 1967, 277). Some of these holdings dated back to earlier decades. For instance, when Santander acquired Banco Mercantil de Santander in 1946, it inherited Mercantil's stake in steel firm Nueva Montaña Quijano; this was its first important holding of stock in a nonfinancial company. The firm delivered handsome profits during the 1950s and 1960s, as it benefited from the expansion of automobile assembly plants. During the 1980s, however, it fell into a severe crisis, and Santander and the other shareholders disposed of their holdings (Hoyo Aparicio 2000). Santander was also unlucky with its acquisition of Cervezas La Cruz Blanca, which could not compete against its larger rivals in the beer industry (Hernández Andreu 2000). The investments in oil and electricity were the result of Santander's collaborative relationship with Banco Central (Tortella and García Ruiz 2003, 90–91).

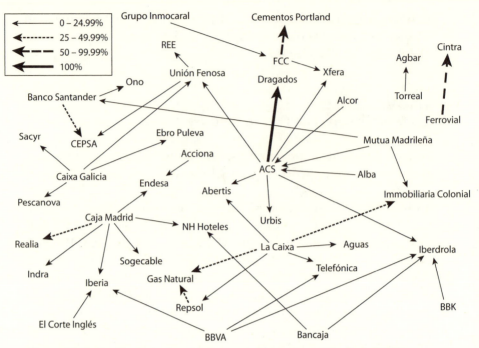

Figure 3.1: Equity Ties in the Spanish Corporate Network. as of the End of 2006
Sources: Company Web sites.

As a result of its relatively small number of equity holdings in industrial companies, Santander was not as heavily interlocked with industrial firms as the other big banks were. As of the end of the 1960s, Santander's board members were involved in 179 interlocking directorships, compared to 478 for Bilbao, 463 for Vizcaya, 390 for Central, 378 for Banesto, 336 for Urquijo, 228 for Popular, and 201 for Hispano Americano. Of the 179 interlocking directorships, Emilio Botín II accounted for 29, his brother Marcelino for 19, and his sons Jaime and Emilio for 11 and 9, respectively. The companies with which Santander shared a director were active in automobiles, cement, beer, dairy, shipbuilding, metals, electrical appliances, electricity, oil, railways, construction, banking, hotels, and water, among others. During the 1960s and 1970s Santander's president, Emilio Botín II, was a director of an average of five major companies in any given year, mostly in electricity and manufacturing (Muñoz 1967, 467, 495–551; Tamames 1977, 239).

There is some dispute as to whether Santander's small role in industry was planned. Some observers note that, though interested, Emilio Botín II never succeeded at making industrial investments, or at least did not do as well as the other big banks. Reportedly, he did not excel at identifying targets, anticipating shifts in industrial development, or focusing his attention on helping the invested companies succeed. Although in the mid-1960s he communicated to Santander's shareholders that "Bankinter would be our industrial bank," he subsequently decided it would focus on commercial banking. In hindsight, Santander's lack of a strong presence in industry would prove to be a blessing when the worldwide crisis of the 1970s struck and Spanish industrial activity went into a tailspin.

The Industrial Crisis of the 1970s and the Banks

By the late 1960s problems had started to occur with the nondiscriminating use of rediscount lines and the lending policies of industrial banks, especially the official credit institutions. A shift in the power balance within the Franco regime enabled economists at the Banco de España to introduce reforms that would give the central bank regulatory authority over the entire private credit market, with the concomitant decline in the influence of economic planners and the end of the cheap-credit policy. Some signs of the precariousness of the bank-industry link had already occurred during the early and mid-1960s in the steel and coal industries, in which most Spanish firms were not internationally competitive. When the banks refused to provide fresh funds, the government assumed these firms' losses and the public sector took over many of their assets (Martín Aceña and Comín 1991; Pérez 1997, 108–9). By the early 1970s, shipbuilding had followed the same path, and the banks also managed to disengage as the state stepped in. During the rest of the 1970s, the role of the banks in nonfinancial firms declined even further. Thus, the banks had remained active in industrial financing only as long as the policy of cheap credit lasted. To bolster their profitability, the big banks initiated their practice of fixing minimum interest rates on loans during their famous monthly luncheons, which they continued to hold until the late 1980s. Competition among the banks shifted from price to distribution and marketing, as one would expect in an oligopoly, leading to an expansion in the branch network. At this time, Spain became a world leader in the number of branches per capita, with about twice the average for the European Union. The banking cartel could easily shift the higher costs onto its customers, namely, households and nonfinancial firms (Casilda Béjar 1997; Pérez 1997, 112–13).

Spanish industrial firms had to deal not only with increasing financial costs but also with two oil shocks and with the wage inflation that took place before and during the transition to democracy starting in 1976. Despite the efforts to shift the burden to the state, the banking sector did not survive the crisis unscathed. Nearly sixty small and medium-sized banks went under between 1977 and 1985, in addition to two relatively large, up-and-coming banking groups (Banca Catalana and Rumasa), altogether representing some 27 percent of deposits. Most of these banks had been created after 1960 and were heavily involved in industry. The state covered four-fifths of the costs of the crisis, and the private banks the rest (Cuervo 1988). Among the big seven, Banco Hispano Americano suffered the most because of its close ties to industry through its intimate partner, Banco Urquijo (Muñoz 1967, 145–47; Tortella and García Ruiz 2003). It was the only top Spanish bank in recent memory forced to skip a dividend, in 1984. Shortly thereafter, in 1985, the accommodation between the government and the banks became even more pronounced as the big bankers invited the president of state-owned Banco Exterior, former economy minister Miguel Boyer, to join their monthly luncheon.

Santander's Recent Strategy in Industrial Holdings

Santander's official policy concerning stakes in nonfinancial firms became clearly articulated during the 1990s. According to Rodrigo Echenique, a board member and former CEO, and his coauthor, a director general, "at the present time, in the midst of full competition in banking and strong exposure to capital markets, the sole criterion guiding investment decisions in nonfinancial companies is profitability.... The goal is to maximize the contribution of such investments to consolidated group profits, including attributable earnings, dividend payouts, and capital gains from sales" (Echenique Gordillo and Grimà Térre 2001, 80).

The two executives referred to the "induced banking business" from owning stakes in large companies as being harder to define and measure. They also pointed out that tax regulations needed to be favorable so that the banks could realize their gains. Lastly, they noted that Santander could not possibly have obtained large profits from nonfinancial stakes without having a team of executives specifically dedicated to the task, who would carefully manage the mix of investments at various stages of development (cash cows, liquidity, and growth).

As a result of the implementation of these investment criteria, Santander has shifted its industrial portfolio considerably over the past twenty years. In 1985, on the eve of Spain's entry into the European Union, most of Santander's investments were in nonfinancial companies in manufacturing or energy, especially chemicals, metalworking, food processing, water, and electricity (see table 3.1). The shift away from manufacturing took place during the late 1980s and early 1990s, as the bank sought to reduce its exposure to low-growth industries. By 2004 Santander had totally overhauled its equity holdings, retaining only a minor presence in manufacturing and heavy industry, with the notable exception of CEPSA, the oil firm, which is a distributor and retailer as well as a refiner. Santander had astutely taken equity positions in some of Spain's fastest-growing sectors, including real estate, construction (e.g., Dragados, later sold to ACS), wholesale and retail (several medium-sized companies), telecommunications and media (Auna and Antena 3 de Televisión), travel and leisure (several medium-sized companies), Internet and e-commerce, and software and data. The bank also held stakes in a number of relatively small service companies. The strategy of targeted investments in high-growth industries has generated large capital gains, which in some cases the bank has realized, as the next sections document.

The Banesto Industrial Holdings

A separate phase in Santander's industrial holdings involved its 1994 purchase of Banesto, a bank with historically large interests in manufacturing and infrastructure (see chapter 4). Immediately after the acquisition, the press began speculating about what Santander

TABLE 3.1

The Fluctuating Number and Diverse Distribution of Nonfinancial Companies in Which Santander Had Holdings, Directly or Indirectly, by Industry and Year (1985–2004)

	1985	1986	1987	1988	1989	1990	1991	1992	1993
Agriculture	0	0	0	1	2	2	0	0	0
Mining	2	2	2	2	2	2	3	0	0
Oil	0	0	0	0	0	0	0	0	0
Industrial goods	13	7	6	7	9	4	2	1	1
Consumer goods	3	3	1	3	3	4	2	1	1
Construction	1	0	0	0	0	1	0	0	0
Real Estate	3	2	1	1	3	5	4	2	2
Wholesale/Retail	1	1	1	1	0	0	0	0	0
Telecom and Media	0	0	0	0	0	0	0	1	0
Electricity	5	5	4	4	5	3	0	0	1
Travel and Leisure	2	3	4	3	4	5	5	3	2
Internet and E-commerce	0	0	0	0	1	1	1	1	0
Software and Data	0	0	1	1	1	1	1	0	0
Other services	9	8	7	3	10	11	10	4	5
Total	39	31	27	26	40	39	28	13	12

Sources: Annual reports.

Notes: Because firms vary enormously in size from industry to industry, the annual totals do not necessarily correlate with the amounts involved in the investments. Companies from the Corporación Banesto are excluded unless they were kept on Banesto's balance sheet.

would do with the Banesto industrial group. For example, the *Economist* (30 April 1994) reported:

> Santander may also sell some of Banesto's assets. Mr. Botín has already asked Bankers Trust, an American bank, to organise the speedy disposal of Banesto's politically sensitive media interests. These include 4 percent of *El Mundo*, a newspaper which has been highly critical of the Socialist government, and Antena 3, a television channel. Eliminating Banesto's rag-bag of industrial shareholdings

1994	1995	1996	1997	1998	1999	2000	2001	2002	2003	2004
0	1	0	0	3	0	1	1	3	3	3
0	0	0	0	0	0	0	0	0	0	0
0	0	0	0	0	1	1	1	1	1	1
8	7	3	3	3	6	3	3	4	3	3
1	1	1	0	0	2	0	0	1	1	2
0	0	0	1	0	1	1	2	1	2	2
1	1	1	4	3	6	7	4	18	18	22
0	0	1	1	0	1	2	2	5	4	4
3	3	1	0	0	0	0	1	4	7	4
1	0	0	0	0	1	2	1	2	3	2
4	2	3	4	3	2	2	1	8	7	8
0	0	0	0	0	0	3	2	21	19	17
0	0	0	2	2	2	0	1	8	6	6
2	3	2	2	1	1	2	1	19	23	24
20	18	12	17	13	23	24	20	95	97	98

will be a far tougher task. Its portfolio includes a clutch of metal bashers and a big zinc producer. Mr. Botín hopes buyers will emerge as the Spanish economy edges out of its worst recession in recent memory.

Most of the Banesto companies had reported losses in 1993 and carried heavy debts.

Botín's team at Banesto, headed by Alfredo Sáenz as president and Santiago Zaldumbide as CEO of the Corporación Banesto (the industrial holding), moved swiftly. By the end of

1994, a mere eight months after taking over the bank, they had sold Tudor (Europe's third-largest battery maker), Carburos Metálicos (an industrial gas company), and 23 percent of Asturiana de Zinc to foreign multinationals. Banco Bilbao Vizcaya's (BBV) wine company bought Bodegas AGE. In early 1995 Banesto reached a complex agreement that put Agromán into Ferrovial's hands, making the latter the third-largest construction company in Spain. By 1998 Santander had sold all other major stakes, including Radiotrónica (a telecom equipment maker), Isolux Wat (an electrical infrastructure company), and the rest of Asturiana de Zinc. Of the original Banesto holdings, the last significant company that remained in the group was Urbis, a real-estate developer, which Banesto agreed to sell in the summer of 2006 in a deal that contributed 778 million to profits. These deals were in line with Santander's stated policy of focusing on commercial banking. Moreover, the companies' balance sheets were so weak that the disposals required extensive provisioning and debt restructuring.

The Case of CEPSA

The case of Spain's second-largest oil firm, CEPSA, illustrates Botín's instrumental approach to the management of external links to nonfinancial enterprises. CEPSA, founded in 1929, originally operated only in the Canary Islands. Banco Central was among its initial shareholders and became the leading one during the late 1940s; Santander also had a modest equity stake. In 1990 CEPSA invited French oil giant Total (today, Elf Total Fina) to become a major shareholder. When Santander merged with Banco Central Hispano (BCH) in 1999, BCH held almost 18 percent of CEPSA. By the time Botín had reasserted his power within the merged bank in 2002 (see chapter 8), Santander held about 20 percent of the oil company. In September 2003 Santander surprised the market by launching an unsolicited tender offer to CEPSA's shareholders for 16 percent of the equity out of the 20 percent that was widely dispersed, in a deal worth 1.2 billion. If successful, the operation would have enabled Santander to control 36 percent of CEPSA, while Total would own about 45 percent. International Petroleum Investment Company of the United Arab Emirates would control a further 9.5 percent.

In addition to its direct stake in CEPSA, however, Santander also owned—together with Total and electrical utility Unión Fenosa—some 59.5 percent of Somaen Dos, which in turn owned 33 percent of CEPSA. Santander actually owned all of the voting shares in Somaen Dos. This arrangement dated back to the mid-1990s in order to avoid charges that a French company was in control of one of Spain's largest companies, and one in a strategic sector of the economy.

Total's reaction was one of disbelief, and it decided to challenge the tender offer in the court of arbitration at The Hague in the Netherlands on the grounds that the private shareholder agreements with Santander precluded any purchase or sale of equity in CEPSA without the other party's approval. Meanwhile, the Spanish Securities and Exchange Commission authorized the tender offer, and CEPSA's board of directors recommended to the small shareholders that they sell to Santander. Even Unión Fenosa suggested at the time that it might sell its 5 percent stake to Santander. Although Santander was successful at attracting slightly more than 12 percent of its shareholders, Total's lawyers scored a victory by obtaining a temporary restriction on Santander's ability to exercise its ownership rights in CEPSA. Meanwhile, CEPSA's shares advanced in price by more than 2 above Santander's offer of 28. By mid-2004 speculation in the market turned to the possibility that Total would want to issue shares and exchange them with Santander for CEPSA's stock. (This had been the outcome when Santander sold Superdiplo to Ahold, and Airtel to Vodafone.)

In April 2006 the arbitration process at the Hague came to an end with a decision in favor of Santander, which had argued that a new transparency law of 2003 made private shareholder pacts invalid if the parties owned more than 25 percent of the equity. Although the court ordered Santander to compensate Total for its legal bills and to sell some 4 percent of CEPSA at just 7 a share, Botín's move seemed to have paid off. The financial daily *Cinco Días* reported on 4 April 2005: "Santander estimated yesterday capital gains of 1.3 billion on the 27.7 percent of CEPSA that it owns after Total's option to buy 4.35 percent, taking into account book value and a market price of 45 per share," some 60 percent more than the price of the tender offer back in 2003. At the time of writing, however, Santander continues to be a major shareholder in CEPSA, thus indicating that realizing the implicit capital gain has proved to be more complicated than initially anticipated.

Extraordinary Profits

With Emilio Botín III at the helm, Santander has obtained handsome capital gains from buying and selling companies, or parts of them. Table 3.2 summarizes the most important deals (note the presence of a variety of financial and service companies but only one manufacturing company, the dairy Puleva). The most impressive aspect of this long list of profitable divestitures is that twice as many of them took place abroad as in Spain, which shows that the gains are not just a consequence of privileged connections in the domestic market. Nor were the foreign deals limited to emerging economies with their less than ideal transparency. For instance, Santander has acquired minority stakes that it later divested in First Union and MetLife in the United States, Royal Bank of Scotland and Vodafone in the United Kingdom, Société Générale in France, and Sinshei Bank in Japan, obtaining combined capital gains in excess of $7 billion. Some of these deals served as the template for the CEPSA operation described previously—for example, the all-share sale of Airtel to Vodafone and the subsequent, three-step disposal of the Vodafone shares. All these successful deals received wide press coverage.

Santander's experience with industrial shareholdings illustrates the advantages and disadvantages of the bank-industry link. Its reluctance—some would say inability—to pursue industrial investments initially constrained the bank's domestic growth. Santander's small role in industry turned from disadvantage to advantage in the wake of the crisis of the 1970s. The bank managed to outgrow its domestic and international peers thanks to its leaner and more solid structure, which enabled it to take the initiative in domestic and foreign mergers and acquisitions while its rivals were burdened by underperforming investments and entangled in difficult restructurings.

TABLE 3.2

Banco Santander's Capital Gains (or Losses) on the Sale of Major Positions

Year	Company	Industry	Country	Sold to	Equity Sold (%)	Sale Price (million euros)	Capital Gain (million euros)
1993	Entel	Telecom	Chile	Chilquinta (3.42%); Sipsa (3.24%); CNS (2.37%); Aetna Chile (0.97%)	10.00	43.5	23.4
1996	Puleva	Dairy	Spain	Caja Gral. Granada; Caja S. Fernando	9.00	...	6.0
1997	First Union	Banking	United States	Market	10.90	1,802.9	1,502.4
1999	Banco Comercial Português	Banking	Portugal	Banco Comercial Português	13.80	...	480.8
2000	Airtel	Telecom	Spain	Vodafone	30.45	...	36.1
2001	Royal Bank of Scotland	Banking	United Kingdom	Market	1.53	...	400.0
2001	Société Générale	Banking	France	Market	4.43	...	185.0
2001	Compañía de Seguros de Vida Santander, and Compañía de Reaseguros de via Soince	Insurance	Chile	MetLife	100.00	284.0	160.0

(continued)

TABLE 3.2 (*continued*)

Year	Company	Industry	Country	Sold to	Equity Sold (%)	Sale Price (million euros)	Capital Gain (million euros)
2001	MetLife	Insurance	United States	Market	3.2	⋯	300.0
2001	Vodafone	Telecom	United Kingdom	Market	1.10	⋯	1,619.6
2001	Superdiplo[a]	Retail	United Kingdom	Ahold	0.86	1,250.0	421.0
2002	Royal Bank of Scotland	Banking	United Kingdom	Market	3.00	1,360.0	809.0
2002	Vodafone	Telecom	United Kingdom	Market	0.56	⋯	274.0
2002	Dragados	Construction	Spain	ACS	22.00	900.0	520.0
2002	Vallehermoso	Real estate	Spain	Sacyr	24.50	568.8	301.0
2002	Société Générale	Banking	France	Market	1.50	⋯	92.0
2002	MetLife	Insurance	United States	Market	0.64	⋯	76.0
2002	Banco Bital	Banking	Mexico	HSBC	27.00	260.0	125.0
2002	Aguas de Valencia	Water	Spain	Banco Valencia (10.61%); Fomento Agricola Castellonense (6.42%); Luis Batalla SA (4.94%)	21.97	32.5	16.0

2002	Patagón América	Internet	Argentina	Wenceslao Casares and Guillermo Kirchner	100.00	10.7	(700)
2003	Antena 3	TV	Spain	Grupo Planeta	8.50	128.0	41.1
2003	Antena 3	TV	Spain	Market	2.98	47.2	16.8
2003	Santander-Serfin	Banking	Mexico	Bank of America	24.90	1,600.0	700.0
2004	Royal Bank of Scotland	Banking	United Kingdom	Market	2.51	1,845.0	472.0
2004	Vodafone	Telecom	United Kingdom	Market	0.46	…	241.0
2004	Shinsei Bank	Banking	Japan	Market	4.00	…	118.0
2005	Royal Bank of Scotland	Banking	United Kingdom	Market	2.57	2,024.0	717.0
2005	Unión Fenosa	Electricity	Spain	ACS	22.00	2,000.0	2,000.0
2005	Auna	Telecom	Spain	ONO; France Telecom	23.49	12,800.0	355.0
2005	Banco Santa Cruz	Banking	Bolivia	Banco Mercantil	96.33	31.7	16.7

Sources: Factiva; various newspapers.

[a] Purchased and sold through Vista Capital, a private equity firm jointly owned by Santander and Royal Bank of Scotland.

Santander has certainly invested in nonfinancial companies, but mostly with a view to obtaining capital gains rather than acting as a long-term, patient shareholder. As the next three chapters demonstrate, however, Santander has engaged in very aggressive growth in retail banking domestically and internationally, frequently using the extraordinary capital gains documented in this chapter to fund that expansion.

4

Survival of the Biggest?

> Spanish banks will have an extraordinarily hard time
> surviving in these conditions [of European integration]. If
> we delay the merger process any longer, we will be forced to
> do it when the foreign banks have already descended on us.

—Carlos Solchaga, economy minister, in *Reuters News*, 11
December 1987

> We are very proud of Abbey, which represents one-third
> of the Santander group today. The takeover of Central
> Hispano was also crucial. But without a doubt the most
> important development in our recent history was buying
> Banesto.... It was a quantum leap for Santander.

—Emilio Botín III, in *Euromoney*, 1 July 2005

> Las fusiones son un follón que tapa otro follón (Mergers
> are a mess that is supposed to cover up another mess).

—Fernando González Urbaneja, banker and journalist, 2006

There are two schools of thought in retail banking, both in Spain
and elsewhere. One point of view holds that only the fittest, that is,
the best-managed banks, survive and succeed. In this view, building
a strong capital base, developing risk management capabilities,
investing in human resources and information systems, engaging
in product differentiation and astute marketing, managing cash
efficiently, and keeping costs low are the keys to high performance.

According to this logic, both small and large banks can attain high levels of profitability.

The other perspective claims that, with the unification and globalization of financial markets, size is becoming ever more important, making it possible for banks to perform more efficiently. Two reasons are mentioned in this regard: the increasing importance of economies of scale, especially in global custody, asset management, back-office operations, and information systems (Walter 2004); and the defensive value of size to prevent hostile takeovers. Still, in almost every retail market around the world, some banks pursue a niche strategy, whereas others seek scale and growth. Relatively smaller banks can identify geographical or market segments on which to focus their competitive efforts.

In Spain, BBVA and Santander have aggressively sought to grow bigger through both domestic mergers and foreign acquisitions. By contrast, Banco Popular Español and Banco de Sabadell have focused on the domestic market and engaged in fewer, more selective acquisitions As a result, they remain about one-sixth the size of their larger rivals but continue to be among the best-managed, better-capitalized, and most profitable banks in the world.

Many of the analysts and experts whom we interviewed for this book raised the issue of a possible trade-off between shareholder returns and corporate growth; they argued that mergers and acquisitions were not necessarily good for shareholders. Mergers of equals, in particular, have frequently led in banking—and in other industries as well—to friction and the eventual dominance of one of the parties. The important point to keep in mind for the analysis of Santander's breathtaking growth over the past two decades is that the competitive dynamics of the Spanish banking sector shifted rather suddenly during the 1980s as the country joined the European Union. The larger size and sophistication of their European rivals led the Spanish banks to look to mergers and acquisitions as a way to put themselves on a more equal footing. The relatively nimble and unscathed Santander was perhaps the bank best positioned to take the initiative in the turbulent period that started with the industrial and banking crises of the 1970s and culminated with liberalization and deregulation during the 1990s. The fact that Emilio Botín III had firmly established himself as the top executive and surrounded himself with a cadre of competent managers enabled the bank to make moves decisively.

A Dormant Banking Sector Facing Liberalization and Deregulation

For several decades, Spanish banks operated in a protected and highly regulated environment that permitted them to enjoy wide interest spreads and to charge large fees. As we noted in the previous chapter, the big seven banks thrived with even the least efficient benefiting from both the cheap-credit policy environment of the 1960s and the cartelization of the credit market that followed the crisis of the 1970s. The only threat to the status quo came in 1965 when the minister of the treasury backed a proposed merger between Banco Central and Banco Hispano Americano. This episode acquired enormous significance because the merger could have upset the competitive equilibrium among the big banks. General Franco, however, blocked the deal out of a fear that the resulting entity would become too powerful. A close collaborator of Franco's quoted him as saying, "I have always been opposed to this merger ... which creates the big monsters that dominate everything, and if you do not work with them then you are lost.... I prefer the nationalization of banks over those monopolies."[1] One must remember that Franco, while certainly autocratic, based his power on an uneasy and continually shifting coalition of forces ranging from the fascist to the traditional and conservative. Thus, the dictator was always very suspicious of any one faction within his regime predominating over the others. While during the late 1950s and 1960s the regime introduced a series of new economic policies aimed at the modernization of labor, capital, and consumer markets, and of economic and financial relationships with other countries, the reforms did not extend to the banking sector, which continued to be a cozy club dominated by the big seven.

The first democratically elected government of 1977 started to liberalize and deregulate banking, supported by the Banco de España. Both actors realized that the country's financial sector was unfit to meet the challenges of Spain's integration into the global economy and eventual membership in the European Union. The initial reforms involved a series of changes related to monetary policy and a rather timid liberalization of interest rates on deposits and of the entry of foreign banks. These measures were too limited to alter substantially the status quo in the credit market. The first wave of foreign entrants—especially the U.S. banks (see chapter 6)—failed to achieve much, which led them to withdraw within a few years (Casilda Béjar 1997; Pérez 1997, 126–28).

The resounding electoral victory of the Socialist Party in 1982 brought almost immediate changes to the financial sector, as the government prepared the country for European Union membership. The first two economy ministers had central banking backgrounds (Miguel Boyer and Carlos Solchaga), and they looked for ways to bring the banks into the reform process. At the Banco de España, the new governor, Mariano Rubio (1984–92), also favored reform, focusing on modernizing deposit and credit institutions. The banks initially did not enthusiastically embrace changes to the regulatory environment and their competitive landscape. Still, as the process of European integration had reached the point of no return, they realized that their best chance was to participate in the reform process and find ways to shape it according to their interests (González Urbaneja 1993; Pérez 1997, 140–47).

The government's first move was to create a short-term market for public debt, which was badly needed at the time in order to finance a yawning budget deficit and to muddle through an era during which unemployment reached as high as 20 percent of the labor force. In 1984 the government put foreign bank entry on hold in a move that reflected the accommodation between the government and the big seven banks. In 1985 the government liberalized the opening of bank branches, a measure that had the potential of unleashing interbank rivalry. But these developments paled in comparison to the changes that European membership would bring about.

Spain and the European Union

Imagine Spain on 1 January 1986. The country had just become a full member of the European Union, joining eleven other states in an ambitious project to create a single market for goods and services by 1 January 1993. In 1989 the European Commission passed a new banking directive that created a "European passport"; a bank licensed to do business in one member country could open branches in any other member country without the need for administrative approval by the regulatory authorities of the host country. Although Spain had negotiated a seven-year transition period for its banking sector

(Pérez 1997), it became readily apparent to everyone that Spanish banks stood very slim chances of survival in a unified European marketplace unless they learned how to compete—and managed to get much bigger. In the mid-1980s, Spain's so-called "big" seven banks were actually tiny by global and even European standards. The largest—Central—ranked only 100th in the world; it was about one-fifth the size of Banque Nationale de Paris (BNP) or Crédit Agricole, and one-fourth the size of Barclays Bank or Deutsche Bank. Santander and Popular were the smallest of the big seven. Tellingly, during the preceding years, dozens of relatively large Spanish firms in manufacturing and insurance had fallen prey to bigger European rivals. Within a few years foreigners came to control more than half of the country's manufacturing base. Spanish bankers were at best apprehensive and at worst frightened. They feared for their jobs, their careers, their privileges; in sum, they feared for their futures. They were determined to ward off any foreign incursion into their domestic turf.

Spurred in part by European requirements, the government moved swiftly to eliminate anticompetitive regulations and to liberalize the market for financial services. In 1987 it removed interest rate ceilings, liberalized commissions, and reduced the compulsory investment coefficients. In 1988 it liberalized brokerage in the stock markets, but established such a high capital threshold for market-making firms that only the banks could effectively operate, once again demonstrating the accommodation between the government and the banks. That same year, it also liberalized entry by foreign banks.[2] In 1989 it deregulated the savings banks, allowing them to open branches throughout the country. The savings banks managed to grab just over 50 percent of deposits by 1994, up from 32 percent in 1977, mainly at the expense of the commercial banks. Two of the savings banks, La Caixa and Caja Madrid, grew so large that they came to rival the banks in size and influence, with La Caixa becoming the largest savings bank in Europe. In 1990 the Banco de España reduced the compulsory cash coefficient to just 5 percent and phased it out by the end of 1992. In 1991 the government liberalized cross-border capital flows. By the beginning of 1993, and in compliance with European rules regarding the single market, capital markets and transactions were completely liberalized. In 1994 the government passed legislation awarding the Banco de España its independence, a reform intended to free its hands in the fight against inflation, but which carried with it one additional consequence.

The Banco de España also is the regulatory authority for deposit and credit institutions, the real source of its tremendous influence. Independence meant not only an enhanced ability to pursue price stability but also greater power in its role as the watchdog of the banking sector.

The late 1980s and early 1990s were truly revolutionary in terms of innovation, with the banks launching new products and services, introducing market segmentation strategies, and upgrading their technology. New products such as certificates of deposit, retirement accounts, mutual funds, credit cards, and insurance became part of a renewed marketing effort to offer comprehensive services to customers. The banks overhauled the ways in which they interacted with the customer, introducing automatic tellers, telephone banking, and interactive television. The banks invested heavily in information technology, control systems, risk management, and electronic data interchange. They also made their marketing effort more sophisticated, spending large amounts on specific product launches and on conveying a unified corporate identity to the customer (Casilda Béjar 1997, 82–88). Unlike British banks, however, the Spanish banks did not use new technology as a substitute for face-to-face contact at the branch, a decision that would prove important at the time of the acquisition of Abbey in 2004 (see chapter 7). In general, the Spanish banks came out of the process of liberalization as relatively strong, well-prepared institutions, equipped with better human and technological resources. Still, they retained many of the more traditional practices, including the priority they had historically given to their branches as the focus of their competitive efforts in a country in which people have always preferred to interact with the human beings who handle their money.

The Merger Craze

Given the comprehensive and rather sudden political, competitive, and technological changes that were taking place during the mid-1980s, it is not surprising that the banks started to jockey for position, with some of them launching the first attempts at consolidation. Table 4.1 summarizes the main merger movements. "Spain's Second-Largest Bank Is Target of Hostile Bid That Ushers

TABLE 4.1

Attempted and Successful Mergers and Acquisitions in the Spanish Banking Sector

Date	Banks Involved	Outcome	Comments
1965	Banco Central and Banco Hispano Americano	Unsuccessful	Although backed by the minister of the treasury, General Franco ultimately blocked it, fearing too much concentration of market (and political) power.
1987	Banco de Bilbao's hostile bid for Banesto	Unsuccessful	Indirectly, it paves the way for the rise of Mario Conde to the presidency of Banesto.
1988	Merger of Banco Central and Banesto	Unsuccessful	The government opposes the merger, which is designed in part to prevent the Alberto brothers (who own 12% of Central) from taking over the bank.
1988	Merger of Banco de Bilbao and Banco de Vizcaya	Completed: BBV	A few months later the president of Vizcaya, Pedro Toledo, dies. Bilbao executives take over the bank, causing an exodus of Vizcaya executives to other banks.
1991	Merger of Banco Exterior, Caja Postal, Banco de Crédito Local, Banco de Crédito Industrial, and other state-owned banks	Completed: Argentaria	Francisco Luzón, president of Banco Exterior, persuades Economy Minister Carlos Solchaga that a state-owned megabank makes business sense.
1991	Merger of Banco Central and Banco Hispanoamericano	Completed: BCH	Central becomes dominant force because it is a larger bank and Hispano Americano has a weaker balance sheet.

(continued)

TABLE 4.1 (*continued*)

Date	Banks Involved	Outcome	Comments
1994	Banco Santander bids for Banesto	Completed	The Banco de España takes over Banesto in 1993 due to its shaky financials and Mario Condé's fraudulent practices. Santander outbids Argentaria and BCH.
1999	Merger of Banco Santander and BCH	Completed: SCH	Although initially structured as a merger of equals, by 2002 Emilio Botín outmaneuvers BCH executives to gain control of SCH.
1999	Merger of BBV and Argentaria	Completed: BBVA	Although initially a merger of equals, BBV executives lose control after entering into a confrontation with the conservative government and after the scandal of the secret pension accounts in tax havens comes to light.
2003	Banco Sabadell bids for Banco Atlántico	Completed	Banco Sabadell wins in a protracted political battle with Portugal's Caixa Xeral do Depósitos.

Sources: Factiva; Tortella and García Ruiz (2003); and Gómez Escorial (2004).

in New Era" read the headline in the *Wall Street Journal* (1 December 1987). Banco de Bilbao had launched a "friendly" bid for Banesto in early November, which eventually turned into a hostile takeover attempt after Banesto's management announced its opposition to the bid, which represented a 40 percent premium above the shares' trading price. Bilbao's president was José Angel Sánchez Asiaín, a technocrat with a solid managerial record and connections in Felipe González's government (González Urbaneja 1993; Rivases 1988). This event shocked bankers and stockbrokers because traditionally such important deals were consummated in private meetings, not by appealing to shareholders in the open market. Bilbao's bid for Banesto went nowhere, in part because the banking establishment—especially Banco Central—reacted strongly against it (Gómez Escorial 2004; Rivases 1988). The governing board of the Madrid stock market turned down the tender offer on a technicality, in a move that reflected the tensions between the stockbrokers, who controlled the exchange in a monopolistic fashion thanks to archaic regulations dating back to the nineteenth century, and the government, which sought to liberalize stock trading.[3] Bilbao's president lamented the outcome: "We will not appeal, but you should know that we have been thrown out. We have not left of our accord. One day someone will have to answer for this historic failure, which halts the modernization of Spain."[4] Sánchez Asiaín was entirely correct in his analysis; his mistake was not to pursue an impossible dream, but rather to choose the wrong means.

The failed takeover, however, had three key effects. The first was to warn bankers that times had changed, that the long period of stability and accommodation struck after the Civil War had come to an abrupt end. The second effect was the signal that some of the big seven banks were better prepared than others to seize the initiative in the new environment. Bankers suddenly realized that they were not all equal; some were more equal than others. The third effect of Bilbao's hostile bid was to debilitate Banesto's top management to the point that such a total outsider as thirty-nine-year-old Mario Conde—who together with the longtime financier Juan Abelló controlled at least 5 percent of the bank and possibly as much as 8 percent—was able to catapult himself into the presidency of Banesto in December 1987, just one month after the announcement of Bilbao's hostile bid. Conde was not the ideal president in the mind of the key families who owned Banesto stock, but they could not agree on any other candidate (Pablo Torrente 2003, 122–24). Conde's rise to the top of Banesto would prove consequential for Santander a few years later, as his mismanagement of the bank forced the Banco de España to intervene, take over the bank, and subsequently organize an auction that Santander would win. Thus, one cannot possibly understand the present configuration of the Spanish banking sector—and by extension of European banking—without the chain of events that began when Sánchez Asiaín launched his unprecedented bid for Banesto.

The government of Felipe González, especially with Carlos Solchaga as economy minister (1985–93), was keen to see the banks merge (Rivases 1988). In the wake of Bilbao's failure to take over Banesto, Solchaga argued that if they were to remain in Spanish hands the Spanish banks would have to merge before the foreign banks arrived.[5] Solchaga was a strong figure within the government, and the relatively good economic data of the late 1980s, especially GDP growth, had boosted his prestige. The government favored mergers because it certainly wished to avoid foreign takeovers, but it had other motivations as well. It was engaged in a long-term effort to restructure the manufacturing sector, especially heavy industry, in which several banks played key roles as lenders and equity holders. In addition, the government wished to remove the old guard of bankers and install a "friendlier" cadre. Conde's rise complicated this goal (González Urbaneja 1993; Rivases 1988). It is important to note that the government and the Ministry of Economy and Finance had a major influence over the viability of mergers and acquisitions because they could approve or deny fiscal credits when it came to accounting for capital gains and the updating of the book value of assets.

At the time the government was especially worried about the rise of the Kuwait Investment Office (KIO) and the Catalan financier Javier de la Rosa as major shareholders of Banco Central, the largest bank in the country. The minister of the economy and the governor of the Banco de España orchestrated a behind-the-scenes transfer of much of KIO's 12 percent equity stake directly or indirectly to Alberto Alcocer and Alberto Cortina, two cousins known as "Los Albertos," active in the construction business and with strong political connections (González Urbaneja 1993, 110–13). However, in May 1988, shortly after being named president of Banesto, Conde agreed with Central's president Alfonso Escámez to merge their two banks. The government's opposition derailed the deal; the merger did not make much sense to the government given the overlapping branch networks of the two banks and the closings and staff cutbacks that would have occurred (Gómez Escorial 2004).

After a behind-the-scenes attempt to merge Banco Central and Banco de Vizcaya fell through, in 1988 Bilbao made a second, friendly move to merge with Banco de Vizcaya. The *Wall Street Journal* put the resulting Banco Bilbao Vizcaya (BBV) in perspective: "The new bank ... will have assets of six trillion pesetas ($53.17 billion) and a 20 percent share of the Spanish banking market. With combined capital and reserves of 230 billion pesetas, it will be Spain's biggest bank, ranking approximately 69th world-wide and 33rd in the European Community" (25 January 1988). Although the merger had been friendly, the immediate postmerger period was difficult, and the frictions and conflicts between Bilbao and Vizcaya managers became public. The two Basque banks were proud institutions, with long histories and entrenched management teams (Pablo Torrente 2003, 126–27). The untimely death of Vizcaya's president Pedro Toledo in December 1989 paved the way for the victory of the Bilbao executives, after the Banco de España tilted the balance of power in their favor. In a sentence that captured well Bilbao's view of the situation, Bilbao's president, Sánchez Asiaín, stated that the merger combined not two *culturas* but one *cultura* and one *incultura*.

Enter Mr. Botín

While its bigger rivals attempted or consummated mergers and were struggling with postmerger integration issues, Santander stood quietly on the sidelines. Emilio Botín III took advantage of two key factors to initiate his own strategy for growth. First, Santander had a nimbler and more solid structure due to its lack of involvement in industry. Second, the bank was run in a decisive way from the top down. Botín made his first bold decision in 1989 with the launch of the *supercuenta* or high-interest checking account, which paid 11 percent on balances of 500,000 pesetas ($4,000) or more (at the time the consumer price index was about 6.8 percent). This action triggered the so-called *guerra del pasivo* or deposits war. Banesto was the only bank that met Santander's challenge head on, about five months later, but given its internal financial problems, its margins deteriorated quickly, which contributed to its near bankruptcy by late 1993, an event that would eventually benefit Santander. BBV and Hispano Americano also launched competing products, though less aggressively. Santander overlooked, however, the market potential of the low-income segment of the population. In 1990 BBV launched its *libretón*, or lottery-linked checking account, an innovative counterstroke that would later prove to be of value in the Spanish banks' expansion in Latin America (see chapter 5). Then, in 1991 Santander introduced a product that would grow in popularity during the 1990s, the investment fund. BBV responded in kind some four months later. The *guerra del activo*, the loans war, started in 1993 when Santander introduced the *superhipoteca*, a mortgage loan with a nominal interest rate of about 12 percent, when the other banks charged 14 percent. It followed this promotion in 1994 by offering the first personal loan product. Massive marketing and advertising campaigns never before seen in the Spanish banking sector accompanied each of these product launches, changing the nature of bank marketing (Bocigas Solar 2001). Santander generally was taking the initiative, leaving the other domestic banks reacting, or attempting to react, to its moves.

At roughly the same time, a new wave of mergers started, with May 1991 taking its place as the most intense month in the history of banking in Spain. On 4 May Economy Minister Solchaga announced the merger of several state-owned banks, including Banco Exterior de España, into the conglomerate Argentaria, a bank that the government would later privatize in stages starting in 1993. Solchaga reiterated his views: "It would be a good idea for Spanish banks to merge if they want to protect themselves from foreign competition. Although they are [of] an acceptable size for the domestic market, their size in the single-market arena is totally insufficient" (*Wall Street Journal*, 6 May 1991). Eleven days later, he broke the news that Central was merging with Hispano Americano, which had been in financial difficulty since the early 1980s, to create Banco Central Hispano (BCH). By that time, Central's president Escámez had managed to defuse the threat posed by Los Albertos—aided in part by Conde's dirty public-relations tricks against them—and Iraq's invasion of Kuwait had turned KIO's attention away from Central. The war also damaged Conde's prospects by making it much harder to attract investors to his newly created Corporación Banesto, which had reorganized the bank's vast holdings in industrial companies. Within a day or two of the BCH announcement, Solchaga again pushed for more mergers, arguing that a combination between Santander and Banesto would be "desirable" (*Textline Multiple Source Collection*, 15 May 1991).

While the country's top three banks—BBV, BCH, and Argentaria—were digesting difficult mergers and Banesto wallowed in its financial difficulties, Emilio Botín's Santander continued to grow organically, taking advantage of its larger rivals' difficulties. In addition, Santander entered into consumer finance in Europe, a most important alliance with Royal Bank of Scotland, and banking in Portugal, Puerto Rico, and the United States.

Santander's moment of truth would come in 1994 with its acquisition of Banesto, following a series of events that Minister Solchaga could not have possibly predicted. In Botín's own words, "without a doubt the most important development in our recent history was buying Banesto. It changed the fabric of the bank. We knew if we wanted to be an international player, we needed to be the number one bank in our home market. Banesto made that possible. It was a quantum leap for Santander" (*Euromoney*, 1 July 2005). Botín also reflected on how much he had awaited the moment: "We have spent years storing up capital to be able to take advantage of opportunities, peseta by peseta, patiently, prudently" (*Financial Times*, 3 May 1994).

Banesto was undercapitalized. The roots of its precarious situation were Conde's daring drive to create a large media group in order to gain political influence, to restructure the bank's industrial holdings, and to match Santander's and the savings banks' aggressive commercial practices. The first Gulf War prevented Conde from carrying out a large share offering orchestrated by JP Morgan that might have kept the bank afloat, at least for a little while longer. On 28 December 1993, Governor Luis Angel Rojo of the Banco de España, a highly respected and competent economist and university professor, followed established legal procedure and removed Conde, his top executives, and the entire board of directors. He replaced them with bankers from the old Vizcaya, which had lost the "civil war" at BBV to reorganize and recapitalize Banesto with a view to its sale. In the auction, which took place in May 1994, Santander outbid BBV by 14 percent. Interestingly, as the *Economist* (30 April 1994) pointed out, "Arguably, the other two bidders were handicapped in the competition for Banesto. Argentaria, which is gradually being privatized, faced political pressure not to bid recklessly and in the end made by far the lowest bid. BBV, itself the product of a merger, is still haunted by the difficulties of mixing banking cultures. Thanks to the presence of some of its managers acting as caretakers inside Banesto, BBV was perhaps in the best position to judge the bank's value." The Banesto auction was the first case of several where Botín demonstrated his willingness to pay well to ensure that he would get what he wanted.

In buying Banesto, Santander achieved its goal of becoming one of the two largest banks in Spain. Furthermore, the deal had the advantage that it was not a merger—with all of the associated frictions and problems—but an outright acquisition. This aspect would prove to be of utmost importance for the future. Also in 1994, Santander beat a consortium led by BBV in the bid for a much-coveted second license in telecommunications, a deal that would help Santander later realize important capital gains. The Banco de España also emerged strengthened from the episode. For instance, the *International Banking Regulator* (2 May 1994) wrote that "the Banesto intervention will probably go down in history as an example of the right way to handle a liquidity crisis."

As a condition for the sale of Banesto, Santander had to keep the brand and branch network for a period of four years. Botín, however, had little interest in integration. Most observers believe that he continues to keep Banesto as a separate bank—which is publicly listed with a float of nearly 12 percent of its shares—to use it as a "training ground" for executives, including his daughter Ana Patricia, and as a possible negotiating or exchange chip in future European cross-border mergers and acquisitions. Analysts calculate that if Santander were to sell Banesto today, it could obtain capital gains in excess of three or four times the acquisition cost, even if one were to adjust for the passage of time. To run Banesto, Botín retained former Vizcaya executive Alfredo Sáenz, whom the Banco de España had appointed as president to prepare the bank for the auction. One interviewee maintained that "the acquisition of Sáenz was even more important than that of Banesto" for Santander's future development.

The socialist governments of Felipe González came to an end in 1996, having completely changed the face of the banking sector in Spain. This period included liberalization of financial markets, de-regulation of various banking practices, two mega-mergers (BBV and

BCH), consolidation of a dozen state-owned banks into Argentaria, and the takeover of Banesto and subsequent sale to Santander. The big seven had become the big four. Even so, they were still small relative to the challenge that the integration of financial markets in Europe posed. BBV, the largest Spanish bank in 1995, was only about one-third the size of the largest bank north of the Pyrenees.

The Conservative Government and the Euro

Like the arrival of the socialists in 1992, the victory of the conservative Partido Popular in the 1996 general election brought enormous change to the banking sector. The greatest impact derived from the decision to ensure that Spain would join the European Monetary Union as a founding member in 1999, which essentially made further banking consolidation even more of a priority. The government moved swiftly to reassert its influence over the banking sector, installing Francisco González, a successful broker, to replace Francisco Luzón at the helm of Argentaria. The government then turned its attention to BBV, which had reportedly angered Prime Minister José María Aznar in a variety of ways (Gómez Escorial 2004). First, both the bank and its president, Emilio Ybarra, indirectly owned part of Tele 5, a television channel that was critical of the conservative government. Second, the head of BBV's economic research department, Miguel Sebastián, was a noted socialist and criticized the conservative government in BBV's reports on the state of the economy. Third, Aznar, being himself a victim of a terrorist attack in his days as opposition leader, was said to dislike the new CEO of BBV, Pedro Luis Uriarte, formerly the Basque Country's economy minister (1980–84) with the Basque Nationalist Party, whose pro-independence policies the conservative government in Madrid abhorred. Over the next few years, Aznar and his government managed to undermine the power of Ybarra and his lieutenant, Uriarte.

This episode illustrates yet another advantage of the Botíns' presence at the helm of Santander. The conservative government did not have any outstanding issues with Emilio Botín, who has always been very discreet and skillful politically, frequently lending his support to the government's economic policy while not commenting about topics unrelated to banking.

After weeks of negotiations—and the helpful implicit endorsement of the government—BCH and Santander announced a merger of equals in January 1999, with the heads of each bank becoming co-presidents of the new entity. Like most mergers of equals, the aftermath was problematic. The tensions between the two factions went on for three years, with Botín eventually reasserting his control over the merged bank (Santander Central Hispano) after a tactical retreat. This move turned Santander not only into Spain's undisputed market leader but—coupled with its simultaneous Latin American expansion—into one of Europe's largest banks.

BBV obviously felt the pressure of replicating Santander's moves, as oligopolistic theory of market competition would predict. BBV not only followed Santander into Latin America but in October 1999 announced its merger with Argentaria—by this time, fully privatized—to create BBVA. In December 2001 the merger of equals turned into a most unforeseen managerial coup by the Argentaria top executives—and, by implication, the conservative government of Aznar—when the president and CEO of the former BBV resigned in the midst of a growing scandal. The displaced executives had used illegal accounts and pension funds on the Channel island of Jersey and later in Liechtenstein to offer additional compensation to some board members (often without their knowledge) and to pay commissions during the purchase of Bancomer in Mexico (Gómez Escorial 2004). Thus, the Aznar government accomplished in two strokes what the socialists had not: the creation of two large banks run by individuals who were either politically friendly (BBVA) or interested in banking rather than politics (Santander Central Hispano).

The Unexpected Outcome

By the time the conservative party lost power to the socialists in 2004, the Spanish banking sector had changed considerably. The domestic market now consisted primarily of two large banks (Santander and BBVA), plus two medium-sized ones (Popular and Sabadell), with all four in fierce competition with the savings banks, which came to account for 40 percent of deposits, compared to 53 for the commercial banks and 7 percent for credit cooperatives and other institutions. Emilio Botín II's prediction from 1983 had come true, though he somewhat underestimated his son's ability to make Santander the market leader: "A widespread opinion is that in a relatively close future there will be only three or four important banks in Spain. If that were true, my collaborators and I are convinced that one of those banks will be Santander" (*Expansión*, 23 September 1993, p. 8). Nobody in the industry or the government could have possibly predicted that Santander would become Spain's largest bank, having acquired or absorbed Central, Hispano Americano, and Banesto. Everyone looked forward to the consolidation of the sector, but the specific combinations of banks that would prevail in the end had been a matter of widespread speculation. The whole process was ripe with intrigue and manipulation, often driven by the egos, desires, and interests of rather colorful individuals. The outcome was the result of many contingencies and unanticipated events, some political, others economic or organizational. Even the clash of cultures played a role

Table 4.2 documents the meteoric rise of Santander since 1985, the year before Spain entered the European Union and Emilio Botín III succeeded his father. Santander then ranked 152nd in the world; by the end of 2005 it had become the world's 10th-largest financial institution, according to *The Banker*. In 1985 Bilbao, Vizcaya, and Exterior were each slightly larger than Santander (without counting industrial holdings); by 2005, after the two-stage merger that created BBVA, they had climbed more than 100 positions in the rankings to become the 33rd-largest bank in the world. Popular and the two largest savings banks (La Caixa and Caja Madrid) also made it into the top 100 list during this period, rising from being in the 100–200 range.

Banks from other countries also grew quickly via mergers and acquisitions, especially JP Morgan Chase and Wells Fargo of the United States, Royal Bank of Scotland and HBOS (the former Bank of Scotland) of the United Kingdom, Mitsubishi Tokyo of Japan, BNP Paribas of France, and Banca Intesa of Italy (the result of a merger between Banco Ambrosiano, Banco Ambroveneto, and other smaller banks). HSBC and Bank of China grew both organically and with acquisitions. Other banks were already large in the mid-1980s and continued to grow apace: Citigroup, Bank of America, Crédit Agricole, Mizuho Financial Group (formerly Fuji Bank), and Barclays. Santander and Royal Bank of Scotland, for many years allied with

TABLE 4.2

The Largest Banks in the World and the Relative Position of the Spanish Banks

| | | 2005 | | 1995 | | 1992 | | 1985 |
Name	Rank	Tier-One Capital	Rank	Tier-One Capital	Rank	Tier-One Capital	Rank	Total Assets
Major banks								
Citigroup	1	79.4	4	19.2	29	7.8	1	167.2
HSBC Holdings	2	74.4	1	21.4	10	11.8	30	68.8
Bank of America	3	74.0	12	14.8	25	8.6	9	114.8
JP Morgan Chase	4	72.5	30	9.6	37	6.8	31	67.6
Mitsubishi UFJ Financial	5	63.9	9	16.7	5	16.0	5	132.9
Crédit Agricole	6	60.6	2	20.4	7	15.6	8	122.9
Royal Bank of Scotland	7	48.6	106	3.3	85	3.1	112	21.1
Sumitomo Mitsui Financial	8	39.6	7	18.6	1	19.5	4	135.4
Mizuho Financial Group	9	38.9	11	15.4	4	17.0	3	142.1
Santander	**10**	**38.4**	**55**	**6.0**	**73**	**3.7**	**152**	**15.0**
China Construction Bank	11	35.6	72	4.8	39	6.4	–	–
HBOS	12	35.6	122	2.9	151	1.7	178	12.0
UniCredit	13	34.0	115	3.1	89	2.9	71	37.2

Barclays Bank	14	32.5	24	11.1	21	9.0	16	94.2
ABN AMRO Bank	15	32.4	14	13.4	15	9.5	48	51.3
Selected smaller banks								
UBS	18	30.4	3	19.9	8	12.8	33	67.2
Wells Fargo	19	29.9	100	3.5	103	2.6	87	29.2
ING Bank	22	27.6	50	6.3	24	8.6	–	–
Deutsche Bank	23	25.8	6	18.9	11	11.3	15	95.8
BNP Paribas	24	25.1	19	11.4	14	10.2	6	123.1
BBVA	31	19.2	–	–	–	–	–	–
La Caixa	68	8.4	105	3.3	113	2.4	205	10.3
Caja Madrid	80	7.7	123	2.9	117	2.3	264	7.7
Banco Popular Español	91	6.7	133	2.7	142	1.8	213	9.8
Merged Spanish banks								
BBV	–	–	47	6.4	43	5.6	–	–
Argentaria	–	–	57	5.6	51	4.9	–	–
BCH	–	–	102	3.4	49	5.1	–	–
Banco Central	–	–	–	–	–	–	100	23.2
Banesto	–	–	–	–	80	3.4	101	23.1

(continued)

TABLE 4.2 (continued)

| Name | 2005 | | 1995 | | 1992 | | 1985 | |
	Rank	Tier-One Capital	Rank	Tier-One Capital	Rank	Tier-One Capital	Rank	Total Assets
Banco Hispano Americano	–	–	–	–	–	–	122	19.2
Banco de Bilbao	–	–	–	–	–	–	130	17.5
Banco Exterior de España	–	–	–	–	–	–	133	17.0
Banco de Vizcaya	–	–	–	–	–	–	137	16.7

Source: *The Banker*, several issues.
Note: Tier-One Capital and Assets expressed in billion U.S. dollars of each year.

each other, stand out as the banks that climbed more positions on the ranking during the past twenty years. At the same time these banks were growing or at least keeping pace, the German banks suffered the most significant loss in relative size. The largest, Deutsche, came down from 6th place in 1995 to 21st in 2004. Clearly, the growth of the Spanish banks to global prominence has been one of the most remarkable developments in global retail banking during this time.

The most significant consequence for the banking sector of Spain's long road toward monetary stability was the rapid decline in interest rates (Mosley 2006), which coincided with an upswing in inflation. Back in 1981, banks would lend money at 18.2 percent for three years, and inflation stood at 14.6 percent, resulting in a 3.6 percent real interest rate. In 1986, when Spain entered the European Union, three-year loan rates were at 15.4 percent and inflation at 8.3 (7.1 percent real). Prior to the liberalization of interest rates, nominal rates went up and real rates stayed between 9 and 11 percent until the mid-1900s. In 1998, on the eve of the advent of the euro, mortgage loan rates, for instance, stood at 5.1 and inflation at 1.4 (3.7 real). And in 2005 real interest rates turned clearly negative for the first time, with loan rates at 3.2 and inflation at 3.7 (–0.5 real). The convergence had both a negative and a positive effect on the banks. The negative effect has been the steady reduction in intermediation margins, which in 1990 hovered around 4 percent and by 2002 had fallen to about 2.2 percent (Berges 2003). The positive effect has to do with the greater ease with which the banks can now expand abroad on the basis of cheap money. These two forces have generated marketing-driven, product-differentiation competitive strategies in the domestic market and an aggressive search for expansion opportunities abroad, especially in underdeveloped banking markets.

The process of banking consolidation in Spain illustrates that smaller, nimbler banks can actually end up becoming the hunters rather than the hunted. Santander clearly benefited from the shaky balance sheets of some of its larger rivals, burdened as they were by underperforming industrial holdings. Santander took the initiative in launching new products and making acquisitions at a moment when its larger rivals were enmeshed in difficult mergers of equals. The bank's unique top management team and corporate governance played a key role in this process of growth. The domestic mergers and acquisitions analyzed in this chapter turned out to be just act 1 in a yet unfinished play. Market liberalization and deregulation triggered banking consolidation and concentration. The resulting oligopolistic rivalry between BBVA and Santander, coupled with intensifying competition from the savings banks, provided the impetus for act 2, namely, the expansion of the two large banks into Latin America, the subject of the next chapter. Without their foreign expansion, the two Spanish banks would not have been able to become so large relative to their peers. Act 3 follows in the wake of the Latin American experience as the banks turned their attention back to Europe at the onset of the twenty-first century.

5

The New World

Spanish firms with a large presence in Latin America are in a better bargaining position with a view to future alliances or acquisitions than those without such a presence."

—Francisco González, president of BBVA, 2001[1]

We made money every year in Latin America. We didn't always make money every year in every country, but altogether the results were always positive.

—Ana Patricia Botín, *Wall Street Journal*, 27 March 2002

Santander expanded in Latin America in two waves (Cardone-Riportella and Cazoria-Papas 2001). The first wave commenced shortly after World War II and ended at the start of the "Lost Decade" of the 1980s. The second wave, which involved Santander in the acquisition of major local banks and brought it to its present position, began in the early 1990s and really accelerated in the mid-1990s. The second wave represented Santander's shift of the focus of its growth strategy toward Latin America. This significant change in focus was a response to a series of rather momentous trends and events that transformed the rules of competition in the Spanish banking sector. The domestic market had become hopelessly saturated, the savings banks were gaining in market share relative to the commercial banks, domestic mergers had produced larger banks in need of greater markets, and the country had entered the European Union. Spain's membership became effective at the beginning of 1986, precisely the year in which the EU committed itself to the creation of a single market for goods and services by 1993. Market saturation and the competitive threats that European integration posed were the dual engines of internationalization. Spanish banks were still small relative to their European counterparts, and this played a key role in their strategic thinking. As one Santander executive put it, "We were a takeover target. We needed to grow. We went on a shopping spree."[2]

Santander was not alone. Following Santander's lead, the other large Spanish banks—BBV, Argentaria, and BCH—displayed a similar sense of urgency. They also pursued growth across the Atlantic, as did banks from other countries facing similar concerns, especially the Dutch bank ABN AMRO and Scotiabank (Bank of Nova Scotia).

How then did a relatively small Spanish bank such as Santander manage to become the largest bank Latin America? This tantalizing question requires a careful analysis of the nature of the opportunities available in the New World, the ways in which foreign banks could enter the region, the possible advantages of being a Spanish bank, the risks of operating in emerging economies, and the intricate ways in which the actions of the various banks interested in the region interacted with each other.

The following pages recount the fast-moving story of Santander's expansion into the New World. It is important to avoid taking for granted that Santander was destined for greatness in the Western Hemisphere. It succeeded only in fits and starts and in stiff competition with other banks. Moreover, one should not assume that gaining a position in each country across the Atlantic was purely a replication of the same model or template of foreign market entry. In fact, each country presented unique combinations of financial, economic, and political peculiarities that required specific managerial attention and extensive strategic and organizational adaptation. In some markets the grapes turned sour, limiting the bank's overall profitability in the region, and even hurting its stock price. Still, what Santander has managed to accomplish in the New World is astonishing.

Spanish Banks Rediscovering the New World

The New World is hardly uniform; the very plural term "the Americas" implies diversity. Patterns of colonization, settlement, and political and economic development have produced what amounts to a mosaic of diverse realities. From the point of view of banking, one can subdivide the region into three main geographical areas, each of which contains substantial internal variation. Latin America comprises the Spanish or Portuguese speaking countries south of the Rio Grande: Mexico, Central America, and South America. This is the largest part of the New World in terms of population, although not economically. Santander's current presence throughout Latin America makes it the largest retail bank in the region in terms of deposits and loans.

The second geographical area—the Caribbean—is perhaps the most heterogeneous of the three. Besides some limited activity in Cuba, Spanish banks have mostly targeted Puerto Rico, which is a unique setting given its Spanish cultural heritage and its financial and monetary association with the United States. In fact, Puerto Rico is the only country in the Caribbean in which Santander has maintained a strategy of foreign growth in retail banking, starting in the 1970s, and it is now one of its core markets in the New World.

The United States and Canada constitute the third geographical area, one in which, its presence in financial centers aside, Santander has over the years had an only episodic presence as a minority partner in an alliance with an aggressive local bank. From the point of view of retail banking, the United States is not one big market, but a collection of fifty statewide markets in which it is difficult to establish a retail presence all at once. Still, the presence of important Hispanic populations concentrated in California, Arizona, New Mexico, Texas, Florida, and New York make these specific states more attractive than others from the point of view of a Spanish bank with a strong presence in Latin America.

While the pattern and timing of Santander's investments in the Americas strongly suggests the importance of a shared language and culture, it is important to note that there were other factors at play. Leaving aside the entry into Chile, Santander's first expansion into Latin America, which primarily took place between the early 1960s and the early 1980s, was not notably successful.

Then, in the late 1980s and 1990s, Santander and the Spanish banks found in Latin America a set of countries undergoing deregulation, privatization, and liberalization of competition. These interrelated processes offered the opportunity of entering high-growth markets hitherto closed to foreign banks. Moreover, the changes in

Latin American retail banking were occurring about five to ten years after they had taken place in Spain (Dietsch and Lozano Vivas 1996), meaning that the experience of dealing with such transformations was fresh in the minds of the Spanish banks. They could easily transfer knowledge, operating procedures, and organizational models from their Spanish operations so as to compete in the region. The cultural and linguistic similarities no doubt facilitated the process of transfer, but they were only one among several factors that coincided in time to make the region very attractive to Spanish banks.

If at First You Don't Succeed: Santander in Latin America

Among banks from countries with a history of colonization, the Spanish banks were latecomers to internationalization. Spain lost most of its colonies early in the nineteenth century and so never developed overseas banks such as the United Kingdom's Barclays (Dominion, Colonial, and Overseas), France's Banque de l'Indochine, the Netherlands' Nederlands Handel-Maatschappij (later Algemene Bank Nederland – ABN), or Portugal's Banco Nacional Ultramarino. At the end of the nineteenth century, banking in Cuba, the Philippines, and Puerto Rico—Spain's remaining major colonies—was in the hands of leading local banks such as the Banco Español de la Isla de Cuba, Bank of the Philippine Islands, and Banco Español de Puerto Rico.[3] The Spanish-American War then cost Spain these colonies too, though money repatriated from Cuba was the foundation of Banco Hispano-Americano and Banco Atlántico, which Banco Sabadell acquired in 2003. Still, despite their origins, for most of their history these banks concentrated on the Spanish market. Santander and BBVA, which today are carrying the Spanish flag into the New World and Europe, were domestic banks that grew into their international roles.

From the first, Santander benefited from the Spanish-American trade flowing through the northern port city of Santander. Even so, the bank did not venture abroad until the 1950s when it opened its first representative offices.[4]

During the first phase of Santander's Latin American expansion from the 1940s to the 1970s, most countries in the region had relatively protected markets and were engaged in import-substitution industrialization. Santander went to Latin America mostly to establish a presence that would enable it to serve its domestic customers with their dealings in the region, just as other European and Spanish banks did, or to establish a limited retail banking presence with a view to acquiring experience. In 1947 Santander established an accord with the Trust Company of Cuba.[5] Santander followed this with a representative office in 1951, an office it maintained until 1960, when Fidel Castro nationalized the banking system, expelling all the foreign banks.

Santander established its next representative office in Mexico City in 1956. For many years Mexican law would block any further investment. That next year Santander opened a representative office in Caracas. That same year Santander took a small equity stake in Banco Intercontinental do Brazil, which it later transferred to a holding company that it had set up (Mobiliaria Internacional – Movinter) in 1968. Movinter sold the shares sometime thereafter.

Santander first entered Argentina in 1960, also with a representative office. In 1963 it purchased Banco el Hogar Argentino, a long-established but relatively small bank founded in 1889, which it renamed Banco de Santander–Argentina. This was Santander's first acquisition in the Americas and, in fact, its first outside Spain. The acquisition made this bank a subsidiary, that is, a majority or wholly owned entity incorporated under local law in the host country.[6] In 1967 Santander also acquired Banco Mercantil de Rosario de Santa Fe and Banco Comercial e Industrial de Córdoba. The Peronist regime nationalized the banks, by then apparently only branches, in 1974; however, the military government that took over in 1976 reversed the nationalization, and Santander recovered these branches.

Santander opened a representative office in Lima, Peru, in 1965 and, in the next year, a subsidiary in Panama, Banco de Santander y Panamá. Shortly thereafter, the Panama subsidiary established a branch in El Salvador.[7] Thus, in the early phase of expansion into Latin America, Santander used all four entry modes into foreign markets—representative offices, branches, affiliates, and subsidiaries—as circumstances and strategy dictated.

Santander's growth in Latin America continued during the 1970s and early 1980s. In 1976 Santander acquired a 30 percent stake in a small bank in the Dominican Republic, Banco Condal Dominicano, which it renamed Banco de Santander Dominicano. The next year it established Banco de Santander Costa Rica and acquired Banco Inmobilario in Guatemala. In 1979 Santander entered

Uruguay, where it formed Casa Bancaria Santander, and Chile, where it formed Banco Santander Chile. It also acquired a 20 percent stake in Banco Sociedad General de Crédito in Ecuador. In 1982 Santander acquired insolvent Banco Español Chile, which in 1989 it would merge into Banco Santander Chile. It also acquired Banco del Litoral Asociados in Uruguay, with its nineteen branches, which it merged with Casa Bancaria Santander to form Banco de Santander Uruguay. Lastly, Santander established a branch in São Paulo, Brazil. It should be noted that Santander did not enter the two largest retail markets in the region—Brazil and Mexico—because local regulations discouraged or essentially prohibited foreign banks from acquiring domestic banks.

By the early 1980s, Santander had a more extensive presence in Latin America than more seasoned banks such as Bank of America.[8] However, as Latin America labored under the Lost Decade, which started in 1982 with Mexico's default on its international debt (Grosse and Goldberg 1996), Santander reconsidered its investments. In 1985 Santander sold its stake in its affiliate in the Dominican Republic to Central Financiera Universal, a local banking conglomerate, which bought all of the bank's fourteen branches in the country, together with its assets of US$30 million.[9] This was only the first of a series of divestments. In 1986 Santander disposed of its minority stakes in the Ecuadorian and Guatemalan affiliates. In 1987 Santander closed the El Salvador branch of its Panamanian branch and disposed of the Costa Rican subsidiary. Lastly, in 1992 it sold to Grupo Financiero del Istmo its subsidiary in Panama and disposed of what was left of its commercial banking subsidiary in Argentina, leaving it with only a representative office in Buenos Aires.[10] That same year, however, it established a significant presence on the investment banking side, which included Banco Santander Argentina (the second-largest intermediary in government securities in the local market), Santander Sociedad de Bolsa (the third-largest brokerage firm), and Santander Investment Asset Management. By 1995 Santander had become the most active brokerage in Argentina and also led in the trading of fixed-income securities.

The two retail banking operations that Santander kept—Banco Santander Chile and Banco Santander Uruguay—were performing well and acceptably, respectively. The Chilean subsidiary had 68 branches, which the bank increased to 100 by the end of

1993, and 176 the year after. The Uruguayan subsidiary remained at 11 branches, down from a peak of 29 branches in 1985.

Expanding in Earnest

Santander's second, and more aggressive, push into Latin America started in the early 1990s. Fortuitously, two developments coincided. The first was that Santander had emerged from the deregulation of the Spanish market as one of the two leading banks in Spain, locked in competition with formidable domestic competitors BBV, BCH, and Popular, among others. Further growth at home would be difficult, absent mergers, something that was not immediately available at the time. If Santander was to escape being swallowed up by some European bank in the new, apparently unifying European banking market, it would have to grow. Furthermore, its experience with deregulation in Spain had made it both more efficient and confident in its abilities not just in banking but also in dealing with deregulating markets. In looking around the world at possible growth markets, it realized that the United States and Europe were too difficult and expensive, that it did not possess any experience in Asia, and that it lacked any entrée into Eastern Europe, which in any case was already drawing the attention of Austrian, German, Italian, and Dutch banks. Some of the banks from the first three countries had extensive ties to the region from before World War II and the descent of the Iron Curtain (Koford and Tschoegl 2005).

The second development was that Latin America was emerging from the Lost Decade. Throughout Latin America, governments were deregulating banking and opening their markets to foreign entry. Santander not only had experience in these markets, but its involvement in investment banking via Santander Investments had brought it into contact with governments and their plans. It was thus in a good position to recognize the opportunity that was presenting itself. The shared language also made entry easier in that it facilitated the transfer of executives and documents between Spain and the host markets and provided some cultural familiarity. Latin America was an attractive market because of the margins and the inefficiencies of the banking systems in the region (see table 5.1).

TABLE 5.1

Comparative Banking Statistics of Selected Emerging and Developed Economies, Early 1990s

	Bank Deposits/ GDP[a]	Bank Share in Financial Intermediation[b]	Share of State-Owned Banks[c]	Share of Foreign-Owned Banks[d]	Noninterest Operating Costs[e]	Net Interest Margins[f]	Non-performing Loans[g]
Argentina	24	98	36	22	8.5	9.2	11
Brazil	21	97	48	9	6.0	6.8	6
Chile	21	62	14	21	3.0	6.1	1
Colombia	9	86	23	4	7.3	8.3	3
Mexico	33	87	28	1	3.9	5.1	15
Venezuela	13	92	30	1	5.7	8.1	18
India	3	80	87	7	2.6	2.9	20[i]
Hong Kong	8	...	0	78[h]	1.5	2.2	3
South Korea	5	38	13	5	1.7	2.1	1
Singapore	6	71	0	80	1.4	1.6	...
Taiwan	6	80	57	5	1.3	2.0	3
Indonesia	8	91	48	4	2.4	3.3	11
Malaysia	9	64	8	16	1.6	3.0	8

Thailand	7	75	7	7	1.9	3.7	8
United States	4	23	0	22	3.7	3.7	2
Japan	3	79	0	2	0.8	1.1	3
Germany	5	77	50[h]	4	1.1	1.4	...
Spain[j]	...	...	...	2	2.5	3.7	4

Sources: Goldstein and Turner (1996); World Development Indicators; OECD.

[a] Average percentage over the period 1980–95.
[b] Assets as a percentage of the assets of banks and nonbank financial institutions in 1994.
[c] Percentage share of assets in 1994.
[d] Percentage share of assets; date not given.
[e] As a percent of total assets, averaged over 1990–94.
[f] As a percent of total assets, averaged over 1990–94.
[g] Average 1994–95; these figures may not be strictly comparable.
[h] Not strictly comparable.
[i] Relates only to public-sector banks.
[j] Excludes savings and cooperative banks.

For its second thrust into Latin America, Santander changed its strategy to one of buying controlling stakes in large domestic banks. It had learned from its earlier experience that neither de novo investment nor the acquisition of small domestic banks would provide an adequate platform for meaningful growth, either in terms of having a viable operation in the host markets or in terms of making Santander into a leading world bank.

Santander initially built its position in Latin America around Santander Investment, its investment banking arm, which it had established in 1984. In 1988 Emilio Botín III brought in his daughter, Ana Patricia Botín, from J.P. Morgan, where she had been working since graduating from college in 1982, to start up a new capital markets group to engage in investment banking with a focus on emerging markets. In 1991 she became director general of Banco Santander de Negocios, and in 1994 CEO. As several of our interviewees pointed out, arguably Santander Investment's most important contribution to Banco Santander's later expansion was the creation of a cadre of young managers who came to know each other and acquired experience around the region. Santander's commitment to Latin America helped it compete against banks with a more diffuse focus for top recruits who had a personal dedication to the region. This cadre then became important to Santander's subsequent acquisitions of retail banks.

In acquiring banks in Latin America, Santander would face little competition from other foreign banks, except for the other major Spanish banks. Banks based in the United States were still recovering from their sour experience with the 1982 Latin American debt crisis. The U.S. banks, which had built up a presence in several key countries starting during World War I, either remained content with their position (e.g., Citibank and BankBoston, though BankBoston has since withdrawn) or retreated (e.g., Bank of America and Chase Manhattan Bank). Moreover, Citibank and BankBoston preferred to focus on the upper end of the market; Santander planned to target the mass consumer market. British and German banks were capable and well-capitalized institutions, but they had their attention focused elsewhere, Asia and Eastern Europe, respectively. Among the British banks, Lloyds withdrew from Latin America, where it had been active since the mid-nineteenth century, and HSBC, which has as its motto "The World's Retail Bank," started to enter that market only around 2000 (Tschoegl 2004a). Japanese, French, and Italian banks were underperforming during the late 1980s and early 1990s and were not considering expansion into Latin America, a region they perceived as volatile. Credit Lyonnais did try briefly, but after its de facto insolvency it disposed of most of its foreign operations, including those in Latin America, as a condition of its rescue. The Italian bank Intesa has been breaking up and disposing of the Sudameris subsidiaries that it acquired with its acquisition of Banca Commerciale Italiana in 1999, ending Sudameris's ninety-year history in Latin America.

As is typical in a situation where two or three banks, or companies more generally, dominate their home banking market, action by one of them will generally meet with a reaction from the others. Thus, when Santander began an aggressive series of acquisitions in Latin America, BBV and BCH followed. BBV, Argentaria, and BCH, like Santander, already had some mix of representative offices, branches, and small subsidiaries in the region. As we discussed in chapter 4, European integration triggered mergers in the home country, and market concentration invited the banks to explore foreign countries for growth. This pattern of international expansion signaled a change in strategy from normal cross-border banking—following trade and home country corporations, and the ongoing opportunistic purchase of small subsidiaries—to a concerted push into retail banking abroad.

In its expansion, Santander generally bought majority stakes in top-tier banks, brought in senior management, and put its brand name on its acquisitions. By contrast, BBV and its successor BBVA were initially content to take minority stakes, though with management control, and were less diligent about creating a common brand. BBVA owes some of this presence to Banco Exterior (later a part of Argentaria), but some it acquired in the late 1990s. BCH, perhaps with fewer resources, usually invested as a more passive shareholder in lesser-quality banks and favored alliances with local business groups.

Santander and BBVA followed a pattern of opportunistic acquisitions and painstaking restructuring following the acquisition to build up positions in numerous Latin American banking markets. For Santander, these fall into three categories: the unsuccessful forays (Bolivia, Paraguay, Peru, and Panama), the question marks (Uruguay, Colombia, and Venezuela), and the four core markets (Argentina, Chile, Mexico, and Brazil).

Some Unsuccessful Forays

Not all acquisitions by the Spanish banks have been successful. Just as BBVA left Brazil, so too has Santander withdrawn from some ventures. Bancosur (Peru), Banco Asunción (Paraguay), and Banco Santa Cruz (Peru) were acquisitions by Banco Central Hispano that Santander inherited from the merger; they had been part of the portfolio of the O'Higgins Central Hispano (OHCH) joint venture, which had owned 89 percent of Bancosur, 78 percent of Banco Asunción, and 67 percent of Banco Santa Cruz. Unlike its treatment of a number of other BCH subsidiaries that it inherited, in each of these cases Santander built up its ownership to more than 90 percent before deciding to exit the ventures.

In 1995 Santander submitted a bid in the privatization of Banco Continental, the third-largest bank in Peru, but lost to BBVA. Santander immediately went on to acquire Banco InterAndino, a relatively small bank, and Peru's Banco Mercantil, and then merged them to form Banco Santander Peru. Banco Mercantil ranked eighth in market share in Peru and had mainly a retail portfolio. By contrast, Banco InterAndino, although it consisted of only one office and ranked ninth, had a strong corporate client list.[11] Together the two banks achieved a market share of about 4.5 percent and ranked seventh. When Santander merged with BCH it also inherited Banco de Sur (Bancosur), Peru's fifth-largest bank, which BCH-OHCH had bought in 1996. Santander merged Banco de Sur into Banco Santander Peru in 1999. In 2002 Santander sold its Peruvian subsidiary to Banco de Crédito del Perú, the country's largest bank.

In 2003 Santander decided to close Banco Asunción and pull out of Paraguay after being unable to find a buyer for the bank. Banco Asunción's market share was less than 1 percent of a particularly small banking market. In 2005 Santander sold its 96 percent stake in Banco Santa Cruz in Bolivia, once it became readily apparent that the populist candidate would win the presidential election.

Santander also found itself again having to withdraw from Panama. In acquiring Colombia's Bancoquia in 1997, Santander also came to own a subsidiary in Panama, which it renamed Banco Santander Colombia–Panamá The merger with BCH also brought with it the latter's Panamanian subsidiary. Santander sold Banco Santander Colombia–Panamá in 2002 and started phasing out Banco Santander (Panamá), the former BCH subsidiary, with the intention of focusing the operations of its remaining branch there on offshore banking. Thus, between 1999 and 2002, Santander had two subsidiaries in Panama. Rather than consolidating the two to form the basis for a renewed effort in the country, Santander has maintained its decision to leave Panama.

The Question Marks: Uruguay, Columbia, and Venezuela

As we discussed earlier, Santander entered Uruguay in 1979 and expanded by acquisition. After shrinking to eleven branches, Santander Uruguay has since rebuilt its network to sixteen branches in the country, nine in Montevideo and seven elsewhere. The country is too small to permit Santander to grow its operation into a core holding, but the subsidiary is performing well enough that there seems to be no rush to dispose of it either. Columbia and Venezuela have a greater potential, but political factors could tip the scale against Santander retaining them.

Santander and BBVA made acquisitions in Colombia and Venezuela at the same time as in Argentina. In 1996 BBV bought a minority stake in Banco Ganadero, which it later upgraded to majority and full ownership. The next year Santander bought 55 percent of Banco Comercial Antioqueno (Bancoquia) under an agreement that had Bancoquia selling its stakes in investment banking, warehousing, and Colsabank first but also buying Invercredito, a Colombia consumer lending company. Today Santander fully owns its subsidiary in Colombia. BBVA and Santander are relatively small players, together accounting for just about 11 percent of banking system assets. Banco Hispano Americano had acquired 26 percent of Banco de Colombia in 1992, but an attempt to acquire it fully fell through and the bank merged with Banco Industrial Colombiano.

In 1997 Santander, forty-one years after establishing a representative office, acquired Banco de Venezuela. In 2000 Banco de Venezuela purchased Banco de Caracas and fully absorbed it in 2002.[12] In 1997 BBV acquired 55 percent of Banco Provincial, which had itself just acquired large minority positions in Banco de Lara and Banco de Occidente. In 1999 Banco Provincial merged in Banco de Occidente and Banco Popular y de los Andes; then in 2000, BBVA merged in Banco de Lara. BBVA and Santander together account for about 30 percent of the assets in the banking system, and their subsidiaries are the second- and third-largest banks in the country, after Banco Mercantil, which is Venezuelan-owned.

The Four Core Markets: Chile, Argentina, Mexico, and Brazil

Entering the First Economic Reformer: Chile

In the second half of the 1970s, Chile became the first major Latin American country to introduce liberal economic policies, leading it to enjoy faster growth than any other economy in the region. Despite its general commitment to these policies, Chile chose, in the context of a very open economy, to moderate inflows of capital by imposing a 30 percent reserve requirement on short-term capital inflows. This policy discouraged short-term borrowing from abroad and kept real domestic interest rates above international levels. Still, solid macroeconomic policies reduced inflation while maintaining economic growth. Even so, during the early 1980s, Chile could not entirely escape the effects of rising interest rates and decreasing prices for commodity exports (copper in particular), the two proximate causes of the Latin American debt crisis of 1982.

The particular policies and conditions accounting for the Chilean "miracle" are the subject of heated debates in both academic and policy circles. These debates extend to Chile's political model, because the country faced long-running problems in consolidating its transition to democracy due to the military's inescapable presence.

Since the 1980s Chile has indeed made progress economically: exports of commodities such as copper and nitrates have lost relative importance while those of fresh fruit, wines, fish, and forestry products have grown at double-digit rates; the private savings rate is among the highest in the world, thanks in part to the privatization of the pension system; its power utilities and the telephone system are among the most efficient in the world; and educational standards are rising rapidly.

Merger activity in the Chilean banking sector was intense during the mid-1990s. Mergers helped the Banco Santiago (50 percent owned by BCH) move into first place in the size rankings and Banco Santander Chile settle into second place. These new leaders heightened the pressure on the previous number one Banco de Chile (then in third place) and Banco del Estado de Chile (fourth place) and on middle-tier banks such as Banco Edwards and Banco Hipotecario de Fomento (BHIF). By the end of 1997, the banking industry consisted of fifteen private locally incorporated banks, including four foreign wholly owned or majority-owned subsidiaries and some with large foreign minority positions, plus state-owned Banco del Estado de Chile. In addition, thirteen foreign banks operated as local branches of their parents. In total, the foreign banks accounted for some 20 percent of banking system assets and loans.

Banco de Chile and Banco del Estado de Chile are solid institutions and either difficult or impossible to acquire. The former was at the time an obvious acquisition target, but a takeover would require a public tender offer as the bank is widely held. Also, the bank had a poison pill in the form of a forty-year loan owed to Banco Central de Chile. (The loan was part of a rescue package during the 1982 crisis and contained restrictive covenants. Any acquirer would wish to pay it off before maturity.) Banco del Estado de Chile was state-owned, and the government had no plans to privatize it. Though profitable, the mature and fiercely competitive Chilean financial sector more closely approaches performance norms of the countries in the Organization for Economic Cooperation and Development (OECD) than those in Latin America in terms of margins and service: return on equity for the financial system fell from 21 percent in 1993 to about 13 percent in 1997.

Santander and other foreign banks saw in Chile not just a profit opportunity but also an opportunity to learn about rapidly deregulating markets. In 1993 Santander acquired Fincard, then Chile's largest issuer of credit cards, and in 1995 it purchased Financiera Fusa, a consumer finance company targeting lower-income customers. In 1996 it bought Banco Osorno y La Unión to become the second-largest commercial bank in Chile. Santander paid well for the bank; its bid valued Banco Osorno at about 10 percent above its market value. As Emilio Botín III had demonstrated in the acquisition of Banesto in Spain in 1994, he showed a willingness to bid aggressively to ensure success over other competing bids. Also in 1996, BCH formed a fifty-fifty holding company (O'Higgins Central Hispano—OHCH) with the Lúksic group, which already owned Banco O'Higgins. OHCH then bought Banco Santiago from the central bank, which had acquired the shares in a rescue, and merged O'Higgins into it. BCH transferred to OHCH its former subsidiaries in Argentina, Uruguay, Paraguay, and Peru. When in 1999 Santander and BCH merged to form Santander Central Hispano

(SCH), Santander bought out the Lúksic group's shares, giving it control of both Santander Chile and Banco Santiago. This acquisition led to regulatory concerns about concentration in the banking sector that now are moot. In 2002 the Banco Central de Chile exercised a put option, selling 35 percent of Santiago to SCH, which already held 44 percent; Santander then merged its two subsidiaries. Today Banco Santander Chile is the largest bank in Chile; it has about a 25 percent market share, and it is highly efficient and very profitable.

BBV trailed Santander in Chile, although the reverse was true in Mexico and Colombia. For years BBV just had a representative office in Santiago. Then in 1998, BBVA bought Banco Hipotecario de Fomento (BHIF) from the Said family, to form what is now BBVA Banco BHIF. Still, its profile in Chile is much lower than Santander's.

The Argentine Banking Roller Coaster

Argentina is one of the most volatile countries in all of Latin America. Decades of instability—twenty-three presidents (nine generals among them) and fifty-two economy ministers between 1943 and 2006—have resulted in erratic policies and continuing economic decline (Guillén 2001). In the midst of the capital flight, hyperinflation, and social unrest of the late 1980s and early 1990s, the newly elected President Menem (1989–99) pushed an ambitious program of reforms comprising deregulation and liberalization, privatization of state-owned companies, and creation of Mercosur, a customs union with Brazil, Uruguay, and Paraguay. A key piece was the April 1991 Convertibility Law that created a currency board (i.e., like the nineteenth-century gold standard, an unmanaged, fixed-exchange-rate regime) with the Argentine peso pegged to the U.S. dollar at parity These reforms resulted in strong economic growth, falling inflation, and huge foreign investment inflows that helped finance a growing trade deficit. The economy expanded vigorously except in 1995, when investors, companies, and consumers overreacted to the Mexican crisis. The *tequila* shock resulted in a 20 percent fall in bank deposits as customers turned to cash or sent money abroad. By March 1995 roughly one in three Argentine banks was technically bankrupt. When the supervisory authority raised capital adequacy requirements and increased required reserves, banks responded by merging or by selling themselves to better-capitalized foreigners.

Brazil's devaluation in 1999 triggered a recession that lasted four years and led to the chaotic events of the fall of 2001 and the default and abandonment of currency convertibility of early 2002. The economy has since recovered thanks to a floating exchange rate, although the country continues to be relatively uncompetitive in many products.

Federal, provincial, and municipal banks—many of which still exist—have traditionally dominated Argentine banking. Today, the largest bank is still the government-owned Banco de la Nación Argentina. "Nonstate" banks were nationalized and privatized several times during the past half century, but the biggest impediment to the development of the financial sector has been instability and hyperinflation. At one point during the 1980s, total deposits fell to US$2 billion (for a country of 33 million people) as people avoided bank accounts. Even today, Argentina is an underbanked market. The provincial and city-owned banks represent a problem in that the central government cannot force the local governments to privatize them and the banks' operations remain highly politicized.

The foreign banks' presence in Argentina dates back to initiatives to exploit natural resources and agricultural development during the late nineteenth and early twentieth centuries, when Argentina was one of the richest countries in the world. Citibank arrived in 1914 and BankBoston in 1917. German and Italian banks also arrived, drawn by the country's large immigrant populations. Since the 1980s, the number of foreign-owned private banks has fluctuated around a slight growth trend, helped by the government's removal in 1994 of operating and ownership restrictions. There were twenty-seven foreign banks at the end of 1980, thirty-two at the end of 1985, twenty-eight by March 1997, and thirty-four at the end of 1997. Of these, some fifteen were branches, five affiliates, and the rest subsidiaries. There were also 103 representative offices, though some of these belong to banks that also had an operating presence.

Santander's current commitment to retail banking in Argentina took off in the wake of the 1994–95 crisis, when many privately owned Argentinean banks became available at reduced prices. In 1996 Santander acquired Banco Río de la Plata, one of the most profitable and best-capitalized banks in the country. Santander also established a strong position through acquisitions and joint ventures in pension fund management. At the same time, BCH acquired 50 percent of Banco Tornquist and 10 percent of Banco de Galicia y Buenos Aires. When Santander and BCH merged, Santander acquired the remaining shares in Tornquist, which it merged into Banco Río. BBV also entered Argentina in 1996 by acquiring Banco Francés de la Río de la Plata, another well-run bank with a compatible culture, together with its foreign operations, including the former Banesto Banco Uruguay, which Santander had divested after inheriting it from Banesto.[13] The following year, Francés acquired the troubled Banco de Crédito Argentino, which it later merged into Francés. Lastly, in 1999 BBV acquired Corp Banca. Although the Spanish banks came to control the largest nonstate Argentine banks, they trail the federal and provincial banks in size. At the same time the Spanish banks entered, Scotiabank, Credit Agricole, and HSBC also made acquisitions, albeit of smaller banks. BankBoston, Banamex, Banca Intesa, Citibank, and Banco Itaú also made additional acquisitions in a bid to expand their existing Argentine operations.

The 2001–2 Argentine financial crisis hit all the foreign banks hard, including Banco Río de la Plata and BBVA Francés. Bank of Nova Scotia and Crédit Agricole left in April 2002. Banca Intesa, Lloyds TSB, and Société Générale all sold their subsidiaries to local banks. What happened was that following the devaluation of the peso, the government imposed an asymmetric "pesification" of bank assets and liabilities. It ordered the banks to convert dollar-denominated loans into pesos at the predevaluation 1-to-1 exchange rate. At the same time, it demanded that the banks convert dollar-denominated time deposits at the rate of 1.4 pesos per dollar. These requirements essentially wiped out the entire capital of the banking system. They also introduced a significant foreign exchange exposure into the banks' balance sheets, as foreign obligations remained denominated in their original currency. Francisco Luzón, who was in charge of all of Santander's Latin American operations at the time, said of the Argentine government's policies, "They broke all the rules of the game."[14]

The Banco de España played a central role in containing the fallout from the Argentine crisis. As the Spanish banks started their expansion in Latin America, it had allocated personnel and resources to assess and monitor the risks. As a result, it had a good sense of the banks' direct exposure throughout the region. It required that the Spanish banks strengthen their provisioning both in advance and after the fact. The Banco de España asked the banks to provision their entire investment in Argentina (including goodwill), as well as cross-border intragroup risk and provisionable cross-border risk with third parties. Santander set aside €1.2 billion (US$1 billion) in provisions on its balance sheet for its banking and pension fund activities in Argentina, and BBVA set aside €1.4 billion (US$1.2 billion). (HSBC set aside US$1.1 billion.) As a result, Santander maintained its nonperforming loan (NPL) ratios and provision cover in 2002 at levels of 2001 (1.9 and 140 percent, respectively). Excluding Argentina, the NPL ratio stood at 1.7 percent (0.9 percent in Spain and 3.1 percent in Latin America), while the cover rate was 152 percent (191 percent in Spain and 140 percent in Latin America). In 2002 the governor of the Banco d'España declared that Santander and BBVA "were managing the impact of the crisis appropriately. We have asked them to manage the risks and to make suitable provisions, and that is exactly what they are doing."[15]

Both Santander and BBVA ended up closing seventy branches each and reducing staff. Their parents wrote down the capital of their subsidiaries on their own books. Still, because of its financial strength, Santander's Banco Río de la Plata was the first financial institution to recommence issuance of personal loans and fixed long-term mortgages after the crisis.

Mexico Opens Its Doors to Foreign Banks

Mexico is a country of extremes. Until the 1980s policies encouraged import substitution in manufacturing, except for the export-oriented *maquiladora* tax-free regime introduced in the border areas during the 1960s. The process of industrialization had historically led to the rise of a relatively large urban middle class enjoying the benefits of a protected domestic market at the expense of the rural peasantry. Also, Mexico borrowed heavily from abroad after new oil deposits were discovered in the early 1970s. When in the early 1980s interest rates rose and crude prices fell, Mexico defaulted on its debt and saw its financial system collapse. The government of President Lopez Portillo nationalized Mexico's banking sector in September 1982, as a response to the Latin American financial crisis. At the time, the banking system consisted of sixty private domestic banks of various kinds. Many of these banks belonged to wealthy individuals or closely held family groups. Following nationalization, the government named political appointees to run the banks under strict orders from the central authorities; the government essentially used the banks to purchase government bonds. Interest rate controls, high reserve requirements, and other restrictions further discouraged bank expansion. These restrictions were temporary, being gradually eliminated during the late 1980s, but the overall effect was to create a banking system that ill-served the public and that consisted of banks without bankers or their skills.

By the late 1980s, the government had consolidated the banking sector into six national and twelve regional banks, together operating more than 4,450 domestic branches. In addition there were fourteen smaller, second-tier banks. In 1990 the government of President Carlos Salinas began the process of reprivatization, which it executed in six auctions of three banks each (Unal and Navarro 1999). To prevent undue concentration, the government forbade any successful bidder in an earlier auction from participating in subsequent auctions. Also, only qualified (domestic) entities could bid. The first auction took place on 7 June 1991 and the last one on 3 July 1992. The process was thorough and left the banking system largely in the hands of Mexican business groups and private investors. Estimates obtained during interviews suggest that the government's restrictions on bidders probably cost it about 20 percent of the possible revenue that it might otherwise have garnered. Having privatized the banks, the government began issuing new banking licenses, the first in decades.

The government of President Salinas got carried away by its apparent economic successes, especially membership in the North American Free Trade Agreement (NAFTA) and the OECD, and by growing international investor confidence. Outward portfolio investment rose sharply after the government abolished capital controls in 1991 and the government held the currency within an increasingly unrealistic band. In spite of the visible signs of economic strain and political turmoil during 1994, President Salinas left office as scheduled without making the necessary macroeconomic adjustments. Within a couple of weeks after the new president was sworn in, speculation mounted that foreign reserves were running out. Investors withdrew their portfolio investments swiftly, and the government and domestic firms found they could no longer roll over their short-term debt with international lenders. The peso collapsed by 45 percent between December 1994 and January 1995, forcing the United States to orchestrate an international bailout amounting to US$52 billion. Although 1995 was a year of economic contraction and increasing poverty and unemployment, the Mexican economy managed to recover from the so-called *tequila* crisis in 1996 and 1997 thanks to an export boom that also allowed for a repayment of the international loan.

When the government privatized the banks, the legal and regulatory framework governing the banking sector did not keep pace, and oversight was inadequate (Unal and Navarro 1999). The government underestimated the necessary investment in regulators and their skills to oversee the return to competition in banking. Furthermore, a period of "hypercompetition" had followed privatization as the owners sacrificed profitability to gain market share and position. Unfortunately, the new owners' skills were mainly in money market trading due to the huge growth of government domestic borrowing, and not in banking, and the banks generally were unable to weather the crisis. The result was that many of the privatized banks ended up back in the government's hands.

In early 1995, in order to alleviate the banks' problems created by the new crisis, the Savings Protection Fund (Fobaproa), a trust under the Banco de México, entered into risk-sharing swaps with the banks—the banks acquired bonds and gave up nonperforming loans. As one of our interviewees at the Banco de México remarked, "our experience with *Mexican* bankers was an expensive one."[16] By April 1998 the government put before Congress a new reform plan for the financial system. The proposal gave the Banco de México full control over exchange rate policy, strengthened banking supervision, and removed restrictions on foreign ownership of Mexican banks.

By the late 1990s, Mexico's banking system included fifty-two commercial and foreign banks. There were also development banks, savings and loans, and credit unions. The *bancos de primer plano* or *multibancos* (first-tier commercial banks) could offer virtually any financial service, including commercial and investment banking as well as securities services.

For a long time, Citibank was the only foreign bank operating in Mexico, a country it entered in 1928, at a time when other foreign banks were withdrawing in the face of widespread hostility to foreigners and the onset of the Great Depression. In 1932 the government banned new entry by foreign banks but grandfathered Citibank and the few other remaining foreign institutions; by 1946 only Citibank remained. After World War II and until 1994, Mexico allowed new entry only via representative offices.

In 1994 Mexico opened its market to foreign banks in a series of hesitant and perhaps even grudging steps. Under NAFTA, Mexico agreed to permit North American banks to establish locally incorporated subsidiaries and then extended the opening to banks from all OECD-member countries By the mid-1990s there were twenty-eight of these affiliates, representing only 4 percent of banking system assets. No foreign bank was allowed at the time to control any Mexican bank whose book capital (at the time of acquisition) exceeded 6 percent of the banking system's total book capital. This blocked foreigners from majority ownership of Mexico's three largest banks: Banamex, Bancomer, and Serfin.

The foreign-controlled domestic banks accounted for 18 percent of total assets; together with the subsidiaries' 4 percent, foreign banks controlled 22 percent of total assets. (Foreign banks also had stakes in excess of 15 percent but less than a majority share in banks that represented 43 percent of banking system assets.) Foreign control of local banks was until recently a politically sensitive topic in Mexico.

Santander's Mexican presence dates back to 1955, when it established a representative office. The key move leading to its present status in Mexico was Santander Investment's entry in 1989. In 1994, following the establishment of NAFTA, Santander was able to create Grupo Financiero Santander Mexico. This consisted of three subsidiaries: an investment banking operation with several offices, which Santander staffed with a small team of highly trained executives; a stockbrokerage; and a fund management company. In 1997 Santander made its major push into commercial banking when it acquired 60 percent of InverMéxico, which included brokerage and insurance companies as well as Banco Mexicano with its 265 branches, 6,300 employees, and a 4.9 percent deposit market share, after it had written off Mexicano's capital and transferred its loans to Mexico's deposit guarantee fund. Santander then merged Banco Mexicano with its affiliate to create Banco Santander Mexicano. In 1997 HSBC acquired 20 percent of Banco Serfin, Mexico's third-largest bank. However, in 1999 Santander beat HSBC with a US$1.56 billion bid for the remaining shares of Banco Serfin in a government auction. At that time HSBC sold its 20 percent to Santander. The latter then merged its holdings to create Banco Santander Serfin. Banco Serfin was Mexico's oldest and third-largest bank; it traced its corporate history back to Banco de Londres y México, founded in 1864.

Unlike in Chile, other Spanish banks were faster to acquire banks in Mexico than was Santander. BBV became the first Spanish entrant in commercial banking when it took an initial 2 percent stake in Banco Mercantil Probursa in 1991 at the invitation of the Mexican investor group that had bought Probursa in the 1980s. The owners had quickly realized that they did not have the skills they needed, so they sought out assistance from BBV. After taking its stake, BBV brought in ten managers from Spain to run the bank. Then in 1995, when Mexican law was changed to permit foreigners to increase their ownership in Mexican banks, BBV raised its stake in Probursa, which in turn acquired Banca Cremi and Banco Oriente in 1996. In 2000 BBVA Probursa merged with Bancomer, which owned Mexico's second-largest bank (Banco Comercial Mexicano), to form Grupo Financiero BBVA Bancomer. The next year Bank of Montreal sold its 20 percent stake in Grupo Financiero BBVA Bancomer to BBVA. (Bank of Montreal had acquired its stake in Bancomer in 1995 but then chose not to commit further.) In 2004 BBVA spent €3.3 billion to acquire the remaining 41 percent of BBVA Bancomer that it did not already own. Next, BBVA bought Hipotecaria Nacional (Hipnal), Mexico's largest private mortgage banking institution, with a US$2.2 billion loan portfolio and about 90,000 clients, for US$375 million. Vitalino Nafria, director of American banking for BBVA, boasted that "Hipotecaria Nacional is not just the biggest but the best managed of the Mexican mortgage lenders." Mexico—Latin America's second-largest economy—now accounts for some 70 percent of BBVA's assets in Latin America.

BCH became the second Spanish entrant into Mexico when it took an 8 percent stake in Grupo Financiero Bital (Banco Internacional de México) in 1992; its affiliate Banco Comercial Português (BCP) took a similar stake. Bital had also acquired Banco Atlántico from the government. In 2002, after it had merged with BCH, Santander bought BCP's 8 percent share in Bital and built up its shareholding to 26 percent of the capital and 31 percent of the voting capital. At the time, Santander CEO Alfredo Sáenz commented, it was a "win-win situation."[17] Santander would either gain control of a major bank in a key Latin American market or, failing that, could perhaps sell its stake later for a profit, which is what indeed transpired. In August 2002 HSBC wholly acquired Bital from Santander, other shareholders, and the Berrondo family (who owned 54 percent).

Mexico is frequently presented as a case study of how foreign banks may contribute to the upgrading of the banking system. Schulz (2005) shows that foreign bank entry has had a positive though limited effect. What the foreign banks accomplished was to recapitalize the banking sector. However, he argues that the low level of competitive intensity so far has limited the transfer of skills, technology, or management know-how.

Joining Latin America's Largest Economy: Brazil

Brazil accounts for about one-third of Latin America's economy. The country enjoyed an economic miracle of sorts during the 1970s, as import-substitution policies were supplemented by a relatively successful export drive in the automotive, chemical, and metals sectors. The 1982 crisis, however, resulted in hyperinflation, instability, and recession. The adoption of the Plan Real of currency stabilization adopted by President Fernando Henrique Cardoso in 1994 has provided a solid macroeconomic and financial foundation for growth, although the economy has failed to grow enough to reduce unemployment and underemployment, and social and economic inequality remains among the worst in the world.

Unlike in Mexico and Argentina, there are strong local players in Brazil, including Banco do Brasil, Banco Bradesco, Unibanco, and Banco Itaú, which are themselves international banks, and family-owned Banco Safra. Due to Brazil's belated adoption of privatization and deregulation, the Spanish banks entered the country relatively late. Santander had had a connection with Brazil for some forty years and had built up its presence from 1982 to include several branches and offices. Still, a more serious incursion began in 1997 when Santander bought Banco Geral do Comercio. Santander followed that with another purchase in 1998 when it purchased Banco Noreste from the Cochrane Simonsen family. Next, in 2000, Santander acquired Grupo Meridional, with its two banks, Banco Meridional and investment bank Banco Bozano Simonsen. The most important acquisition to date is Banco do Estado de São Paulo (Banespa), in a privatization that took place in 2001 in Brazil's most important state. Santander paid well for the bankrupt bank, which had a market share of about 6 percent, but in 2002 was able to report that net income in Brazil rose 21 percent to just over $800 million, exceeding Santander's forecast by one-third. Similarly high profit figures were reported between 2003 and 2005. In that year Emilio Botín III would say, "We have invested $5 billion in Banespa. It was a big price but it was worth it."[18]

BBVA was less successful than Santander in its Brazilian expansion, focused as it was on Mexico. It bought Banco Excel-

Economico in 1998 for one Real but sold it five years later to Bradesco when BBVA realized that it would be too expensive to achieve a profitable scale. As part of the sale price, BBVA received a small equity stake in Bradesco, the country's third-largest bank. So far, foreign banks in general have not been as successful in Brazil (Cardim de Carvalho 2000; de Paula 2002) as elsewhere in Latin America.

Lose Some, Win One: Santander in the Caribbean

We have already mentioned Santander's unsuccessful ventures into the Dominican Republic and Cuba. Even though Cuba was the venue for Santander's first venture outside Spain and several Spanish banks currently have operations in Cuba, Santander has not returned.

When Cuba tentatively reopened to foreign banks, the first to enter was Banco Exterior de España, which established a representative office in 1995. In the same year Banco Sabadell also established a representative office in Havana, and a fifty-fifty joint venture—Financiera Iberoamericana—with Cuba's Grupo Nueva Banca. Caja Madrid, Spain's second-largest savings bank, did not enter until 1998. In addition to opening a representative office, however, it formed a majority joint venture with Cuba's state-owned Banco Popular de Ahorro to offer corporate financing services primarily to Spanish companies looking to invest on the island. Lastly, Caja de Ahorros del Mediterráneo has a representative office; this appears to be the continuation of an earlier joint office for a group of Spanish banks and an Argentine bank.

Still, the Caribbean, in the form of Puerto Rico, is today the site of one of Santander's core markets in the New World. Santander made its first acquisition in Puerto Rico in 1976 when it acquired First National Bank of Puerto Rico, which it renamed Banco Santander de Puerto Rico. Santander proceeded to grow its presence via a series of further acquisitions: Banco Crédito y Ahorro Ponceño in 1978, which brought thirteen branches in Puerto Rico and one branch in New York;[19] Bayamón Federal Savings Bank from the FDIC in 1989, with some twenty branches, which it renamed Santander National Bank; and Caguas Central Federal Savings Bank and its thirty branches from the Resolution Trust Corporation (RTC) in 1990, which turned Santander into the second-largest bank in Puerto Rico. Three years later, Santander Mortgage, a unit of Banco Santander Puerto Rico, bought Chase Manhattan Bank's US$800 million mortgage portfolio there. In 1994 Santander merged Santander National Bank into Banco Santander de Puerto Rico and two years later it bought Banco Central Hispano's subsidiary, Banco Central Hispano-Puerto Rico with its US$2.8 billion in assets and twelve branches, after BCH had sold four branches to Roig Commercial Bank and six branches to Western Federal Savings Bank.[20] BCH had bought the failing Banco Economias, then Puerto Rico's fourth-largest bank, in an emergency takeover. The merger with BCH increased Santander Puerto Rico's assets to US$6.8 billion and its branches to seventy-two and gave it some 18 percent of the Puerto Rican market. Since 2005, however, Santander's Puerto Rican operations are not doing as well as they used to, perhaps because of managerial turnover.

BBVA too built up an operation in Puerto Rico. BBV began in 1979 by buying Banco Commercial de Mayagüez, which a group of local traders and manufacturers had established in 1967. Like Santander, BBVA expanded via acquisition. In 1992 BBV bought Royal Bank of Puerto Rico, Royal Bank of Canada's Puerto Rican subsidiary, with its seventeen branches, which BBV added to the ten it already had.[21] Then in 1999 BBV bought Banco de Ponce and its twenty-eight branches. That same year BBV bought Chase Manhattan Bank's Puerto Rican operations. Currently, BBVA Puerto Rico is the third-largest bank in this U.S. commonwealth, behind Banco Popular de Puerto Rico and Banco Santander.

With an Option to Buy: Santander in the United States

It is no secret that Santander sees the United States as a market for future growth. The bank opened an agency in New York in 1977 and upgraded it to a branch the next year, when it also opened an agency in Miami. In 1979 it added to its presence in Miami by establishing an Edge Act subsidiary, Banco de Santander International.[22] Miami was of interest because of its role as a financial center for Latin America.

In 1982 Santander opened a branch in Nassau in the Bahamas to complement its operations in New York and to deal in the Eurodollar market. In 1988 it replaced this with a subsidiary, Banco Santander

Trust & Banking Corporation (Bahamas). Then in 1992 Santander complemented this with another, albeit short-lived, Bahamian subsidiary, Banco Santander Investment Bank.

Santander's first major investment in the continental United States was the purchase in 1991 of 13 percent of First Fidelity Bank in New Jersey. After a nine-month search, Santander had winnowed eighty possible targets to one, whose focus on consumer banking and services to small and medium-size enterprises was similar to Santander's own. Its location in the U.S. Mid-Atlantic region appeared to offer the most economic potential. Still, Santander chose a strategic alliance because it believed that the U.S. market was so large and so competitive that this made more sense than an acquisition.

By 1995 Santander had increased its stake in First Fidelity to 30 percent. At the same time, First Fidelity proceeded to buy several smaller banks, including Bank of Baltimore in 1994. In 1995 North Carolina's First Union Bank made a bid on First Fidelity, a merger that Emilio Botín III and Santander enthusiastically backed. The merger converted Santander's stake in First Fidelity into an 11 percent stake in First Union. When the press asked whether he would retain the stake in First Union, Emilio Botín III reportedly said, "While our initial investment, made in 1991 in First Fidelity Bancorp, was a strategic move for us, our current investment in First Union is not strategic in nature." Santander's stake had cost it about $650 million; when it sold its shares, the secondary offering in 1996 brought Santander an amount in excess of $2 billion. It then used the proceeds to amortize the goodwill of its acquisitions of banks in Argentina, Chile, Colombia, Mexico, Puerto Rico, and Venezuela.

Two of Santander's Spanish competitors did establish subsidiaries in the United States, but these were never of any importance and are now gone. In 1980 Banco Central bought United Americas Bank and renamed it Banco Central of New York. The subsidiary operated until 2001, when Santander sold it as part of its tidying up after acquiring BCH.[23] Banco Exterior created Extebank in 1980 by acquiring and combining Century National Bank and Suffolk County Bank, both also in New York State. In 1995 Banco Exterior sold Extebank's eight branches to North Fork Bancorporation of Long Island and Suffolk County, but transferred the international assets to the branch in New York City that it had just opened. Neither of these operations appears to have had any compelling logic behind it, such as tapping Hispanic populations or as an option on further growth in the United States.

Santander's most recent move in the U.S. retail banking market is a reprise of its acquisition of First Fidelity. In 2005 Santander paid US$2.4 billion to acquire a 20 percent stake in Sovereign, a Pennsylvania bank with a strong customer base between Baltimore and Boston. Two years earlier Jay Sidhu, the CEO of Sovereign, had said that he was willing to sell the bank. At the time, Royal Bank of Scotland (RBS) apparently considered the possibility but then backed off. Between 1993 and 2003, RBS made nineteen acquisitions in the United States, including Commonwealth Bancorp in Pennsylvania, through its Citizens Financial Group, based in Providence, Rhode Island, which RBS had purchased in 1988. Before its 2004 acquisition of Abbey had brought it into competition with RBS in the United Kingdom, Santander and RBS were strong allies. Forced to dismantle the alliance, Santander was now free to compete directly with RBS in retail banking on the U.S. eastern seaboard. Despite having been able, through the alliance, to monitor RBS's apparently successful strategy in the United States, Santander chose to reprise its own first and equally successful entry.

The Santander-Sovereign deal ran into shareholder opposition and required some changes in order to gain acceptance. Relational Investors, an activist hedge fund, had opposed Sidhu's acquisition of Independence Community Bank, among other measures. Sidhu used a variety of tactics to retain control, the last being the agreement with Santander. The initial agreement both diluted the existing shareholders' stake and committed Santander to supporting Sidhu. It was not enough. After extensive negotiations, Santander agreed to a series of terms that actually gave it a freer hand into the future. Sovereign used the proceeds of the sale of the equity to purchase Independence Community Bank, becoming the ninth-largest bank in the Metro New York deposit market. Sovereign now has US$83 billion in assets and is among the top 10 banks in the northeastern United States and the top 20 banks in the entire country.

As part of the deal, Santander got two seats on Sovereign's board of directors, which Emilio Botín III and Juan Rodríguez Inciarte took up. In addition, the agreement provided procedures under which Santander could in the future acquire Sovereign. If and when Santander acquires 100 percent of Sovereign, it agreed that for a period of ten years Sovereign would be its exclusive vehicle for acquisitions and growth, that Santander would contribute to Sovereign all existing businesses it might then own in the United States or its territories, and that it would maintain the corporate headquarters of Sovereign in Wyomissing, Pennsylvania, or in a mutually agreed location, for a period of five years. In 2006 Santander increased its holdings in Sovereign to 25 percent, and it will be able to acquire Sovereign wholly in 2008, should it choose to do so.

In October 2006 a boardroom uprising forced Jay Sidhu to resign. At the time Santander stated that it would not try to block the dissident board members but that it would vote with the majority. Among the complaints against Sidhu were that he had emphasized growth over profitability and that he had rebuffed offers to buy the bank. The question now is what Santander will do with its stake in Sovereign. Should Sovereign's board seek a merger with another U.S. bank, the situation could readily develop into a reprise of the First Fidelity alliance, which yielded Santander a healthy capital gain but no enduring presence in the United States.

The Hispanic Market in the United States

Currently, the U.S. Hispanic population numbers about 41 million people, or 14 percent of the total U.S. population, even without the inclusion of an estimated 8 million immigrants without papers. The Hispanic population's average household income, while 20 percent lower than the national average, is growing fast. If U.S. Hispanics had their own separate country, that country would rank as one of the world's ten largest economies. Hispanics are a rather heterogeneous group with diverse ethnic and national origins, and very different occupational and educational backgrounds. From the point of view of a bank, this segment is interesting for two reasons. First, many Hispanic subgroups are underbanked: in some of these groups no more than half the population has a checking account and just about 10 percent has a credit bureau rating. Second, they participate disproportionately in the US$15–17 billion annual market for remittances, which has very high margins.

The Hispanic market had been only minimally attractive to the Spanish banks. Despite their operations in Puerto Rico, neither Santander nor BBVA tried to build links to the Puerto Rican population in New York, for instance. This was probably due in part to the dominant position in this market of Puerto Rico's largest bank, Banco

Popular de Puerto Rico. Banco de Ponce and Popular, then Puerto Rico's two largest banks, had both had branches in New York since 1961. The two merged in 1990 to form the largest bank in Puerto Rico. Popular now is the largest Hispanic bank in the United States, as it has acquired banks and branches where Hispanics, including those not of Puerto Rican origin, live. By 1991 Popular had operations in the primary states with Hispanic populations: New York, Illinois, California, New Jersey, Florida, and Texas.

No Latin American banks tried to tap the Hispanic market either. After 1982, during the decade or so in which the Mexican banks were nationalized, the Mexican banks focused on the domestic market. Although Banamex acquired California Commerce Bank in 1981, it made no major effort to reach out to California's population of Mexican origin. Similarly, in 1982 Bancomer purchased Grossmont Bank in California but took only two seats on the board of directors. Grossmont made some further acquisitions but never targeted the Hispanic market; in 1997 Bancomer sold Grossmont to Zions Bancorp, a Utah-based bank.

Still, in recent years the Hispanic market in the United States has become a matter of interest for Santander and BBVA, although they have followed quite different strategies. Santander has used an alliance, whereas BBVA has built up a U.S. subsidiary.

Santander is taping the Hispanic (Mexican) market indirectly, through an alliance between its Mexican subsidiary, Santander Serfin, and Bank of America. In 2003 Santander sold 25 percent of Santander Serfin to Bank of America.[24] Bank of America already had a large Hispanic customer base and was willing to pay dearly because it wanted to compete with Citigroup, which owns Banamex, the largest bank in Mexico. In the United States, Bank of America has some 16 million Mexican clients (40 percent of the total Hispanic population). In discussing the deal at the time of its announcement, Emilio Botín III said, "We see this as a superb opportunity to better serve our customers in Mexico as well as Bank of America's vast client coverage in key states across the border." The alliance strategy is congruent with Santander's historic caution toward actually owning a subsidiary in the United States.

By contrast, BBVA is building its position in the Hispanic market around subsidiaries. In Mexico it controls Bancomer, and in the United States it acquired small banks in California and Texas in 2004: Valley Bank of California (now BBVA Bancomer USA) and

Laredo National Bancshares in Texas. In 2006 BBVA bought two more Texas banks, Texas Regional Bancshares and State National Bancshares. Francisco González, president of BBVA, termed the acquisitions a "decisive step" in its expansion into the United States, which is an integral part of the bank's global strategy. The acquisitions in Texas, the second most populous U.S. state, and growing at twice the U.S. average, tripled BBVA's presence there to US$12.6 billion in assets, US$10.1 billion in deposits, and 166 branches. In 2007 BBVA paid US$9.6 billion to wholly acquire Compass Bankshares, the parent holding company of Compass Bank, which is based in Birmingham, Alabama, and has US$34 billion in assets and 417 branches in Alabama, Arizona, Colorado, Florida, New Mexico, and Texas. This acquisition is BBVA's largest in its history. BBVA plans to merge its U.S. banking subsidiaries with Compass, and when the acquisition is complete, BBVA will have US$47 billion in assets and 622 branches in the United States. BBVA USA also includes BBVA Puerto Rico and Bancomer Transfer Services, which provides fund transfer services between the United States and other countries, particularly Mexico, where it accounts for about 45 percent of the estimated US$15–17 billion remittance market between the United States and Mexico.

As Walter (2004, 56) points out, Santander and BBVA do not, however, have the Mexico-U.S. cross-border banking market to themselves; HSBC and Citibank are as well positioned. HSBC owns not only Bital but also HSBC USA, the largest foreign bank in the United States. Citibank, for its part, owns both Banamex and Citibank West in California. The competition between the four, together with the presence in the remittance market of nonbank remittance providers such as Western Union, may quickly erode the market's profitability.

Entering the Consumer Finance Market

In late 2006 Santander announced that it would pay $465 million to buy 64.5 percent of the shares of Texas-based Drive Financial Services from HBOS (Halifax Bank of Scotland; Bank of Scotland had merged with Halifax Building Society in 2001). Drive Financial specializes in buying auto loans that auto dealerships offer to subprime (i.e., high-risk) buyers. The company operates in thirty-five states, but currently half its business comes from Texas, California, Florida, and Georgia. Drive Financial's management owns the rest of the company and has agreed to sell another 25.5 percent to Santander for about $200 million, which brings Santander's ownership to 90 percent. Santander also has an option to buy the remaining 10 percent of the shares between 2009 and 2013. In purchasing Drive Financial, Santander is extending the reach of its consumer finance division (which has a strong presence throughout Europe; see chapter 7) to the United States.

Was Latin America Worth It?

To provide a basis for considering whether Santander's entry into Latin America was worthwhile, we must first address why banks go abroad. Furthermore, in assessing a strategy one must be careful to separate ex ante and ex post assessments. A good strategy may have an unfortunate outcome and a poor strategy may have a fortunate outcome. The initial discussion of why banks go abroad addresses the reasonableness of the Santander's strategy and the subsequent discussion evaluates the outcome.

Banking is a mature industry, albeit to different degrees depending on the country. All the countries Santander entered in its push into Latin America have well-established banking sectors with many indigenous banks. The question then is, why did Santander go where it did? The answer has to do with the characteristics of the banks and of the banking markets.

In his pioneering article on foreign direct investment in banking, Grubel (1977) distinguished three markets: the wholesale, the corporate, and the retail. Banks seeking to operate in the wholesale foreign exchange and money markets necessarily must have a presence in the major world financial centers such as London, New York, Tokyo, and Hong Kong (Tschoegl 2000); with a branch in each of the first three, the parent bank can span 22.5 hours of the 24-hour day and have a presence in the financial centers of the three most important economic areas in the world. Banks seeking to serve corporate clients—domestic customers moving abroad or host country firms either seeking or willing to deal with foreign banks—necessarily also locate in regional financial centers such as Miami or Panama, or national financial centers such as Buenos Aires, Miami, Santiago, or São Paulo. Until recently, foreign banks have generally avoided the retail market abroad. Where retail banking is well developed and competitive, there is no reason to expect foreign banks in general to be better than local banks (Tschoegl 1987).

Foreign banks are like fast-growing, opportunistic plants that respond to the upturned, fertile soil that liberalization, crises, or economic transitions create. The foreign banks that respond to these opportunities are often willing to enter retail banking as well as traditional international banking, and they can respond quickly because they are well capitalized, efficient, and have surplus managerial resources (Kindleberger 1969; Tschoegl 2004b). Even in mature markets, foreign banks tend to enter in the aftermath of financial crises (Tschoegl 2002a, 2002b, 2005) Papp (2005) too has documented the increased presence of foreign banks after a financial crisis. The reason foreign banks enter these newly opened markets has to do with the opportunities the situations present, now that the banks are free to enter. One source of opportunity can be the foreign banks' efficiency relative to that of the domestic banks. In the Czech Republic and Poland, foreign-owned banks were more efficient than domestic-owned banks, and this was not due to scale differences or the structure of activities (Weill 2003). Dopico and Wilcox (2002) found that foreign banks are more pervasive in countries where banking is more profitable, such as in a previously closed market, and where the banking sector is smaller relative to GDP, as in many developing countries such as Mexico (Lopez-de-Silanes and Zamarripa 1995). Similarly, Demirgüç-Kunt and Huizinga (1999) and Claessens et al. (2001) found that foreign banks tend to have higher margins and profits than domestic banks in developing countries. Similarly, Dopico and Wilcox (2002) showed that foreign banks have a greater market share in underbanked countries, that is, markets in which a relatively small percentage of the population is a bank customer.

Another factor that can help one understand banks' foreign direct investment in particular cases is strategic interaction between firms. This approach has its origins in the literature on oligopolistic reaction or "follow-the-leader" behavior (Flowers 1976; [1960] 1976; Knickerbocker 1973). The broader phenomenon, of which oligopolistic reaction is simply one outcome, is that a firm's strategy of foreign direct investment depends not only on its own capabilities but also on the behavior of its chief competitors. Oligopolistic reaction has historically characterized the international expansion of banks from such countries as Germany, Scandinavia (Boldt-Christmas et al. 2000; Engwall and Wallenstäl 1988; Jacobsen and Tschoegl 1999), Singapore (Tschoegl 2002b), and Spain (Guillén and Tschoegl 2000), and surely others as well.

Santander's initial foray into Latin America had to do with classic international banking: representative offices and branches in places of interest to its home country customers, plus the occasional opportunistic acquisition of a small retail bank. It was only decades later that the bank began more systematically to acquire subsidiaries and equity stakes throughout the region, only to scale back dramatically during the Lost Decade of the 1980s. Santander's big thrust in the 1990s broke with both traditional international banking and its earlier approach. Instead, Santander committed itself to acquiring full ownership of large domestic banks throughout Latin America. This new strategy reflected a fortuitous timing: Santander had emerged as a lean, efficient survivor of the restructuring of the Spanish banking market (Maudos et al. 1997) at the same time as Latin America emerged from its Lost Decade. Santander was willing to take on the risk because of its long familiarity with the region, plus its recent involvement with government debt via the activities of Santander Investment. Santander's second thrust into Latin America beginning in the mid-1990s triggered the predictable reaction from the other large Spanish banks, which followed suit. The pattern of oligopolistic reaction is visible in table 5.2, which summarizes Santander's, BBVA's, and BCH's rush to acquire subsidiaries in Latin America between 1990 and 2005. Moreover, table 5.3 shows that the Spanish banks were not alone in seeing an opportunity in Latin America and attempting to seize it.

Santander internal documents, investor-relations presentations, press releases, and annual reports highlight Latin America's attractions: "a region with high growth potential," "two familiar languages, Spanish and Portuguese," "a natural market for Spanish companies and banks," "a set of markets under deregulation," and "an underbanked market." BBVA executives have over the years echoed these assessments. In our interviews and conversations with executives of the bank and its competitors, these themes came up time and again. Still, our argument is not that these explanations are erroneous or misleading but that growth has been—and continues to be—Santander's primary goal, in part driven by European and domestic events. In this context, Latin America was

TABLE 5.2
Acquisitions of Banks in Latin America by Spanish Banks, 1990–2005

Country	Acquirer	Bank Acquired	% Stake[a]	Acquisition Date
Argentina	Santander	Banco Río de la Plata	35	1997
	BBV	Banco de Crédito Argentino	100	1997
		Banco Francés del Río de la Plata	52	1996
		Corp Banca	100	1999
	OHCH[b]	Banco Tornquist	100	1996
Bolivia	OHCH	Banco Santa Cruz	100[c]	1998
Brazil	Santander	Banco Noroeste	80	1997
		Banco Geral do Comercio	50	1997
		Grupo Meridional	97	2000
		Banespa	76	2001
	BBV	Banco Excel Economico	55[c]	1998
Chile	Santander	Banco Osorno y La Unión	51	1996
	BBV	Banco Hipotecario de Fomento (BHIF)	55	1998
	OHCH	Banco Santiago	43	1995
Colombia	Santander	Banco Comercial Antioqueño	55	1997
	BBV	Banco Ganadero	59	1996
		Banco Nacional de Commercio	54	1998
Mexico	Santander	Grupo Financiero InverMéxico	61	1997
		Banco Serfin	80	1999
	BBV	Banco Oriente & Banco Cremi	100	1996
		Probursa	70	1991–96
	BBVA	Banco Comercial Mexicano	30	2000
		Hipotecaria Nacional	100	2004

(continued)

TABLE 5.2 (continued)

Country	Acquirer	Bank Acquired	% Stake[a]	Acquisition Date
	BCH	GFBital	8[c]	1992
Paraguay	OHCH	Banco Asunción	78[c]	
Peru	Santander	Banco Interandino & Intervalores	100[c]	1995
		Banco Mercantil	100[c]	1995
	BBV	Banco Continental	60	1996
	OHCH	Banco del Sur	49[c]	1995
Venezuela	Santander	Banco de Venezuela	93	1996
	BBV	Banco Provincial	40	1996

[a]Initial stake.
[b]OHCH was a h olding company jointly owned by Banco Central Hispano (BCH) and the Luksic family through its holding in Banco O'Higgins.
[c]Since sold.

a convenient opportunity that presented itself at the right moment. Santander needed and wanted to grow, and at the time other parts of the world were less attractive relative to the opportunities in Latin America: the United States and Europe were too competitive and expensive, the Spanish banks had little comparative advantage in the transition economies of Eastern Europe relative to the Austrian and other banks focusing on that region, and Asia was too far away and too different.

Despite difficulties in some countries, especially Argentina, both Santander and BBVA, continue to maintain extensive operations in Latin America, and HSBC and Citibank are also continuing to expand. Santander did learn two key lessons from its problems in Argentina and some of the other countries. The first was the need to manage country risk, in great part by reducing the vulnerability of the bank's profits to events in any one country. The second lesson was that the bank did not need to be everywhere in Latin America but instead could and should focus on Latin America's larger, more promising markets.

Santander has gone through several phases of reorganizing its presence in Latin America. In a first stage, it dealt with the investments inherited from Banesto and BCH through local mergers or disposals. It then decided to focus its efforts on some key markets

TABLE 5.3
Some Major Acquisitions of Banks in Latin America by Foreign
(non-Spanish) Banks, 1990–2005

Country	Acquirer	Bank Acquired	% Stake[a]	Acquisition Date
Argentina	HSBC	Banco Roberts	70	1997
	Bank of Nova Scotia	Banco Quilmes	25	1995
	Citibank	Banco Mayo Cooperativo	100	1998
Brazil	HSBC	Bamerindus	100	1997
	ABN AMRO	Banco Real	100	1998
		Bandepe	100	1998
		Paraiban	100	2001
		Banco Sudameris	95	2003
Chile	HSBC	Banco O'Higgins	10	1993
Colombia	Standard Chartered	Banco Extebandes	>50	1998
Mexico	HSBC	Banco Serfin	20	1997
	Bank of Nova Scotia	GFInverlat	55	1992
	Bank of Montréal	GFBancomer	16	1996
	Citibank	Confia	100	1997
	Citibank	Banco Nacional de México	100	2001
	Banco Comercial Português	Bital	8	1992
	HSBC	Bital	100	2002
Peru	HSBC	Banco Sur	10	1997
	Bank of Nova Scotia	Sudamericano	25	1997
	Standard Chartered	Banco extebandes	>50	1998

[a] Initial stake.

and to leave others. It has identified Argentina, Brazil, Chile, Mexico, and Puerto Rico as core countries, while still evaluating three other markets, Colombia, Uruguay, and Venezuela. Now the task has moved to cross-border coordination of image and brands, and unification of back-office systems to bring about cost savings. These are the traditional management challenges of "doing the right thing" and "doing the thing right."

Expanding in Latin America was but the first step that Santander took in its quest to become one of the world's top ten financial institutions. Executives at both Santander and BBVA made it clear to us that, subject to some constraints of profitability and shareholder returns, growth was their *main* consideration. This the Latin American acquisitions achieved. That growth in turn thrust Santander into the league of major international banks. Santander (and also BBVA) now competes head-on in retail banking with such banks as Citibank and HSBC in many places throughout Latin America, where before they met only tangentially in a number of national and international financial centers. Its growth has also reduced Santander's vulnerability to takeover bids and positioned it for its subsequent European expansion.

Since the mid-1990s, Santander has paid $12.3 billion for twenty-seven banks in nine different Latin American countries. BBVA spent $7.8 billion to complete thirty-four major acquisitions in the region. Santander is the largest bank in the region, and BBVA the second-largest, although it leads in pension fund management and project finance. Santander executives emphasize that their Latin American retail operations are profitable, which they are, albeit to different degrees. In interviews, however, the executives also recognized that each completed acquisition became the stepping-stone for the next purchase; each iteration enabled Santander to target ever bigger banks in the next round.

In 2006 both *Euromoney* and *Global Finance* voted Santander the "Best Bank in Latin America." Latin America (including Puerto Rico) accounted for 4,368 of Santander's worldwide total of 10,852 branches (40 percent) and 66,889 of its 129,196 employees (52 percent). Santander attributed 35 percent of its €6.6 billion group attributable profits to Latin America, compared to 11 percent for Latin America and 33 percent for Mexico at BBVA. The difference in the relative importance of Latin America to attributable profits at the two banks has occurred primarily because Santander has been more aggressive than its rival in its European expansion, the subject of the next two chapters.

6

Alliances and Their Limits

> The Royal Bank [of Scotland] alliance has worked like a charm, perhaps because we are both northerners.
>
> —Emilio Botín III, in *Euromoney*, January 1995

If Santander disposed of most of its stakes in industrial firms while enjoying large capital gains in the process, its policy during the 1980s and 1990s of signing alliances with other European banks, which in some cases involved equity cross-shareholdings, has also resulted in substantial financial payoffs. The banking and financial services alliances we discuss in this chapter differ from the industrial stakes that we discussed in chapter 3 in that banking alliances are with firms in related businesses and so offer opportunities for learning, cost reduction, and future options; because industrial alliances are alliances with firms in unrelated businesses, they cannot offer these benefits. While industrial and banking alliances can both afford the strategic benefit of mutual support, banking alliances also offer the strategic benefit of mutual nonaggression pacts, a frequent feature when mergers are not possible in law or in fact or are simply not practical for the limited purposes the partners are trying to achieve.

Santander entered into numerous banking and financial services alliances, all of which contributed something, perhaps an option to acquire or at least an opportunity to learn (even if the lesson was that the direction was a dead end). More importantly, one extremely successful alliance, that with Royal Bank of Scotland

(RBS), gave Santander the knowledge of the British market, which prepared the ground for the eventual acquisition of Abbey National, a deal that (amicably) ended an alliance that both partners valued.

A Reluctance to Join Banking Clubs

Starting in the mid-1960s, many of the large banks, especially in Europe, participated for a while in banking clubs, and a few clubs still exist. The clubs generally had as members no more than one bank from any country and were initially a response to the then forthcoming formation of the European Free Trade Area and the aggressive entry of U.S. banks in Europe. Many internationally inexperienced European banks sought to work together because they were not ready to establish their own international network of branches, especially as that would entail establishing operations in each other's countries. Cross-border mergers were also not an option. The solution, which Ross (1998, 2002) has correctly characterized as a flawed strategy, seemed to be to form clubs that were more than alliances but less than full mergers. Because the clubs were also mutual nonaggression pacts, they had some effect in moderating bank interpenetration in each other's markets (Choi, Park, and Tschoegl 1996, 2003; Choi, Tschoegl, and Yu 1986). In time, the clubs became much less ambitious in response to the pressure of conflicts of interest and competition, and now most are gone or are simply loose associations of banks.

Similarly, the leading banks from the Nordic countries entered into two to three cross-border alliances during the period from the late 1960s to the early 1990s (Jacobsen and Tschoegl 1999). The Nordic alliances were stable as long as prohibitions on the entry of foreign banks prevented members from defecting by invading each other's home markets, but they crumbled when these barriers fell.

The Spanish banks were not major participants in alliances because until the mid-1980s they had little to fear from foreign bank entry. Banco Hispano Americano, however, was a member of Europartners, one of the most tightly knit of the clubs. In 1970 Commerzbank and Crédit Lyonnais established an alliance. Banco di Roma joined in 1971, and the club took on the Europartners name in 1972, with Hispano Americano joining the following year.

The basic goal was to form what today one might call a virtual corporation in which the four parties would present a common front to the world while maintaining separate legal identities. The partners established a jointly owned subsidiary in the Netherlands and a securities firm; Commerzbank took over the former in 1984 and the latter in 1988. Also in 1988 Commerzbank took a 10 percent share in Hispano Americano. In 1990 Crédit Lyonnais offered to buy 20 percent of Hispano Americano, an offer the bank rejected because it feared that the French bank wanted control rather than an alliance. Later that year the members disbanded the club. The alliance between Commerz and Hispano Americano persisted though, and in 1991 they established a joint-venture bank in Gibraltar to conduct private banking.

Two surviving examples of clubs are the Mediterranean Bank Network and the InterAlpha Group. Four Euro-Mediterranean Banks—Bank of Valletta (Malta), Türkiye Garanti Bankası (Turkey), Nova Ljubljanska Banka (Slovenia), and Banque Internationale Arab de Tunisie (Tunisia)—established the Mediterranean Bank Network late in 1996. Now its members represent eleven Mediterranean countries out of a possible twenty-one, and some banks from locations outside the Euro-Mediterranean area are affiliates. The other members of the network are Israel Discount Bank (Israel, 1997), Banco Sabadell (Spain, 1997), Bank of Jordan (Jordan, 2000), Zagrebacka Banca (Croatia, 2001), Banco Popolare di Verona e Novara (Italy, 2003), Commercial International Bank (Egypt, 2004), and Hellenic Bank (Cyprus, 2004). All the member banks are relatively small and pose no threat to one another. The club is open to having more than one bank from each country, provided it is not in direct competition with an existing member, which in any case has a veto. The club maintains technical subcommittees that address matters related to banking activities, business development and opportunities, economic information and data exchange, and benchmarking.

Since 1998 Santander has been a member of the InterAlpha Group of banks. Founded in 1971, the group now comprises one bank from each of thirteen countries.[1] The group's early aspirations included the possibility that ultimately the banks would merge. Now the group represents simply a loose agreement to exchange information. The Permanent Coordinating Committee, which consists of executives from the banks' international divisions, meets several times a year. Because cooperation to bring about technological improvements and cost savings is among its members' objectives, ad hoc specialist committees that address specific issues meet more sporadically. Another objective is education, which has given rise to the establishment of the InterAlpha Banking School and the InterAlpha/INSEAD Banking Management Programme. On occasion, InterAlpha's member banks take a common position on issues that affect European banking in order to lobby the European Union (EU). At various times, the group has set up joint representative offices in the United States, Latin America, Tokyo, Hong Kong, Singapore, Tehran, and Moscow. Today, only the last two survive; in the other markets, member banks were able to generate sufficient business to establish their own operations. From 1986 to 1998, BBV was the Spanish member of the group; when BBV resigned in 1998, Santander replaced it.

Working with Bank of America

In 1965 Santander and Bank of America founded two fifty-fifty joint-venture banks in Spain: Banco Intercontinental Español (Bankinter) and Banco Comercial para América (BCPA). Bankinter, originally conceived of as an industrial bank, listed on the Madrid Stock Exchange in 1972 and became a commercial bank focusing on upper-middle-class customers and operating independently of its owners. Santander paid for its share of the joint ventures by contributing Banco Soler y Torra, which it had acquired in 1956, and which operated in Catalonia. In 1979 Bank of America bought out Banco Santander's stake in BCPA and renamed it Bank of America–España. When the two banks established BCPA, Bank of America had retained an option to take full control if and when the Banco de España would give permission to foreign banks to enter, which it did that year. By 1984 Bank of America's ownership in Bankinter was down to 22 percent; shortly thereafter, Bank of America withdrew completely, while Santander permitted its stake to shrink further, though it still retained a seat on the board of directors. In 2004, two years or so after his brother had resigned from the presidency of Bankinter, Emilio Botín III too resigned from the board. Board members currently include Alfonso Botín–Sanz de Sautola y Naveda, representing Cartival S.A., and his brother Marcelino Botín–Sanz de Sautola y Naveda. Cartival, the largest shareholder in Bankinter, which has recently built up its stake to more than 16 percent, is Jaime Botín's investment company.

Although Santander and Bank of America never concluded a formal alliance, they remained in contact. When Bank of America wanted to sell its some of its operations in Germany in 1987, it was Santander that bought them. Then in 2003 Santander sold 25 percent of Santander Serfin to Bank of America, which enabled both banks to tap the market for remittances to Mexico by the Hispanic population in the United States. That same year, Santander bought Bank of America's Polish banking license. In 2006 Bank of America transferred its relationships with 6,000 high-net-worth customers in Latin America to Santander Private Banking.

Trying to Gain a Foothold in Italy

Compared to other countries, Italy has been relatively closed to entry by foreign banks. What complicates the situation is that the Italian government or charitable trusts own most of the large banks. Although Santander was interested in pursuing a Mediterranean strategy, the problem of establishing a presence in Italy was not trivial. At the same time, Santander sought to disencumber itself of some banks in Spain that it had acquired in the past but did not want to merge into Santander itself. One of these was the Catalan bank, Banca Jover, which Santander had acquired in 1978.

In 1988 Santander approached Cassa di Risparmio delle Provincie Lombarde (Cariplo) with a proposal to buy a 30 percent stake in Cariplo's subsidiary, Istituto Bancario Italiano (IBI). After lengthy negotiations, the final agreement was reached in 1990: in a share swap, Santander would get its desired stake, and Cariplo would acquire 30 percent of Banca Jover, pay 2.5 billion pesetas (€15 million), and also take a 1.25 percent stake in Santander. The deal had to get approval from both central banks, which was forthcoming. Shortly thereafter, Santander lost interest in developing the alliance. It bought back 0.5 percentage points of the shares it had sold Cariplo in order to transfer them to Nomura Securities, with whom it was establishing an alliance, too. It then offered Cariplo another 65 percent of Banca Jover, but the two parents could not agree on a valuation. Santander then offered Banca Jover to Crédit Lyonnais, which agreed to buy the entire bank. Santander and Cariplo reversed their share swap, and Santander bought back its shares still in Cariplo's hands.[2]

Testing Unfamiliar Waters

Alliances are often a way to learn about new areas. For Santander, this motivation caused it to ally at various times with Metropolitan Life, a U.S. insurance company; Kemper, a fund management company; and Nomura Securities. Part of Santander's strategy was to prepare itself for the single European market and the advent of a common banking market in 1993.

Metropolitan Life: Bancassurance

One of the coming developments in European financial markets was bancassurance, the combining of banking with insurance, which would allow banks to sell consumers life, auto, and other insurance products. To explore the possibilities, Santander established an alliance with Metropolitan Life (MetLife), an American insurance company, in 1987. MetLife took about a 0.5 percent stake in Santander and received one seat on the board of directors. Because MetLife was a mutual insurance company, that is, its policy holders owned the company, Santander could not acquire any shares in it.

The first manifestation of the alliance was a joint venture that the two partners established in Spain to offer an array of insurance and pension products. The new company, which took the name Genesis, started operating in 1989 after MetLife had trained some 3,000 Santander staff to sell its products through the bank's branch network. Subsequently, the two set up several other Genesis companies in Mexico and Portugal. In 1993 Santander and MetLife took a 49 percent stake in a pension fund management company in Argentina. Banco de la Provincia de Buenos Aires, controlled by the provincial government, held the other 51 percent. In 1994 MetLife also took a small position (about 0.5 percent) in Banesto (as did First Union and Royal Bank of Scotland). Apparently the three Santander allies bought the Banesto shares at prices ranging between 762 and 850 pesetas per share and saw their shares nearly double in value under Santander's ownership. In 1998 MetLife took a short-lived 25 percent stake in Santander Global Investors, Santander's asset management arm.

In 2000 MetLife demutualized, conducting an initial public offering. In a separate, private transaction, Santander bought a 3.9 percent stake in MetLife, as did Credit Suisse. What was perhaps more critical for the alliance was that the merger between Santander and BCH had caused a conflict of alliances. BCH had an alliance with Italy's Assicurazioni Generali, which took the form of 51 percent stakes in BCH subsidiaries BCH Vida, BCH Pensiones, and BCH Seguros Generales. The solution was the creation of a new holding company in which Santander held 60 percent, and Generali and MetLife each held 20 percent. Santander and MetLife contributed the entire Seguros Genesis bancassurance portfolio that was sold through Banco Santander's branches. Generali contributed a reduction in its share in the three joint ventures with BCH. Generali also took about a 1 percent stake in Santander and dispatched a director to the board. All Seguros Genesis's other businesses sold through multiple distribution channels would remain part of Seguros Genesis, with Metropolitan Life holding 80 percent of Seguros Genesis, and Banco Santander reducing its equity ownership to 20 percent. Banco Santander also absorbed the portfolio of Seguros Genesis's branch in Portugal. At the time, it was ranked among the top three life insurance companies in Spain with gross written premiums of more than $1 billion.

Shortly thereafter Santander and MetLife effectively parted company. Around 2001 MetLife sold its shares in Santander and Santander its shares in MetLife. MetLife gave up its seat on Santander's board of directors, though a MetLife executive continued to serve on Santander's international advisory board. That same year Santander sold to MetLife 100 percent of its Chilean insurance affiliates Compañía de Seguros de Vida Santander and Compañía de Reaseguros de Vida Soince-Re. Santander Chile wished to sell the two units because it could sell insurance directly through the bank and did not need a separate insurance subsidiary. Santander reportedly made a capital gain of $173 million on the sale. In 2003 MetLife announced that it was selling its Spanish operation, MetLife Iberia, together with its subsidiaries Seguros Genesis S.A. and Genesis Seguros Generales to Liberty Mutual Insurance, another U.S. insurance company.

Kemper: Fund Management in the United States

In 1989 Kemper Financial Companies and Santander signed "an agreement of general cooperation." The two firms announced that they would work together to develop financial services in Spain, the United States, Europe, and Latin America. Santander also took about a 3 percent stake in Kemper Corporation, the parent of Kemper Financial Companies, making it one of the largest single shareholders in Kemper; it also received four seats on the board of directors. In 1994 Santander supported Kemper management in the face of a hostile takeover bid from GE Capital. Conseco, an Indiana-based life-and-health group, made a more generous bid that then failed when Conseco could not raise the requisite funding. In 1995 Zurich Insurance Group acquired Kemper for about $51 per share, substantially less than GE Capital's initial $55 offer, and Conseco's failed $67 offer. That ended the alliance with Santander.

Nomura Securities: Ephemeral Cherry Blossoms

In the late 1980s Japan's stock market and economy were booming. Santander opened a representative office in Tokyo in 1987, which it upgraded to a branch the next year. It also decided to pursue a listing on the Tokyo Stock Exchange, which brought it into contact with Nomura Securities. In 1989 Nomura and Santander agreed on an alliance that would act as a bridge between Spain and Japan. Nomura sought to sell Japanese securities in Spain and Spanish mutual funds and securities in Japan. Nomura International, the London-based arm of Nomura Securities, took a 1 percent stake in Santander and a 10 percent stake (in the form of convertible bonds) in Banco Santander de Negocios (BSN). Nomura International also dispatched a director to BSN and some employees, and Nomura International (HK) took a 0.5 percent stake in Santander. Nomura paid ¥13.2 billion for the shares and convertible bonds. Santander provided its own shares by unwinding its alliance with IBI. In December 1989 the Tokyo stock market peaked and began a long slide, and by the early 1990s the Japanese economy essentially stopped growing for more than a decade. It is not clear if and when the partners formally terminated their alliance.

Back to Banking: Alliance Rather Than Merger

From the late 1980s on, both Santander and BBVA pursued a strategy of acquiring small stakes in several European banks. Santander allied with San Paolo IMI, Commerzbank (Commerz), Société Générale (SoGen), and Royal Bank of Scotland (RBS). Push-and-pull considerations motivated the alliances. The push factor was a concern about hostile takeovers from abroad. The pull factor was the desire to benefit from the move toward an open EU-wide banking market. Still, the push factors were probably more salient in the general thinking

In 1989 Deutsche Bank bought Banco Comercial Trans-atlántico in Spain. Some three years earlier Deutsche had acquired Bank of America's subsidiary, Banca d'America e d'Italia, which A. P. Giannini, the founder of Bank of America, had established in Italy in 1922 by taking over Banca dell'Italia Meridionale. More threat-eningly, in 1988 Carlo de Benedetti had tried but failed to acquire Belgium's largest holding company, Société Générale de Belgique. Had he succeeded in his six-month battle, he would also have ac-quired 12 percent of Générale Bank, Belgium's largest commercial bank. To derail the takeover, Générale established an alliance with the Netherlands's AMRO Bank, with each bank taking a 10 percent stake in the other, plus warrants on bonds that would permit each to acquire up to 25 percent. Thus the two banks were cooperating in a mutual defense pact.

The perceived need for allies led many banks, Santander included, into alliances that aimed at preserving the partners' autonomy. At the same time, Emilio Botín III, among others, was not enamored of the idea of cross-border mergers of equals. Combinations were difficult enough within a country, let alone across countries where one would face the hurdles of the absence of any EU-wide regulations or harmonization of taxation. Hence, in a meeting with reporters in 2000 to discuss the alliance with SoGen, Botín said, "Speaking frankly, cross-border mergers of equals is a cock-and-bull story as far as European banking is concerned."[3]

For Santander, the strategy led to a set of essentially pairwise cross-border alliances, which in turn led to a number of relatively small, technical joint efforts. Thus, in 2000 the five partners (Santander, RBS, Société Générale, San Paolo IMI, and Commerzbank) announced a plan to launch an e-marketplace for treasury and capital markets products. Although Santander had some hopes of creating a broader alliance much like a banking club, this never developed. Part of the problem was conflicting alliances. One legacy of the Euro-partners club was that Commerzbank was also a core shareholder with a 4 percent stake in SoGen's rival Crédit Lyonnais. At the same time, San Paolo was a shareholder in SoGen's other rival in France, BNP Paribas. For these and other reasons, the alliance with RBS proved to be the most successful, by far, of all of Santander's alliances.

Royal Bank of Scotland: Two Northerners, Seeing Eye to Eye

Santander's alliance with Royal Bank of Scotland began in part as an anti-takeover measure. RBS had been the target of a failed bid by HSBC in 1981, and Santander was concerned about developments in Spain because of the still-wide margins in banking there that might draw European predators after the 1993 arrival of a single banking market. Initially, in 1988, each of the two banks exchanged shares and board seats. Emilio Botín III and Juan Rodríguez Inciarte joined RBS's board, and RBS's chairman, Lord Younger, and CEO, George Mathewson, joined Santander's board. RBS acquired 1.4 percent of Santander, which it raised to 2.5 percent. Santander bought some 9.9 percent of RBS, much of it from the Kuwait Investments Office. (Because RBS had just bought Citizens Bank in the United States, under the American Bank Holding Company Act Santander could not have acquired more than 10 percent without the approval of the U.S. Federal Reserve, even if RBS had been willing to grant Santander a larger stake.) One of the first fruits of the alliance came that same year, when the banks established Royal Bank of Scotland (Gibraltar) as a joint venture. The alliance also had RBS stationing bankers in some 50 Santander branches in Spain to serve both U.K. tourists and businesspeople in Spain.

In the technology area, Santander and RBS collaborated in the creation of IBOS (Interbank On-Line System), a cross-border payment system that enabled clients to effect real-time transfers of funds between accounts at the partner banks by using terminals at the banks' branches. Crédit Commercial de France joined in 1990, as did Banco de Comercio e Indústria (BCI), which Santander owned (together with RBS; see chapter 7). Two other banks joined IBOS, First Fidelity in 1994 and Belgium's Kredietbank; however, the system's charter limited membership to one bank per country. Santander and RBS joined with EDS (Electronic Data Systems; 32 percent) of Texas, together with Goldman Sachs (5 percent) to form an IBOS operating company. Although IBOS tried to expand its remits to include cash management for corporate treasuries, the system never developed the number of transactions its founders had hoped for. Still, in 1995 Denmark's Unibank, Italy's Instituto Bancario San Paolo di Torino, and the Netherlands' ING also joined the system. Chase Manhattan not only joined but paid a substantial sum to acquire 24 percent of the operating company, a share coequal to that of Santander, RBS, and EDS. Chase brought with it its correspondent banking network, the world's largest. At the same time, Santander started to distance itself from IBOS, which had also became less ambitious in its aims. In 1998 EDS and Chase withdrew from the system, and the operating company, through First Chicago NBD and Bank of Nova Scotia, together with its Mexican subsidiary Banco Inverlat, joined the system. Fuji Bank and Bank of Ireland followed in 1999.

Santander and RBS proceeded to work together in a number of ways in addition to technology. Senior executives from the two banks would meet every six weeks to discuss strategy and the banks would come to cooperate on corporate finance deals in Europe. The banks also formed other joint ventures, in particular in Germany and Belgium. Then when Santander made its takeover bid for BCI in Portugal, it did so with RBS's and MetLife's approval. (The two owned 14.9 percent and 3.6 percent respectively of BCI.) Then in 1994 Santander acquired Banesto. RBS supported the bid by buying 2 percent of Banesto's shares from Santander, and in 1997 it sold this stake back to Santander for £75 million, for a pretax capital gain of £30 million.

After Santander merged with BCH, it left the alliance with Banco Comercial Português that it had inherited from BCH. BCP therefore disposed of its 2.7 percent holding in Santander. RBS bought enough of the shares to raise its stake to roughly the same level as it was before the Santander merger with BCH, which had diluted RBS's holdings from 3.4 percent to 2.3 percent.

In 1999 RBS made a bid for National Westminster Bank (NatWest). RBS's bid was a "white knight" counteroffer to a hostile takeover bid from RBS's rival, Bank of Scotland (BoS). (NatWest's preferred bidder was HSBC, but that would have raised many more regulatory issues, and such a bid was not forthcoming.)

Santander's support was critical to the success of RBS's bid for National Westminster, completed in March 2000. Santander pledged its votes in favor of its ally's offer and agreed that it would purchase more equity in RBS, funding the purchase by a private placement share issue. Following the success of the takeover, Santander's almost 10 percent shareholding dropped to 7 percent, of what had become the second-largest banking group in the United Kingdom.

In response to suggestions that RBS's bid for NatWest was the result of manipulation by Santander, Sir George Mathewson replied:

> For the implication to be given that we were somehow being led around by the nose by Santander is quite frankly nonsense. It would be totally wrong to think of Emilio Botín sitting like a spider in the middle of a web pulling strings to which we will jump. We are just not in the business of jumping when people say jump. Santander can't even vote their shares. We vote their shares. That was the very basis at the very beginning of the association some 12 years ago. We have never ever had to refer back to that piece of paper because we have a very close working relationship with each other.[4]

In 2003 Santander and RBS engaged in a bout of mutual organizational restructuring. On the one hand, Santander sold to RBS the credit card and personal loan portfolio that had belonged to Frankfurt-based Santander Direkt Bank. RBS already had a large credit card operation in Europe and was well positioned to benefit from the cards and loans business. On the other hand, RBS sold to Santander the Miami-based Latin American private banking operations of the Coutts Group, with its $2.6 billion in assets under management for more than 1,400 clients. (RBS had acquired the Coutts Group, which specialized in private banking, as part of its acquisition of NatWest.) The purchase permitted Santander to improve its private banking operation in Latin America, where the bank was, as we have seen, already strong, and Coutts to give priority to the

United Kingdom, Europe, and Asia. At the time Santander CEO Alfredo Sáenz, commented: "We are delighted to once again reach agreement with our partners at The Royal Bank of Scotland Group, underlining again our ability to work together for the benefit of our shareholders."

The alliance with RBS had to end after Santander acquired Abbey in 2004; in 2005 Santander sold its remaining 2.6 percent stake. Although RBS retained a 2.8 percent share in Santander, the two banks unwound the exchange of directors. The alliance with Royal Bank of Scotland had lasted some sixteen years and had paid off in many ways, including financially. "We earned 23 percent return on income on an annualized basis from our stake in RBS over the past 17 years," Emilio Botín III reported. "That is a total return to shareholders of about €4.5 billion."[5]

Emilio Botín III stated that the strong personal relationships that developed have endured and that he felt sadness at the necessity of severing the formal relationship between the two banks. A telling indicator of the nature of the alliance is that even as Santander became a direct competitor of RBS, RBS made representations to the European Commission in support of the Abbey acquisition when the commission appeared to be delaying its approval.

Furthermore, in early 2007, when ABN AMRO entered into merger discussions with Barclays Bank, RBS and Santander, joined by Fortis, a Belgian-Dutch bank, quickly made a joint counterproposal. The strategic logic of their bid was that after the consortium acquired ABN AMRO they would split it up with RBS acquiring LaSalle Bank, ABN AMRO's Chicago-based subsidiary, and merging it with Citizens Bank; Santander acquiring Banco Real in Brazil and merging it with Santander Banespa; and Fortis acquiring ABN AMRO itself and merging with Fortis's operations in Belgium and the Netherlands.

San Paolo IMI: Italy's Tantalizing Prospects Frustrated

After its failure to establish a beachhead in Italy through the acquisition of IBI in 1995, Santander bought 2 percent of Instituto Bancario San Paolo di Torino; by 1997 Santander had built up its share to 6.8 percent. The next year (1998), San Paolo bought Istituto Mobiliare Italiano (IMI), which created what was for the moment Italy's largest bank, but it diluted Santander's stake to 4 percent.

Santander rebuilt its stake to 7 percent by buying additional shares in the open market.

In 1996 Santander acquired 5 percent of the shares of Inter-Europa Bank in Hungary, with an option to buy another 4.999 percent, which it shortly exercised. San Paolo had, in 1989, bought 22.5 percent of Interinvest Külkereskedelmi Hitelintézet, which forty-three Hungarian foreign trade companies had created in 1981 to finance export development projects. San Paolo increased its ownership to 32.5 percent and renamed the bank. Then in 2003 San Paolo IMI bought out almost all the other shareholders other than Santander, which still retains almost 10 percent of the shares.

In 2000 Santander and San Paolo signed a mutual coopera-tion agreement that provided for, inter alia, the creation of a Latin America desk in San Paolo and an Italian desk in Santander, to promote each bank's services to the other's customers and to signify the two banks' commitment to acting in concert. The formal agree-ment did not last long.

One year later Santander announced that it would sell some or all of its shares in San Paolo IMI, saying that it was frustrated with the opposition of the Italian banking authorities to foreign investment in the banking sector. Santander announced it intended to withdraw from the agreement and that it would treat its share-holdings as a financial investment rather than a strategic holding. It also withdrew its two directors on the board of San Paolo IMI. Still, the formal change in the status of the alliance did not lead to the abandonment of all ongoing joint activities.

In 2003 Santander and San Paolo dissolved one joint venture but created another. Santander bought out San Paolo's 50 percent share in Finconsumo, a consumer finance venture in Italy. At the same time, San Paolo acquired 50 percent of Santander's subsid-iary, Allfunds Bank. Allfunds, which had a 40 percent share of the Spanish market, specialized in offering access to third-party funds to institutional clients such as commercial banks, savings banks, bro-kers, and asset managers, which would then distribute them to their clients. At the time Santander owned 5.3 percent of San Paolo, which owned 3 percent of Santander. San Paolo did flirt briefly with the Belgian bank Dexia, though nothing came of this. Still, the flirtation may or may not have been the trigger (accounts vary) that caused Santander to reclassify its shareholdings in San Paolo as financial investments in "companies which have no lasting relationship with the group and over which no significant influence is exercised." Despite this, rather than reducing its stake in San Paolo, it increased it from 5.2 to 8.6 percent.

In 2005 BBVA made a bid to buy Italy's Banca Nazionale del Lavoro but gave up in July of that year after Italian insurer Unipol made a rival and slightly worse bid. While BBVA was making its bid, ABN AMRO made a bid for Banca Antonveneta. The Bank of Italy stated that ABN AMRO's bid was within its guidelines, but Antonio Fazio, the governor of the bank, may have tried to engineer a domestic takeover to keep Antonveneta under Italian ownership. At the time, the European Union's single market commissioner, Charlie McCreevy, wrote to Governor Fazio to warn him that the commission would not tolerate any attempt to block the merger. Still, allegations surfaced that the governor had tried to help Banco Popolare Italiana (BPI) buy Antonveneta, over the objections of several other senior regulators. The Bank of Italy permitted BPI to buy 30 percent of Antonveneta, while stalling ABN AMRO's attempt to acquire an equivalent stake. Finally, it emerged that the governor had privately informed BPI's head of his decision to approve BPI's bid before announcing it publicly. The scandal caused BPI's bid to collapse, and in the wake ABN AMRO's bid succeeded. Governor Fabio, protesting his innocence, resigned his position in December. Prime Minister Berlusconi had backed Governor Fabio, and the scandal may have contributed to the prime minister's subsequent election defeat.

In late 2005 Mario Draghi, who was less nationalistic than his predecessor, was appointed governor of the Bank of Italy. In January 2006 the Bank of Italy rejected Unipol's bid. Almost immediately thereafter, in February, the French bank BNP Paribas made a successful bid for Banca Nazionale del Lavoro.

Santander reportedly was interested in strengthening its ties with San Paolo IMI after Draghi's appointment but felt it could not move before April 2007; until then, a shareholders' pact controlled the bank, which would have hampered its bid. In late 2006, before Santander made any move, Banca Intesa of Milan bought San Paolo IMI for €29.6 billion (US$37.8 billion). There is much speculation about what this implies for the relationship with Santander, which at the end of 2005 owned 8.4 percent of San Paolo IMI and was its second-largest shareholder. Now the merger with Intesa diluted Santander's ownership and possibly marginalized its position to being the fourth- or fifth-largest in the merged entity, to say nothing of reducing the possibility of a merger. What may soften the blow is that, at current market prices, Santander is reaping capital gains as it reduces its shareholding. It now owns only 1.7 percent of San Paolo IMI.

Commerzbank: A Foothold in Europe's Largest Market

The merger in 1999 with BCH gave Santander a stake in Commerzbank, Germany's third-largest bank. Rather than dispose of the shares, Santander invited Commerzbank to form an alliance. (Interestingly, Commerz had had a long-standing cooperation agreement with SoGen and with NatWest to assist small businesses with their cross-border business and to reduce the cost of transactions.) Following the merger with BCH, when Banco Comercial Português disposed of its shares in Santander, Commerzbank acquired some of them, bringing its stake in Santander to about 3 percent from 1.8 percent.

That same year Santander entered into negotiations with Commerzbank to double its shareholding to 10 percent. Santander intended to raise the funds for this by selling CC Bank to Commerz for the necessary shares plus cash. Commerz had asked Santander to raise its stake as part of a strategy to ward off a hostile bid from CoBRa Holdings, a German investment group and then the largest shareholder in Commerz with a 17 percent stake. The talks quickly broke down over a disagreement about the value of CC Bank. Commerz apparently valued CC Bank at €675 million, whereas Santander valued it at €800 million.[6]

Santander continued to maintain a stake in Commerz that declined slightly from some 4.8 percent to 3.4 percent. In its 2003 annual report, Santander changed the categorization of its holdings in Commerz (and San Paolo) to financial investments in "companies which have no lasting relationship with the group and over which no significant influence is exercised." During 2005 Santander finally disposed of its shares.

Société Générale: The French Connection

Santander and SoGen began working together in 1994. In 1999 Santander initially bought about 0.15 percent of SoGen, quickly building up its stake to a little more than 3 percent. Then Société

Générale attempted to merge with Banque Paribas, only to face a hostile takeover bid from Banque Nationale de Paris. Santander increased its stake to 5 percent and declared its support for SoGen's management and against the takeover. Regulators blocked BNP's bid, though BNP did wrest Paribas away from SoGen.

After the crisis had passed, in 2000 the two banks decided to deepen the alliance through a mutual share exchange that envisaged SoGen taking a 3 percent share in Santander and Santander upping its stake in SoGen to 7 percent. The two banks signed a formal agreement to cooperate in five areas: asset management, specialized financial services, wholesale and investment banking, retail banking, and Internet banking and brokerage Furthermore, the parents agreed that they would share fifty-fifty in the ownership of any joint ventures that they might establish under the agreement. (As it turned out, they established none.) At the time, the two banks characterized their agreement as a "strategic alliance between equals." At a news conference announcing the alliance, Emilio Botín III again made it clear that, "We think there are no advantages for shareholders from a cross border merger of equals."[7]

The alliance appears to have been essentially stillborn. Although at the onset there was discussion of combining SoGen's strength in Asia with Santander's strength in Latin America, nothing came of this. By 2001, rather than reaching 7 percent, Santander's stake in SoGen had fallen to 1.5 percent. In 2002 Santander sold this stake, too. SoGen retained its 2.7 percent share in Santander until 2004.

Why Alliances in Banking?

Alliances between companies have become one of the most frequent ways of accessing new markets, creating new capabilities, or reducing costs. One may consider alliances from three different perspectives: organizational learning, transaction cost reductions, and strategic motivations (Kogut 1988). All three have something to contribute to our analysis of alliances in banking.

The *organizational learning* approach provides some insight. Santander used alliances to gain knowledge of markets, mostly product markets such as insurance and, to some degree, geographic markets. This approach is consistent with Mody's (1993) view of alliances as flexible organizations that allow firms with complementary strengths to explore new realms. The most important type of organizational learning involves preparing the ground for taking further steps, following Johanson and Vahlne's (1977) model of internationalization as a process of sequential stages based on incremental learning. In this model, alliances enable a parent firm to test the waters but are ultimately dispensable once experience has grown. Mody (1993, 162) points out that one benefit from an alliance could be that it leads to a greater competence in managing further alliances. There is little sign of this in Santander's experience. The alliance with RBS, one of its earliest, was the most durable and fruitful. Its subsequent alliances were generally short-lived and less productive.

The *transactions costs* approach is better at helping explain some of the outcomes of alliances, although it has little to say about the decision to create an alliance and perhaps nothing about the choice of partner. Several of Santander's alliances gave rise to what Hennart (1988) called scale joint ventures. The scale joint venture solves problems of indivisibility; when there are scale economies, pooling ownership of the relevant assets can be more efficient than attempting to maintain separate ownership of portions of the assets. Some joint ventures were link joint ventures that the parents created to facilitate interactions between them. The Inter-Bank Online System (IBOS) joint venture had both scale and link elements.

The transaction costs perspective does help explain why Santander and some of its partners engaged in alliances. In some cases, the alliances enabled the partners to maintain a relationship with its clients abroad. Relationships are firm-specific and provide a basis for scope economies. One can extend one's relationship with one's client at home to one's relationship with the client abroad. Also, one cannot rent out a relationship, and one would be unwilling to introduce a client to a potential competitor. In an environment in which other ways of delivering services to one's clients were not feasible for reasons of scale, cost, or regulation, aiding one's clients by drawing on the services of an alliance partner provided an alternative.

The *strategic motivations* approach is perhaps the most useful for our purposes of understanding Santander's banking alliances because it accounts for the choice of partner. As Mody (1993, 163) suggests, "alliance formation is higher when the costs of merging are greater." Equivalently, alliances, and their manifestations such as clubs, joint ventures, and consortia, are an alternative to mergers.

Regulatory, tax, and legal barriers to cross-border merger in effect made the cost of mergers infinite, raising the probability of alliances. In looking at the French experience, Marois and Abdessemed (1996) point out that a key element in alliance design was "no competition in one's own home market and cooperation elsewhere." This combination of forbearance and cooperation also manifested itself in mutual defense pacts in which the partners agreed to support each other against hostile takeovers, while themselves pledging not to launch a hostile takeover against each other. Lastly, Nakamura et al. (1996) argued that stability in a joint venture appears to require that the parents specialize in complementary organizational skills. An evolutionary divergence in the product or technology realms is unlikely to come about among large commercial banks. Instead, Santander's alliances relied on a geographical specialization and became untenable as this foundation eroded, as the acquisition of Abbey National illustrates.

A common way of "cementing" alliances is to set up cross-shareholding arrangements. The decision to swap equity stakes is consistent with what Perotti (1992) has called a hostage exchange. In his model, the partners exchange sufficient shares to establish a mutual threat of capture or control; each firm then may make a credible commitment to future efficient cooperative actions. In equilibrium, no punishment is necessary. This is not, however, descriptive of any of Santander's alliances. The partners undertook not to increase their shareholdings in each other without the other's agreement. Instead, the cross-holdings acted as symbols of commitment; although they involved the allocation of real resources in the form of capital, the mutuality reduced the net cost. More importantly, they provided a basis for the exchange of delegates to boards of directors, ensuring the transparency to the partner of strategic decisions. Rather than an exchange of hostages, the structure was more an exchange of ambassadors.

The Value of Alliances

In general, Santander appears not to have lost financially from its many alliances. Most were short-lived but still generated capital gains, suggesting that Emilio Botín III had a good eye for investments. Even when the alliance ended, the contacts they had created may have facilitated later transactions. There were numerous examples of former alliance partners engaging in transactions that they could just as well have offered to someone else.

Those alliances that Santander entered to acquire a foothold in new financial fields such as insurance seem to have been the least successful in that Santander mostly exited these areas. If Santander entered banking alliances with a view to gaining allies to fight off takeovers, it ended up being the protector more than the protected. Even in mutual assistance when the partner was the acquirer rather than the acquired, it helped RBS in the battle with Bank of Scotland over NatWest but did not require much help from RBS in its two big deals, BCH in Spain and Abbey in the United Kingdom.

The alliance with RBS appears to have followed Doz's (1996) model of cycles of learning, reevaluation, and readjustment. Learning reinforced the partners' positive assessment of the alliance and led them to make further commitments, enlarging its scope. Still, the key to the durability and the depth of this most successful of all of Santander's alliances is almost surely due to personal chemistry at the top. The top executives were able to transcend any initial instrumental calculus and to develop a trust that then permeated the two organizations, enabling them to work together at many levels and in many areas. In assessing the value and contributions of the alliance with RBS, Emilio Botín III has pointed out: "You cannot overestimate the importance of this relationship. Each time we met, we challenged each other, shared ideas and offered our support. We learnt a lot from each other. And we were there to support each other when help was needed. Analysts cannot understand the importance of such relationships."[8]

7

Back to Europe

> Once its expansion throughout Latin America has been accomplished and it has exited from First Union, Banco de Santander "faces," according to its President [Emilio Botín III], "the challenges and opportunities of European Economic and Monetary Union. The strengthening of the group's capital base is fundamental to our strategic positioning towards the euro."
>
> —*El País*, 20 September 1997[1]

Spain entered the European Economic Community in 1986, the same year that the Single European Act was adopted, a program of market integration and liberalization to come into affect on 1 January 1993. These events triggered much speculation about the future prospects of large Spanish firms in general and the banks in particular. As we explained in chapter 5, Spanish companies reacted by expanding throughout Latin America so as to grow in size and avoid unwanted takeovers. By the mid-1990s, the momentum toward the creation of a single currency accelerated, and in 1996 the conservative José María Aznar defeated the social-democrat Felipe González at the polls. As premier, Aznar embarked on an ambitious program of deregulation, privatization, and fiscal discipline, which culminated in 1998 with Spain's successful bid to be one of the founding member countries of the European Monetary System, which came into effect on 1 January 1999. Large Spanish companies—including Santander—benefited immensely from the demise of the peseta. Within a few months, interest rates had converged on the much lower German levels, and

Spanish companies and consumers could borrow money at rates that nobody had ever dreamed of.

The beginning of Santander's expansion into Europe actually predated its foray into Latin America, but for a long time it was a more modest affair. The first step was a tentative entry into consumer finance on the Continent; the second, a move into Portugal's retail banking sector. Albeit worthy, both of these expansions represented only incremental international growth. Furthermore, its alliances had not yielded Santander much success in penetrating any part of Europe. What Santander required to make an impact on Europe was another of Emilio Botín's bold, path-breaking strokes. This came in the form of Santander's acquisition of Abbey National Bank in the United Kingdom, at the time the largest cross-border banking acquisition in the world.

The acquisition of Abbey grew out of Botín's and Santander's past bold moves. The acquisition of Banesto gave Santander the scale to be able to take the risks inherent in creating its Latin American operation. A large presence in Latin America gave Santander the scale to be able to acquire BCH. The acquisition of BCH gave Santander further experience with large mergers as well as the scale to acquire Abbey, while Santander's alliance with RBS had given it knowledge of the U.K. market.

Representative Offices, Branches, and Consumer Finance

Santander's initial expansion in the rest of Europe took shape in the form of a network of representative offices and branches. It opened a representative office in London in 1955, which it later upgraded to a branch. Its next move came twenty-five years later when it opened a representative office in Frankfurt in 1970 and converted it to a branch in 1973. It also had a handful of branches in France, starting with one in Paris in 1972, which it upgraded from the representative office it had established in 1969. However, Santander did not particularly target France, perhaps because several Spanish banks, most notably BBV, had already built up a presence there, targeting Spaniards resident in France and individuals and companies with links to Spain. Banco de Bilbao had opened a branch in Paris in 1902, making it the first Spanish bank to do so. Toward the end of the 1930s, Banco de Vizcaya participated in founding the Banque Française et Espagnole. Banco Popular Español established a representative office in Paris in 1968 that it soon upgraded to a branch. This, in turn, grew to some fourteen banking offices in Paris, its environs, and elsewhere in France. In 1991 Popular incorporated this network as a joint-venture subsidiary with Banco Comercial Português (BCP), under the name Banco Popular Comercial. In 2001 the partners split, with Popular taking full control of now Banco Popular France. Banco Central Hispano had a network of some ten branches, but it had cut this back to one (in Paris) prior to the merger with Santander.

Santander also had representative offices in Brussels (1970 on), Vienna (1971–85), Geneva (1970 on), as well as a finance arm in Geneva in the 1970s. However, all of these offices, including the Frankfurt and Paris branches, primarily engaged in international banking activities, not retail banking. The bank was establishing European operations in support of its Spanish customers' needs.

The first step in what is today a large and profitable consumer finance operation was Santander's acquisition in 1987 of Bankhaus Centrale Credit (CC Bank) with its thirty-one branches in Germany from Bank of America, which had run into financial difficulties at home and was in the process of restructuring and reducing its overseas presence. CC Bank specialized in consumer credit, especially for automobiles. As part of the transaction, Santander also acquired Bank of America's Visa credit card franchise, at the time the only one in Germany. Point-of-sale consumer credit was an attractive business for several reasons. First, it required at most only a limited physical presence; in the case of financing auto purchasing, it is the auto dealers themselves that sell the products. Second, acquisitions in the sector were less likely than acquisitions of regular commercial banks to draw regulatory resistance. Lastly, as Walter (1997) points out, commercial banking in Europe suffered from overcapacity; hence, it would be hard to expand via organic growth. The consumer finance sector was thus a good way for Santander to expand into Europe and learn about the market, albeit in a way that was outside its original corporate strategy.

Not surprisingly, the relatively opportunistic approach to European markets translated into a series of acquisitions, restructurings, and disposals. In 1988 Santander acquired Credit du Nord Belge, the Belgian subsidiary of Paribas's subsidiary, Credit du

Nord, and named it CC-Banque Belgique. This gave Santander a ready-built network of twenty-two branches, but the acquisition had more to do with commercial banking than with consumer finance. The alliance with Royal Bank of Scotland led Santander to sell its ally a 50 percent stake in both the German and Belgian ventures. The partnership in Belgium, however, was short-lived. In 1992 Santander swapped shares in Banco de Comércio e Indústria de Portugal with RBS for RBS's shares in CC-Banque Belgique. The next year Santander disposed of the Belgian operation, transferring its activities to Kreditbank, Crédit Générale, and Gesbank, and then gave up the banking license early in 1994. RBS bowed out of CC Bank in 1996 when Santander acquired RBS's 50 percent stake in CC Holdings, the company the two banks had created to own CC Bank and CC Leasing. The Santander-BCH merger of 1999 returned Santander to Belgium. BCH had a subsidiary there, BCH Benelux, which specialized in corporate banking. Santander kept it, and now it is Santander Benelux.

The next major move in Germany occurred in 1995 when Santander established SantanderDirekt, a direct banking operation. This meant that Santander had three separate consumer-oriented operations in Germany—CC Bank, the Visa credit card business, and SantanderDirekt—with little or no overlap in their customer bases or cross-selling. In 1997 CC Bank opened CC Credit in Budapest and CCB Leasing in the Czech Republic. (In 2003 CCB Leasing merged with CCB Credit to form CCB Finance, which changed its name to Santander Consumer Finance.)

Also in 1997 CC Bank and San Paolo each took 50 percent stakes in Finconsumo Banca in Italy, buying out the previous owners, the Italian banks that set up this operation in 1988 to lend money for car purchases. In 1993 San Paolo transferred its consumer finance activities to Finconsumo, in return for a 13 percent stake that it built up to 50 percent by 1997. At the same time, San Paolo also acquired from Santander a 50 percent stake in Allfunds Bank, which allowed Spanish domestic banks to sell foreign mutual funds directly to institutional investors. (Allfunds is an asset management platform, and the deal included the right for Sao Paolo to use it in Italy.) In 2006 Santander renamed Finconsumo Banca as Santander Consumer Bank.

In 2000 Santander tried to sell CC Bank to Commerzbank, but the two banks could not agree on a valuation. Unable to sell CC

Bank, Santander decided to make it the foundation for a push into consumer finance. Consumer credit was a profitable niche business but not an obvious fit for the bank's global strategy; the solution was to make it part of the strategy. CC Bank would go on to acquire or establish further subsidiaries in Austria, the Czech Republic, Hungary, Italy, Poland, and Norway. The first step was the creation in mid-2001 of a cooperation deal between CC Bank and AKB Bank, part of the German holding company Wilh. Werhahn. The eponymous Werhahn is a 150-year-old family owned company with investments in building materials, manufacturing, and financial services. The agreement included an option for Santander to buy AKB at a later date for €1.1 billion and for AKB and CC to swap some board members. AKB was Germany's largest independent financier for car dealers and buyers and, with assets of DM5.1 billion (US$2.19 billion), was the larger of the two banks. Then in early 2002 Santander issued new shares to fund its acquisition of AKB. Combining AKB Bank with CC Bank gave Santander a company with a market share of 70 percent among Germany's independent financers of automobile purchases, and about 13 percent of the overall market for financing automobile purchases, where CC Bank ranked second only to Volkswagen Bank.

Anticipating the European Union's expansion to the East, in late 2003 Santander bought Bank of America's banking license in Poland, which became CC Bank Polska; and it was negotiating to acquire Gornoslaski Bank Gospodarczy, but the talks fell through. Santander also bought San Paolo's 50 percent share of Finconsumo Banca, giving itself full ownership. At the same time, Santander sold to RBS SantanderDirekt Bank's credit card and personal loans portfolio for €486 million. RBS's Retail Direct unit was now the number three credit card provider in Germany, with about half-a-million accounts; this significantly strengthened RBS's position in Germany's consumer finance market, while permitting Santander to focus on the auto financing business.

In early 2004 Santander bought Polskie Towarzystwo Finansowe (PTF), Poland's largest auto finance company, from Bank Millennium, controlled by Banco Comercial Português. PTF was Poland's fourth-largest credit broker, with a portfolio of €469 million, but more importantly it was the leader in the auto loans market. Santander then merged PTF with its own automotive bank, CC Bank Polska, forming PTF Bank.

A month later, Santander spent €400 million in Norway to acquire DnB Nor's consumer finance division, Elcon Finans. Santander then sold Elcon's leasing and factoring business to Société Générale for €160 million to maintain the focus on consumer finance. Later that year, Santander paid €22 million to buy Abfin, which was an auto financing company belonging to the Dutch retail bank and insurance group SNS Reall. In 2005 Santander spent €54 million to acquire Bankia Bank in Norway, a new bank that had been established in 2001 with a focus on consumer finance. Santander then merged Elcon and Bankia to create a new Norwegian bank, Santander Consumer Bank, which had about a 30 percent market share in auto financing. Santander is also cooperating with Fragus Warranty, part of Sweden's Fragus Group, since 2004. Now Santander will market in Norway Fragus's warranties for used cars.

In the United Kingdom, Santander set up Santander Consumer Finance UK, which too focused on financing purchases of automobiles. Currently this is a de novo operation with a five-year objective of becoming a market leader, although achieving that goal may require additional acquisitions.

Recently, Santander allied with SAG (Soluções Automóvel Globais), an automobile distributor in Portugal. In January 2006 SAG, which owned 50 percent of Interbanco, a Portuguese consumer and auto financing company, exercised its option to buy BCP's 50.01 percent share in the company. SAG then turned around and sold the stake to Santander for the same €118 million it had paid BCP. The third phase of the exercise consisted of Santander contributing its consumer finance operation in Portugal to Interbanco; in return, Santander's ownership of Interbanco climbed to 60 percent. Interbanco now has about a 15 percent market share in auto financing in Portugal and is the market leader. Santander and SAG are also establishing another sixty-forty joint venture to engage in auto rentals. In Italy, Santander acquired 70 percent of the shares of Unifin for €43 million, with a three-year option to buy the remaining 30 percent. Unifin has a 7 percent share in the market for loans secured by clients' salaries.

Its most recent consumer finance acquisition has taken Santander to Russia. Apparently Santander spent about €40 million to wholly acquire Extrobank, a small Russian company, which is involved in the financing of automobile purchases in the Moscow and St. Petersburg regions.

Santander is now one of the top five pan-European providers of consumer finance, from Portugal to Poland, and from Italy to Norway. Its chief competitors are Cetelem (a subsidiary of BNP Paribas), Citigroup, GE Consumer Finance, and Sofinco (which belongs to Crédit Agricole). Of these, the largest is GE Consumer Finance, which has €60 billion in assets and a presence in twenty-four countries, versus Santander Consumer Finance's €36 billion in twelve countries. In 2006 Santander acquired Texas-based Drive Financial Services from HBOS. Drive Financial, too, specializes in automobile finance, where it buys contracts for high-risk consumers from car dealerships. This purchase extends Santander Consumer Finance's reach to the United States.

Santander Consumer Finance constitutes a stand-alone business. Santander established a wholly owned subsidiary that owns many of the Santander Consumer Finance country operations and that borrows in its own name to fund them. Furthermore, the operations are moving to a uniform brand under the Santander Consumer Finance name. Ultimately, Santander Consumer Finance will be an operation that Santander could sell as a unit should it decide to do so. In the meantime, it is delivering steady profits (some 9 percent of the group's total; see table 7.1).

Portugal: Establishing the First European Retail Presence

Although Portugal shares a long border with Spain, the two countries did not engage in much economic exchange until both countries became members of the European Union in 1986. Portugal's banking sector was very different in structure and ownership (Nunes et al. 2002). When it took power in 1975, Portugal's revolutionary government nationalized the domestic banks but permitted the four foreign banks, none of which was Spanish, to continue to operate. In the mid-1980s the government reopened commercial banking and insurance to private initiative to supplement the government-owned banks. This resulted in the creation of four domestically owned commercial banks: Banco de Comércio e Indústria (BCI), Banco Internacional de Crédito, Banco Português de Investimento, and Banco Comercial Português (BCP). BCP quickly established itself as Portugal's leading and fastest-growing private commercial bank.

TABLE 7.1

Performance of Santander's Banking Operations, by Business Unit,
2005 and 2006

Business Unit	Percentage of Operation	Attributable Income (million euros)	Growth (percent year-on-year)	Efficiency[a] (percent year-on-year)
2005				
Consumer finance	9	487	46.3	34.3
Portugal	6	345	35.7	49.4
Abbey	14	811	n.a.	62.2
Santander network[b]	23	1,285	44.1	44.0
Banesto	9	498	24.1	48.2
Latin America	32	1,776	20.8	52.8
2006				
Consumer finance	9	565	16.0	34.6
Portugal	6	423	22.6	47.3
Abbey	15	1,003	23.7	55.1
Santander network[b]	23	1,505	17.1	41.0
Banesto	9	585	17.5	45.3
Latin America	35	2,287	28.8	47.0

Sources: Santander's 2005 and 2006 annual reports.
[a]Without amortization.
[b]Retail banking in Spain.

The government also permitted foreign banks, though for several years not Spanish ones, to establish branches. The first Spanish bank to receive permission to establish a branch was the relatively small Banco Exterior in 1988.

Santander first invested in Portugal in 1988, taking a 10 percent stake in Oporto-based Banco de Comércio e Indústria and proceeded to build up its stake as the Portuguese government relaxed its controls. By 1990 Santander owned 26 percent of BCI, while RBS owned 17 percent and MetLife owned 5 percent, giving Santander effective control. The next year BCI expanded from twenty-five to eighty-two branches as it increased its presence in the Lisbon area. By 1993 Santander had raised its direct ownership to 78 percent, while RBS's ownership had fallen to 13 percent. That same year, Santander established its Portuguese investment bank, Banco Santander de Negócios Portugal (BSNP). (In 1998 Santander changed BCI's name to Banco Santander Portugal or BSP.)

Banesto moved more aggressively. The Portuguese government started privatizing Banco Totta e Açores in a series of tranches, beginning in 1989, ultimately retaining 13 percent. Banesto, under Mario Conde, its president, acquired 25 percent, the maximum legally permissible, directly. However, Conde proceeded to acquire another 25 percent through a series of companies controlled by Carlos Menezes Falcao, the Portuguese partner of Mariano Gómez de Liaño, Mario Conde's personal lawyer. Conde's plan was to build the first pan-Iberian banking group.

The Portuguese government wanted to return majority control of Totta to Portuguese owners, and parliament held an inclusive hearing into the legality of the 25 percent indirect stake. Conde's ownership was embarrassing to the Portuguese government for two reasons. First, Banesto had effectively sidestepped Portuguese law. Second, Conde was in trouble in Spain (see chapter 4).

In 1995 Banesto, by then owned by Santander, sold both the 25 percent direct holding and the 25 percent indirect stake in Totta to Antonio de Sommer Champalimaud, Portugal's richest individual. The government that overthrew the Salazar dictatorship in 1974 had in 1975 nationalized Champalimaud's financial (Banco Pinto e Sotto Mayor; BPSM) and industrial (steel and cement, inter alia) empire. He then retreated to Brazil, where he built a new business conglomerate centered on cement. Just prior to acquiring the 50 percent holding in Totta, Champalimaud had reacquired 80 percent of BPSM.

BBV, too, was an early entrant into Portugal when in 1991 it bought Lloyds Bank's retail network. Then in 2000 BBVA also bought Crédit Lyonnais's retail banking interests, thereby having absorbed two of the pre-1984 foreign banks.[2] Lastly, the merger with Argentaria that same year brought BBV the branch network in Portugal that Banco Exterior had established. Banco Exterior had eighteen branches in Portugal when in 1994 it acquired another thirty in return for the sale of its subsidiary Banco Simeon, with its sixty branches, to Portugal's largest savings bank, the government-owned Caixa Geral de Depósitos (CGD), which wanted to build up its presence in the Spanish areas that bordered Portugal. It already owned Banco de Extremadura, based in western Spain. Simeon had a strong presence in Galicia, in northwest Spain.

Banco Central Hispano established an alliance with Banco Comercial Português (BCP) in 1993, acquiring 10 percent of its shares, a stake it quickly built up to 20 percent. At the same time, it sold to BCP a 50 percent stake in the capital of Banco Banif de Gestión Privada, its subsidiary specializing in private banking—banking services to "high-net-worth individuals," that is to say, the rich. It also sold to BCP its small investment bank, BCH-Portugal, and agreed not to compete with BCP in Portugal, while BCP agreed not to compete in Spain. In 1995 BCP and BCH changed Banif's name to Banco Banif Banqueros Personales. Banif's established its branches in luxury premises and made its services available twenty-four hours a day, 365 days a year. Service extended to delivering currency to clients in their homes.

In 1993, when BCP bid for Banco Português do Atlântico (BPA), the second-largest Portuguese bank, the Portuguese government vetoed the transaction. Part of the reason may have been the government's concern over the growing Spanish ownership of Portugal's banking industry as exemplified by the Banesto-Totta affair. Still, the acquisition eventually took place in 1995 when BCP joined with Companhia de Seguros Império in a joint bid. Império subsequently took over BPA's subsidiary União de Bancos Portuguêses, which it renamed Banco Mello Comercial. The transaction made BCP Portugal's second-largest bank, after Caixa Geral. In 1998 BCP sold to BCH the Spanish branches it inherited from its acquisition.

When Santander merged with BCH, a conflict of interest ensued. As just mentioned, BCH's alliance with BCP included an agreement not to compete in each other's market, but Santander had a subsidiary in Portugal that it was unwilling to divest. Santander therefore sold BCH's (by then) 14 percent stake in BCP, and BCP sold its 3 percent stake in Santander. For the time being, BCP retained its 50 percent share in Banif.

In 1999 Santander established an alliance with Champalimaud, who agreed to sell his family's 52 percent stake in the insurance company Mundial Confiança, which in turn controlled a financial group comprising, inter alia, four Portuguese banks: Banco Pinto e Sotto Mayor, Banco Chemical, Totta, and Crédito Predial Portugués The plan was comprehensive, including cross-holdings for Champalimaud in BSCH Portugal and BSCH Brazil. For Santander, the deal not only pulled it ahead of BBVA in terms of creating a pan-Iberian presence but also would enable it to reduce the relative importance of Latin America in its assets and profits.

Unfortunately, the socialist government of António Guterres, originally elected in 1995, objected to the deal. It accused Champalimaud of breaking a "gentlemen's agreement" that he had made with the Socialist Party leaders and presidents of the largest Portuguese banks to give them the right of first refusal should he sell his holdings. Portuguese finance minister Antonio Sousa Franco vetoed the deal, declaring it against Portugal's national interest, and launched a parliamentary inquiry.

Santander appealed to the European Commission, which cleared the deal and ordered the Portuguese government to lift its veto, but the Portuguese government was obdurate. The government argued that its veto had nothing to do with blocking competition but rather that the deal violated insurance regulations. At the same time, BCP launched a hostile bid for the group. Eventually, after almost six months or so, Champalimaud, Santander, and the Portuguese government came up with a compromise solution. The final settlement gave Champalimaud a 4 percent stake in Santander in return for his 52 percent share of the Confiança financial group. Caixa then bought the group from Santander, but immediately sold back to Santander Confiança's 94 percent holding in Banco Totta e Açores and its 71 percent holding in Crédito Predial. The acquisition of Totta gave Santander about a 12 percent share of the Portuguese market. Santander then bought back the 50 percent of Banif that BCP still owned. Santander could now merge Banif and Banco Santander de Negocios. The merger gave Banif-BSN about a third of Portugal's market for private banking. Caixa Geral sold the 53 percent of Banco Pinto e Sotto Mayor that it owned to BCP but retained the merchant bank Banco Chemical.[3] Santander had retained an option to buy Chemical but let the option lapse. Chemical took over Caixa Investimentos and changed its name to Caixa—Banco de Investimento (CaixaBI), to become CGD's investment banking arm. Still, the acquisition of BPSM made BCP Portugal's largest banking group.

In 2002 Champalimaud took a seat on Santander's board of directors, serving as an ally of the Botín family. By this time, his stake in Santander had shrunk to a little more than 2 percent due to subsequent capital increases in which he had not participated. In 2004 Champalimaud died at the age of eighty-six.

In the three years that followed the acquisition of Totta, Santander engineered a turnaround: net operating profit grew by 35 percent, net income by 63 percent, and the cost-to-income ratio fell almost 10 percentage points to 43.7 percent. This performance was the strongest of the major banks in Portugal, and the cost-to-income ratios became one of the lowest in Europe.

Santander now owns four banks in Portugal: Banco Totta e Açores, which operates as a universal bank; Crédito Predial, which specializes in mortgage lending; BSP, which focuses on high-net-worth and urban customers; and BSNP, its Portuguese investment banking arm. In 2002 Santander made Portuguese one of its then two official languages.[4] In 2003 Santander bought Royal Bank of Scotland's 13 percent stake in Banco Santander Portugal, bringing its ownership to 98 percent.

Santander restructured Totta after acquiring it. Its ownership of Banco Totta gave Santander a branch each in Luanda, Guinea-Bissau, and Cape Verde, a subsidiary in Mozambique, and management and an interest in the partially government-owned Banco Internacional de Sao Tomé e Principe (BISTP). In Asia it gained Totta Asia. At some point early on after Santander took over the bank, Totta disposed of its interest in BISTP to CGD. In 2002 Totta closed the branch in Guinea-Bissau and Banco Totta Asia. It converted the branch in Luanda to a subsidiary, Banque Totta Angola, in 2002. In 2003 it sold the subsidiary in Mozambique to Standard Bank of South Africa and in 2004 it disposed of the branch in Cape Verde. In 2006 Banco Santander Totta and CGD agreed to create a fifty-fifty joint venture that would become the majority owner of Banco Totta de Angola. The joint venture further reduces Santander's already reduced exposure to sub-Saharan Africa, while giving CGD a presence in the one former Portuguese colony in Africa where it was not already present. Santander's disposal of acquired operations peripheral to its strategic aims echoed the disposals that followed the acquisitions of Banesto and BCH.

Currently attributable profit in Portugal is growing more rapidly than at Banesto or in Santander's retail network in Spain (table 7.1). Efficiency is improving but lags that at Banesto and the retail network, suggesting room for further profit gains. In 2006 *The Banker* voted Santander Totta the best bank in Portugal, as did *Euromoney* for the fifth straight year.

Abbey National: Santander Comes of Age

In 2004 Santander acquired Abbey National Bank in the United Kingdom in the largest cross-border retail banking deal in Europe to that date. This was an unprecedented move. In spite of the Maastricht Treaty and Economic and Monetary Union, there has been little cross-border merger activity in banking in Europe (Buch and DeLong 2003; Tschoegl 2003). Despite "European Passport" legislation entitling banks in one European country to operate in any other member country, the major banks have limited their cross-border presence. The relevant national markets are mature and have well-entrenched competitors, which in itself was a factor leading Santander to target consumer finance. Other reasons for the lack of enthusiasm for cross-border acquisitions include differences in legal and tax regimes, as well as cultural barriers. Lastly, national central banks and regulators have often been hostile to foreign banks seeking to acquire a major domestic bank. Thus the press heralded the acquisition as a possible harbinger of other such acquisitions.

Abbey is a vintage British bank. In 1944 Abbey Road Building Society and the National Building Society merged to form Abbey National Building Society. In 1987 Abbey National formed an alliance with Friends Provident, which enabled it to offer its customers its own branded life insurance products; later it cut its links with Friends Provident, buying Scottish Mutual instead. Abbey National continued to expand its geographical reach and range of services, leading it to decide to demutualize in 1989. Six years later it moved into the consumer finance market when it purchased First National Finance. In 1999 Abbey National launched a digital television banking service on Sky Digital's interactive Open channel that enabled customers to view the company's complete range of mortgages and savings accounts, request product information, and arrange to receive a call from an Abbey National financial adviser. That same year the company responded to the coming of the euro by launching its euro business. The next year it acquired Porterbrook, a train-leasing firm, from Stagecoach to develop its wholesale banking operation. Unfortunately, Abbey National got in over its head, and a £1 billion loss at Abbey National Treasury Services devastated its balance sheet.

In 2001 Lloyds TSB put Abbey National into play by making a £19 billion bid for the bank, a deal that Bank of Scotland (presently HBOS) trumped by offering £27 billion. However, the Bank of Scotland merger quickly fell through, and then the regulatory authorities blocked the Lloyds TSB takeover. The next year National Australia Bank entered into talks with Abbey National, which however finally broke them off. In September 2002 Abbey National announced that it intended to sell First National, its consumer finance subsidiary. Early in 2003 GE Consumer Finance, the consumer credit services business of General Electric, agreed to pay £848 million for First National. Selling First National enabled Abbey National to signal to the stock market that it was serious about refocusing on its core retail banking operations after having underinvested in the business over the previous five years. Still, late in 2002 Abbey National briefly entered into merger talks with the Bank of Ireland, which would have resulted in the new entity having its headquarters in Dublin but with its primary stock market listing in London. Abbey National quickly broke off the talks, reporting that the deal undervalued it. Late in 2002 Abbey National got a new CEO, Luqman Arnold, who arrived with a mandate to pull the company out of the ditch it had fallen into.[5] As the problems at Abbey became clearer, the share price almost halved within a year.

In the summer of 2003 Juan Rodríguez Inciarte, the head of Santander Consumer, flew into London.[6] With an expert in British retail banking in tow, Inciarte spent three days visiting Abbey branches posing as a prospective customer. He investigated Abbey's branch distribution, product lineup, and the quality of customer services. On his return to Madrid, Inciarte reported that Santander could apply its expertise in retail banking to turn around Abbey's declining profitability. His arguments proved persuasive, and Santander made an offer for Abbey.

In July 2004, Abbey National agreed to a £8.5 billion (US$15.5 billion) all-stock takeover offer by Santander, plus a special dividend payment. Reportedly, Santander took the view that the Abbey deal gave it two benefits. First, it enabled Santander to diversify geographically, ensuring that future fluctuations in any one part of the world, such as Latin America, would not hit the bank as hard as they had in 2001 and 2002. Second, it increased Santander's market capitalization, making it the fourth-largest bank in Europe in 2005, after HSBC, UBS, and Royal Bank of Scotland, and hence not an easy takeover target.

HBOS tried to block the deal. Its campaign highlighted issues of governance, focusing on Santander's family-led character, including Emilio Botín's dominance and Ana Patricia Botín's leading role in the bank Although HBOS considered a rival £10 billion bid, ultimately it pulled back. On 14 October 2004, 65 percent of Abbey's shareholders (95 percent by value) voted in favor of Santander's offer. The final deal price valued Abbey at £8.9 billion (US$16.2 billion). One hundred eight days after its initial offer Santander completed the acquisition.

In acquiring Abbey, Santander faced two great obstacles with respect to gaining shareholder approval. Because the deal involved payment in shares, rather than being all cash, shareholders faced tax implications and liquidity issues. First, if they exchanged their Abbey shares for Santander shares, the British shareholders would be taxed twice on dividends, once in Spain and then in Britain, because the tax treaty between the two countries did not fully correct for the double taxation. Fortunately the British Inland Revenue came up with an ad hoc solution before the banks finalized the deal in November 2004. However, shareholders would have to pay the higher of the Spanish and U.K. tax rates. U.K. taxpayers in the higher brackets would see their tax rate climb to 32.5 percent from 25 percent because dividends from a Spanish firm do not qualify for a tax credit that applies only to U.K. firms. All other U.K. taxpayers would face a Spanish withholding tax of 15 percent, whereas on Abbey shares they paid nothing. Second, at the time of the bid Santander's shares did not trade in London. To enable small shareholders, those with fewer than 2,000 shares, to cash out if they so desired, Santander offered them a facility that would enable them to sell their shares without paying dealing fees or foreign exchange charges, should they want to sell their shares after the acquisition but before Santander's shares would begin trading in London a few months later. Third, shareholders who wanted to sell out completely might be subject to Spanish capital gains taxes. Santander therefore filed a collective tax document on behalf of all shareholders who used their free facility so that they would be subject only to U.K. capital gains tax, which would apply only to those with gains in excess of £8,000. Still, at the crucial vote, many small shareholders heckled Abbey's chairman with slow clapping and calls for his resignation. These and other obstacles to European cross-border banking deals stand in sharp contrast with the "official" reality of a single market for financial services.

After the takeover, Abbey National sold Abbey National France, which provided mortgages to British residents buying homes in France, to BNP Paribas. The search for a buyer had started before Santander bid as part of Abbey's drive to create a company solely focused on U.K. personal financial services. The year before, Abbey National had sold its Royal Saint Georges Banque, a small unit based in Nantes which it had bought only about two years earlier, to GE Capital Bank France. Incidentally, Abbey had itself briefly invested in Spain. It had entered in 1988, but then in 1994 it had sold its operations to Caja de Ahorros del Mediterráneo.

When Santander acquired Abbey, it promised to slash costs by £100 million in the first year and by £300 million in three years. At the end of the first year, it had reduced costs by £224 million, or 75 percent of its three-year goal. The reason it was able to do so was that Abbey was highly inefficient. Juan Rodríguez Inciarte pointed out in a presentation in mid-July 2005 that Abbey's back-office staff represented 33 percent of its employees, versus 6.5 percent at Santander's best-practice operations. Abbey had sixteen employees per branch, compared to eight at Santander's best operations. Lastly, information technology (IT) costs were 12 percent of net operating income versus 6.9 percent at Santander.

To achieve its cost improvements, Santander cut 4,000 staff in 2005, and another 2,000 in 2006. It has also stopped existing IT projects and renegotiated key software and telecommunications contracts. The result was an improvement in the efficiency ratio (costs as a percentage of revenues) from 62.2 percent in 2005 to 55.1 percent in 2006. Already slightly better than the U.K. average (see table 7.2), it is still noticeably worse than the general level of performance in Spain, to say nothing of the level at Santander (see table 7.1), which has set itself a three-year goal for Abbey of achieving an efficiency ratio of 45 percent.

By early 2007, Santander had already achieved its entire target of £300 million in cost savings, even though it had not yet

TABLE 7.2

Average Efficiency Ratios in the Banking Sector, 2003

Country	Cost as a Percentage of Revenues
Spain	56.8
United States	59.6
Netherlands	60.5
United Kingdom	60.5
Germany	62.1
France	64.3
Italy	67.3
Belgium	67.8
Japan	81.6

Source: Presentation by Juan Rodríguez Inciarte, Santander, Spain, 15 July 2005.

migrated Abbey to its Partenón software platform. Currently Abbey is still running six separate customer databases that contain duplicated information. In 2007 Santander will introduce Partenón in a process that it plans will take eighteen months. This should both enable Abbey to improve its cross-selling of products and reduce its costs. Incidentally, Banesto developed Partenón and in the mid-1990s dispatched a senior IT manager to Santander to help transplant the system there. However, the transplantation failed, due in large part to opposition in Santander. However, when in 2002 Alfredo Sáenz came from Banesto to become CEO of Santander, he was able to champion the introduction of the software.[7]

One open question with the cross-selling is how Santander will deal with a major difference between the Spanish and English institutional environments. In Spain, all residents have a unique identification number because every adult must have a national identify card, which also serves as the identification number for tax purposes. This makes it easy to link their accounts regardless of which Santander products they use or which Santander subsidiary they interact with. In the United Kingdom, however, there is no such ID number. Hence, it is harder to establish that the John Smith of Leeds who has a stockbrokerage account with the bank is also the John Smith with a mortgage and bank account, but is not the John

Smith of Leeds who also has a bank account but in a different branch. While acknowledging the difficulties, top management expressed confidence that it will be able to use other information to get around the absence of an ID number and so improve its ability to cross-sell.

Banking Foreign Investment in Mature Markets

As Tschoegl (1987) and Dufey and Yeung (1993) argue, where markets are well developed and competitive, there is no reason to expect foreign banks in general to be better than local banks at retail banking. Thus retail banking across borders should be fairly rare in developed markets. For foreign direct investment to succeed, the investor must be doing something different, or something better than the competition in the host country. Tschoegl argued that, in general, in retail banking the foreign bank would most likely operate along similar lines as its host country competitors, who would be equally capable. In the 1970s and early 1980s, several U.S. banks acquired retail banks in Europe and elsewhere, only to sell them in the late 1980s and early 1990s as they found that the acquisitions were not profitable. More recently, Demirgüç-Kunt and Huizinga (1999) and Claessens et al. (2001) found that foreign banks tended to have lower margins and profits than domestic banks in industrialized countries. Similarly, Dopico and Wilcox (2002) showed that foreign retail banks had a smaller presence in mature markets than in emerging markets. This is consistent with Santander's limited success and its lack of interest in retail banking in Continental Europe and explains its indirect entry into the United States.

There are two clear exceptions to the argument that foreign banks should avoid developed retail banking markets. The first involves ethnic banking, whereby banks follow migration patterns; doing so can often lead banks to neighboring countries and would represent a case of doing something different from host country competitors. In the past two decades, however, intra-European immigration has tended to be too limited to give rise to much ethnic banking. Santander's expansion into Portugal certainly does not represent ethnic banking.

The second exception arises when a bank can no longer grow rapidly at home, perhaps because it is so large that regulators forbid further domestic acquisitions on antitrust grounds. For instance, in 2000 ten foreign banks owned the twelve largest U.S. subsidiaries of foreign banks, which together accounted for more than 92 percent of the assets of all subsidiaries in the United States (Tschoegl 2002, 2004b). As one would expect, the parent banks were large and tended to be from English-speaking countries. However, the intriguing fact was that the parent was often *the* largest bank in its home country, suggesting that domestic limits to growth were a factor in the foreign direct investment decision. The foreign banks could continue to grow substantially in the United States through acquisition because even the largest subsidiaries were *de minimis* with respect to antitrust concerns. BBVA's acquisition of Compass Bank in the United States, though BBVA's largest acquisition to date, makes it only the twentieth-largest bank in the country.

When the foreign bank seeks to grow but can no longer do so more rapidly than its overall home market, it may come to possess what Kindleberger (1969) has called "surplus managerial resources." It may then decide to grow abroad when it sees an opportunity arising out of combining these surplus resources with what Berger et al. (2000) refer to as a global advantage; they argue that some U.S. banks succeed in the competition with local banks elsewhere in the world simply by being better managed. More generally, the literature clearly shows that firms differ in their productivity and that differences may persist for years (and Doms 2000). However, U.S. banks are not the only well-managed banks in the world. The intense rivalry of the late 1980s and the 1990s made the Spanish banks highly competitive too (Pastor et al. 2000). Table 7.2 indicates that Spanish banks on average are among the most efficient in the world, perhaps a consequence of the intense competition that developed in Spain in the late 1980s and early 1990s, a competition that Santander had in great part instigated. History further shows that foreign banks eager to apply their management skills to the retail sector in the host country frequently believe that it is more cost-effective to improve a larger, local acquisition than to build up an operation entirely from scratch. The acquirer's strategic task is to identify large, poorly managed banks, acquire them for a price that does not fully give up the gains from the acquisition, and then successfully execute the turnaround. This is a difficult task as the legendary U.S. investor Warren Buffet's dictum suggests: "When a management with a good reputation takes on a company with a bad reputation, it is usually the company's reputation which survives."

One study that looked at bank mergers in Europe between 1989 and 1996 (Tourani Rad and Van Beek 1999) found that domestic (intramarket) mergers benefited the acquirer more than did cross-border (intermarket) mergers but the effect was slight and not statistically significantly different from zero. Furthermore, while the shareholders of the takeover target clearly benefited, the return to the shareholders of the acquirer, albeit positive, was much smaller and not statistically significantly different from zero. Lastly, more efficient banks gained more from acquisition than did less efficient banks, but again the difference was not statistically different from zero.

Regardless of the merits of cross-border diversification and acquisition in general, for Santander to be able to compete against domestic banks in its host markets it must be doing something different or better, and either of these possibilities can justify its presence, even if there are costs to operating at a distance and in an unfamiliar market. What appears clear is that, although Santander may not generally be offering different products in the markets in which it has acquired banks—though, as we have remarked earlier, in some markets in Latin America it has— it is running those banks more efficiently than their managers ran them before acquisition. One can see this most clearly in the case of Abbey.

For the year 2005, Abbey's efficiency ratio averaged 62.2 percent (table 7.1), but this is an average of results that improved from 68.1 percent in the first quarter to 56.6 percent in the fourth. In 2006 Abbey's efficiency ratio reached 55.1 percent. Santander's ambitious three year-goal of a 45 percent efficiency ratio would put Abbey between the current values of 47 percent for Santander's Latin American operations and 47.3 percent for Portugal, on the one hand, and the Santander retail networks' 41 percent, on the other. Of course, according to Santander's plans, by then both Latin America and Portugal will have improved also. Clearly, that improvement is possible is evident from the 41 percent efficiency ratio for Santander's retail banking network in Spain, and the 45.3 percent for Banesto.

In 2005 *Euromoney* voted Santander the world's best bank, in "recognition of the leadership shown by SCH in the acquisition of UK bank Abbey National and the strong growth of SCH in the last 20 years." Santander is the first Spanish bank ever to win first place.

The previous winner was HSBC, and the 2006 winner was Société Générale. In 2005 *Euromoney*, *The Banker*, and *Global Finance* voted Santander Best Bank in Spain, and *The Banker* voted it Best Bank in Western Europe. In 2006 *Euromoney* voted Santander (with Banesto) the best bank in Spain.

An Assessment of Santander's Geographical Diversification

With the acquisition of Banco Totta, Abbey, and numerous consumer finance companies throughout Europe, Santander has achieved a geographical diversification of its operations in the sense that no one country accounts for more than a third of Santander's profits. From table 7.1 we can see that even the Iberian Peninsula (including Banesto, the Spanish retail banking network, and Portugal) now accounts for only 38 percent of attributable profit in 2006. Latin America accounts for 35 percent, and Abbey and Consumer Finance in Europe for 24 percent.

Although management has pursued geographical diversification to enhance the stability of the bank's profit stream, the value of this diversification to shareholders is debatable. The first argument against geographical diversification is that it adds value only if the firm can do it more cheaply than shareholders can by themselves. For assessing Santander's strategy the evidence here is ambiguous. It would have been extremely costly in terms of transactions costs such as gathering information and paying brokerage fees for Santander's shareholders to buy the shares of Latin American banks and European finance companies. It would have been less costly to buy the shares of Portuguese and U.K. banks. The problems that Santander faced in getting small shareholders in the United Kingdom to accept the Abbey deal suggests that (1) even within Europe transactions costs on cross-border shareholding for small shareholders are large, but (2) many shareholders do not necessarily welcome the diversification. Abbey shareholders could quite rightly have complained that if they had wanted to own shares in Santander they could have bought them by themselves. The diversification does add value to stakeholders who have concentrated a large part of their assets in Santander. These stakeholders would include senior managers in Madrid and large shareholders such as the

Botíns. For both these groups fluctuating fortunes could mean loss of difficult-to-replace jobs or wealth. As far as the managers are concerned, they can, in theory, compensate shareholders for any costs due to diversification by accepting lower compensation for what are now presumably safer jobs. For large shareholders there is no way to compensate other shareholders for unwanted diversification. We explore this issue further in chapter 9.

The second argument against diversification is an empirically based one. Denis et al. (2002) examined the diversification of U.S. multinational companies over the period 1984 to 1997 and found that increases in global diversification destroyed excess value, while reductions in global diversification increased excess value. They argued that their findings supported the view that the costs of global diversification outweighed the benefits. The reasons for such an effect include the greater complexity of a globally diversified firm relative to a purely domestic firm, which leads to high costs of coordination, difficulties of monitoring, and the possibility of inefficient cross-subsidization by successful operations of less profitable operations as managers seek to increase the assets under their control. Bodnar et al. (2003) examined U.S. corporations from 1984 to 1998 and found a small premium for international diversification that increased with the scope of the diversification and fluctuated with exchange rates. More recently, Doukas and Kan (2006) used cross-border acquisition data to arrive at a more nuanced assessment. They found that shareholder value loss is directly related to a firm's leverage; near-all-equity firms did not exhibit value loss from global diversification. Furthermore, global diversification helped bondholder wealth, while decreasing shareholder wealth. The argument is that geographical diversification reduces volatility, and hence the value of equity, which one can think of as a call option on the value of the firm, while reducing the risk to bondholders of default. Doukas and Kan's results are subtly inconsistent. Near-all-equity firms should still exhibit some loss of value.

None of these studies, however, focus on banks. Banks are, by their nature, highly leveraged firms, but they are also highly regulated. The introduction of regulatory considerations could affect banks' optimal strategies through the effect of the strategies on relations with regulators. Firms can counteract the effect of diversification on reducing volatility and the risk of bankruptcy and its associated deadweight losses by accepting a higher level of debt on the liability side of its balance sheet, or riskier investments on the asset side. Whether in response to the concerns of the Banco de España or its own preferences, Santander has capital adequacy ratios well in excess of Basle II requirements, and its annual reports suggest the bank has been diligent in controlling nonperforming loans. These facts suggest the bank has been conservative in its leverage and careful in its lending rather than aggressive, and therefore has not moved to counteract the consequences of diversification. All of this would suggest that any pursuit by Santander of geographical diversification has probably been of limited value or interest to the bulk of Santander's shareholders, though it may have mattered somewhat to top management.

What Next in Europe?

Although Santander still has far to go in transforming Abbey, market rumors suggest that Emilio Botín III is looking for further acquisitions both in the United Kingdom and on the Continent. The U.K. name the press has mentioned most frequently is Alliance & Leicester, the former building society. However, some observers report that Santander has already reviewed that option only to reject it. Other names mentioned include National Australia's two subsidiaries, Clydesdale Bank or Yorkshire Bank, and Allied Irish Banks, Ireland's second-largest bank.

As we have discussed in the previous chapter, Italy is a logical next target. Italy has one of the most fragmented banking systems in Europe, which provides many potential takeover targets. Some estimates put the market share of the five largest Italian banks at 45 percent, compared with more than 75 percent in France or Britain. Under Mr. Draghi's governorship of the Bank of Italy, the way is now clear both for foreign banks to acquire Italian banks, and for Italian banks to merge, which could reduce the number of targets. However, Santander has reduced its stake in San Paolo IMI to 1.7 percent. In December 2006 it sold a 4.8 percent stake for gross capital gains of €705 million. Whatever Santander's plans for Italy are, they do not seem to center on San Paolo IMI.

Asia beckons, but Santander has already tried and failed to establish itself in the Philippines. In 1995 Santander established a subsidiary in the Philippines, after failing to obtain authorization from the government to establish a branch. In 2003 it sold its Philippine operations to a local bank.

A number of foreign banks have made investments in China, including BBVA, though Santander has not. In 2006 BBVA acquired 5 percent of China Citic Bank, and 15 percent of Citic International Financial Holdings in Hong Kong. One of the key stumbling blocks for Santander is that, unlike the situation in Latin America when Santander started its push, in China the bank lacks a cadre of qualified managers who know both Santander and the target market and around whom it could build an operation. So far it has not been willing simply to establish an alliance with a Chinese bank.

In an interview with a reporter from the capital markets monthly *Euromoney* (Horwood 2005), Emilio Botín III reflected that "Twenty years ago I would never have dreamt that we would be the ninth-largest bank in the world." Half-jokingly, ten months earlier he had closed a meeting with stock analysts and investment bankers in London in the wake of the announcement of the Abbey deal with the rather revealing words, "See you at the next acquisition."[8]

That acquisition was the RBS-Fortis-Santander consortium acquisition of ABN AMRO. For Santander, this brought with it Banco Real in Brazil, which Santander can merge with Banespa. It also brought Banca Antonveneta, ABN AMRO's retail banking arm in Italy, and Interbanca, its merchant bank there. Although this would finally have given Santander the foothold in Italy it had sought for two decades, within a month of the acquisition Santander had sold Antoveneta to Monte dei Paschi di Siena. Santander had valued Antonveneta at US$8.6 billion, so Emilio Botín III jumped at the almost instantaneous US$4.6 billion capital gain that Monte dei Paschi's offer of US$13.6 billion represented. Monte dei Paschi wanted an acquisition to keep it competitive in size with UniCredit and Intesa Sanpaolo and so was willing to pay well for a bank it was already interested in. The offer was unexpected but welcome. As a result, Santander cancelled the €4 billion capital increase it had planned to fund its share of the consortium's payment for ABN AMRO. Though the outcome was fortuitous, once again, Emilio Botín III's eye for an acquisition had proved itself.

8

Managerial Style, Governance, Succession

> Many, many people take part in the bank's decision-making process.... I merely set an example.
>
> —Emilio Botín III, in *Euromoney*, January 1995

> Now, now.... Let's not boast. Every family has its weak points.
>
> —Antonie Buddenbrook to her brother Thomas, in Thomas Mann, *Buddenbrooks: The Decline of a Family* [1901] 1994, p. 115

From the point of view of corporate governance, Banco Santander represents a puzzle. It grew rapidly to become one of the world's top ten banks while members of a family owning about 2.5 percent of the equity influenced strategic decision making by virtue of occupying the top managerial position and several board seats. The Botín family has managed to exercise influence over decision making well in excess of ownership not because of obscure legal provisions, pyramid schemes, or dual-class shares, but rather through a web of alliances and cross-shareholdings. This has in turn provided the bank with a measure of stability in its ownership and control structure, an aspect that many observers believe explains why Santander was able to take advantage of the rapidly deregulating Spanish banking sector during the 1980s and 1990s, and to embark on an audacious pattern of internationalization. Decisive decision making at the top may have distinctively contributed to the bank's ability to seize the initiative at crucial moments in time, such as the breakup of the domestic banking cartel beginning in 1987, the acquisition of Banesto in 1994, the struggle over control at the merged Santander Central Hispano between 1999 and 2002, or the purchase of Abbey National Bank in 2004.

Although Santander is a modern bank with professional management, industry observers and competitors alike consider it to be family-led. If we follow Landes's (2006) definition of a dynastic family firm as one that has survived through three generations of family leadership, Santander clearly qualifies. Members of three successive generations of the same family have influenced its board of directors and the strategic decision-making process for more than half a century. In this chapter we examine the impact of Santander's family character on decision making, growth, corporate governance, and managerial succession. We use a variety of sources—interviews, news reports, and stock analyst reports—to assess the ways in which Santander is and is not a family bank. We conclude that, in line with the perceptions of industry observers and competitors, Santander has benefited from the stability and decisiveness provided by the long-standing influence of the Botín family.

The Debate over Family Firms

The family firm is a controversial form of organization. Its supporters point out that family firms possess certain advantages vis-à-vis other types of firms in terms of personal incentives, commitment, loyalty, reduced agency costs, and even altruistic behavior. Its critics assert that family ownership, control, and management tend to come hand in hand with paternalism, patrimonialism, cronyism, and nepotism. They also point out that family firms are generally unable to reach the scale necessary to be able to operate efficiently or to be technology leaders. Family firms, some argue, are incompatible with a modern, technology-driven, knowledge-based, and meritocratic economy. Various observers on occasion have even pronounced that family firms are in danger of extinction because of their competitive disadvantages. Yet in virtually every country around the world, family firms continue to be one of the most common forms of organization. Even among the largest firms in the major economies, family firms are well represented. The empirical fact is that family ownership, control, and management have survived the two industrial revolutions, the managerial revolution, and the information revolution. This resilience indicates that they are not intrinsically disadvantaged relative to other types of firms.

Family firms continue to dominate the corporate landscape around the world. Some have become large and successful within their respective industries. In the United States, the birthplace of the managerial revolution, as many as one in three of the largest 500 corporations on *Fortune* magazine's annual ranking are family firms (Villalonga and Amit 2006). In Spain, also about a third of the thirty-five companies represented on the blue-chip Ibex-35 stock index are family firms, including three presently or historically associated with the Botín family, namely, Santander, Banesto, and Bankinter.

We define family firms as companies in which members of a family exercise ownership, control, and/or strategic decision making and have the desire to transmit their ownership, control, or management from one generation to the next. This definition is relatively broad in that a family firm can have part of its equity listed, as long as the family retains effective control over the top managerial positions and the board of directors Most importantly, we do not impose the requirement that the firm's top management consist exclusively of family members. Thus, a family firm can have professional management cadres with or without a family member at the top. Under this definition, family firms account for more than half of GDP and employment in most countries around the world (Jones and Rose 1993; Landes 2006; Snodgrass and Biggs 1996).

Economists, development scholars, business historians, and social scientists in general have long expressed skepticism concerning the prospects of family management and control in the modern economy. The most common argument against the viability of family firms is their alleged inability to grow big enough to take advantage of technology and economies of scale. Many experts assume that family firms are victims of a vicious circle, in which their limited ability to raise capital prevents them from growing and from acquiring or developing the best technology. In this formulation, insufficient scale and lack of leading-edge technology puts the family firm at a cost disadvantage relative to firms with other governance structures. Higher costs and shrunken earnings, to close the circle, make it hard for the family firm to accumulate enough capital to grow.[1]

Economists have frequently argued that "family firms are detrimental to economic development because they are based on nepotism and paternalism which foster inefficiency" (Benedict 1968). During the 1950s, modernization scholars argued that traditionalism (including family ownership, control, and/or management) was the main impediment to economic growth and that development could occur only if modernizing elites—social, political, economic, and financial—acted as agents of change (Kerr et al. [1960] 1964; Rostow [1960], 4–12, 26, 31). These scholars were adamant that "technology and specialization ... are necessarily and distinctively associated with large-scale organizations" (Kerr et al. [1960] 1964, 21; see also Rostow 1960, 9–11, 40). They predicted that the growth of large-scale enterprises would undermine family management and control: "The family enterprise is usually most effective in small and relatively simple organizations such as retail and wholesale trade, craft industries, and small or medium-sized industrial plants" (Kerr et al. [1960] 1964, 121). "The more advanced industrial countries place less emphasis on family connections and greater emphasis on competence, although family influence is certainly not unknown.... Preference for family members .. is, however, criticized as 'nepotism'" (Kerr et al. [1960] 1964, 68). Moreover, the scholars associated family firms with "patrimonial management" or "management in which ownership, major policy-making positions, and a significant proportion of other top jobs in the managerial hierarchy are held by members of an extended family. The effective decision-making authority is centered in the family, and the goals of the enterprise are oriented toward the interests and the aspirations of the family" (Kerr et al. [1960] 1964, 120). They also tended to see family firms as displaying a "paternalistic concern for the 'dependent' workers" and criticized the "professional manager [being] subordinated to the authority of the family" (Kerr et al. [1960] 1964, 138–39). Thus, family firms are frequently regarded in the economics literature as not being modern and therefore likely to be relegated to the background as countries develop.

Other types of development scholars have also cast doubt on the viability of family firms. Dependent development theorists, although ideologically and theoretically opposed to the modernization paradigm, argued that the powerful combination of a "triple alliance" among foreign capital, large-scale domestic capital, and the state would swallow the small-scale local bourgeoisie (Evans 1979; see also Cardoso and Faletto [1973] 1979, 163, 174, 213; Frank 1967). In their view, family firms were too small to be economically or politically relevant in the wake of industrialization. They did not predict the demise of family firms but suggested they would play only a subordinate role in the economy.

Late-industrialization scholars—who proposed the cases of Japan and South Korea as models for other countries to emulate—also raised doubts about small-scale enterprises. However, they did not take issue with family control per se, as long as an "autonomous" state could readily impose its logic and controls on them. In fact, they argued that family ownership and control were compatible with the development of both light and heavy industry (Amsden 1989; Amsden and Hikino1994). Neoclassical economists, with their emphasis on comparative advantage, specialization, and free exchange within and across borders, have criticized both "industrial gigantism" and family or worker ownership (e.g., Sachs 1993, 18–20, 82–83). Lastly, prominent business historians have attacked the "conservative" and "personal" character of family firms as the root causes of their inferior performance relative to managerially run firms, at least during the "higher" phase of technologically driven economic development characteristic of the twentieth century (Chandler 1990; Landes 1951; Lazonick 1991).

While economists, development scholars, business historians and many other types of social scientists predicted the demise of family firms, or at the very least their subordination to larger industrial enterprises, a small group of scholars, often working at the edges of mainstream social science, developed a very different framing of the basic issues (for an early example, see Benedict 1968). In a famous article, Ben-Porath (1980) argued that families—like firms—can become effective and efficient ways of allocating resources and conveying goodwill, honesty, fidelity, and skill to the other party in a business transaction. If so, family firms are not necessarily inferior to other types of organization when it comes to arranging production, consumption, or insurance under conditions of uncertainty and market failure. Research by anthropologists (e.g., Benedict 1968) and business historians (Colli and Rose 2003; Jones and Rose 1993) has established that family firms continue to make important contributions to economic growth and technological development even after a country has developed. Not surprisingly, they continue to be one of the dominant forms of organization.

In comparing firms operating in similar industries in Britain, the United States, Germany, and Japan, Church (1993) concluded that variation in the prevalence of family ownership, control, and/or management per se cannot explain the international competitiveness of firms and countries. Rather, it is firms' strategic decisions, independent of their ownership or governance, that drive relative performance. Seeking to avoid facile distinctions and contrasts, the more recent literature has thus moved beyond the dichotomy between family and managerial firms to recognize that family ownership, control, and management do not necessarily lead to inferior performance (Colli and Rose 2003).

Over the past two decades, financial economists and organizational theorists seeking to identify the conditions under which large equity holdings translate into higher market valuations have pursued a new line of research on closely held corporations, including family firms (Burkart et al. 2003; Shleifer and Vishny 1986). The standard argument—based on principal-agent theory—is that family governance is inefficient in countries in which minority shareholders' rights are well protected, such as the United States. Yet, the evidence indicates that, under certain circumstances, family ownership, control, and/or management can contribute to firm value, even in the United States. In a comprehensive study of the Fortune 500 companies in the United States during the 1990s, Villalonga and Amit (2006) found that family ownership created shareholder value, though only when the founder was the CEO or the chair of the board of directors. They also found, however, that descendants serving as CEO or as chair of the board of directors destroyed value. Moreover, family control in excess of ownership—through mechanisms such as multiple share classes, pyramids, cross-holdings, alliances, and voting agreements—tended to reduce shareholder value, although the opposite was true when the firm had a third-generation descendant as CEO. Santander seems to conform to some of these general patterns. The Botín family certainly influences decision making in excess of ownership, primarily through cross-holdings, alliances, and voting agreements that the bank has with other entities, but the presence of a skillful descendant as top executive has delivered relatively solid results over the past two decades, as the next chapter documents.

Using data on the Standard & Poor's 500 from the 1990s, Anderson and Reeb (2004) also found that family firms create more value in general, especially when their boards have fewer family representatives relative to independent directors, who act as a countervailing force that protects the interests of other share-holders. Their empirical results indicate that the optimal mix is two independent directors for each family director, precisely the ratio at Santander (see table 8.1). Other organizational and finance scholars have used stewardship theory (Davis et al. 1997) to argue that family shareholders may care more about the firm than others, thus contributing to better performance (Anderson and Reeb 2003). Research using U.S. data has established that family-member CEOs receive less compensation than nonfamily CEOs (Gomez-Mejia et al. 2003), indicating that family members are more interested in intrinsic rewards and feel more identified with the firm. In our field interviews, several equity analysts and journalists argued that Santander's family character could have beneficial effects given the Botíns' long-standing devotion to the bank.

The Family Character of Santander

The case of Santander is one of many large firms that seem to defy the argument that family governance is doomed to disappear from industrialized economies. The growth of many family firms to global prominence also challenges the assumption that they can compete effectively only if they join forces with other similarly small firms. Santander has become one of the ten largest financial institutions in the world under the guidance of the third generation of the same family, and there are strong prospects for control and top management being transferred to the fourth generation. Our analysis here provides evidence to the effect that, in the specific institutional and competitive circumstances of Spanish and European banking over the past two decades, family governance may well have given Santander a distinct advantage over its competitors.

As we noted in chapter 2, Banco Santander did not begin as a family bank. The origins of its intimate association with the Botín family date back to the 1920s and unambiguously to the 1950s, about 100 years after the bank's founding. Today, a third-generation president continues to make Santander's most important decisions, with the assistance of a small group of close and loyal top managers. More observers than not predict that Ana Patricia Botín, Emilio Botín III's daughter, will eventually become the top executive.

TABLE 8.1

Composition of the Santander Board of Directors, End of 2006

Name	Type of Director	Appointed in	Shares[a] (%)	Background
Emilio Botín III	Executive	1960	2.506	President of Santander
Fernando de Asúa	Independent	1999	0.001	Former president of IBM España
Alfredo Sáenz	Executive	1994	0.026	CEO of Santander
Matías Rodríguez Inciarte	Executive	1988	0.011	Vice president of Santander
Manuel Soto Serrano	Independent	1999	0.004	Vice president of Indra
Antoine Bernheim	Shareholder rep	1999	1.303	Representing Assicurazioni Generali
Antonio Basagoiti	[b]	1999	0.008	Former president of Unión Fenosa
Ana Patricia Botín	Executive	1989	0.000	President of Banesto
Javier Botín	Shareholder rep	2004	0.000	Represents the Botín family shares
Lord Burns (Terence)	[b]	2004	0.000	Former Chairman of Abbey

Name	Type	Year		Description
Guillermo de la Dehesa	Independent	2002	0.000	Former CEO of Banco Pastor
Rodrigo Echenique	b	1988	0.011	Former Santander CEO
Antonio Escámez	b	1999	0.009	Former BCH executive
Francisco Luzón	Executive	1997	0.021	Former president of Argentaria
Abel Matutes	Independent	2002	0.002	Businessman. Former minister and European commissioner.
Luis Rodríguez Durón	Shareholder rep	2004	1.171	Representing Mutua Madrileña Automovilista
Luis Angel Rojo	Independent	2005	0.000	Former governor of the Banco de España
Luis Alberto Salazar-Simpson	Independent	1999	0.002	Former president of Auna

Source: Annual Report, 2006, www.gruposantander.com.

[a]Includes direct, indirect, and delegated voting rights. All shares are of the same class.

[b]External directors not otherwise classified by the bank (Echenique was CEO in the 1990s).

Above all, people inside and outside Santander see it as a family bank especially in terms of its management style. In the sections that follow, we examine the managerial style of the key Botín family members, the bank's corporate governance practices, and the issue of managerial succession.

The Last Traditional Banker: Emilio Botín II

When Emilio Botín II died in 1993 at the age of ninety, the Spanish financial community marked the passing of an era. He had joined the bank in 1929, was appointed managing director in 1934, and became president in 1950, a position that he held until 1986. During his tenure he transformed a tiny provincial bank into one of Spain's Big Seven, albeit the smallest. His life as a banker spanned six decades, four political regimes (two dictatorships, a republic, and a constitutional monarchy), and four economic regimes (autarky, import substitution, indicative planning for export-led growth, and open economy).

In spite of his growing prominence as a banker within Spain, Emilio Botín II avoided publicity, although occasionally he would speak his mind about important political affairs. For instance, in 1967, while General Franco was still solidly in power, Botín caused somewhat of a stir when he declared in an interview with leading daily *ABC* that "in a market open to international trade, firms need to be in a position to produce competitively, something that will be difficult to attain if they do not enjoy the freedom to arrange their work forces as they see fit. Naturally, such freedom should be accompanied by two others: the workers' right to strike and generous unemployment insurance" (quoted in *ABC*, 23 September 1993). During the difficult transition to democracy in the late 1970s, he was among the very first to envision the correct course of action to ensure a peaceful dismantling of the dictatorship and a return to democracy. In the summer of 1976, less than a year after Franco's death, he was the first leading businessperson to suggest publicly the legalization of the Communist Party before the first general election because, although "the Communist Party is totalitarian and antidemocratic [which it proved not to be], I think that the smart thing to do is to legalize it" (*El País*, 1 August 1976). Another example of his rare appearances in the spotlight occurred in 1983, when he sent a telegram of support to Economy Minister Miguel Boyer after the nationalization of the troubled conglomerate Rumasa, which included several banks. The nationalization was a controversial—though appropriate—action that averted a major bankruptcy.

Emilio Botín II espoused liberal economic and political ideas, something that was not exactly common among the ruling elite in Spain during the 1950s, 1960s, and 1970s. As a banker, he had some touches of a revolutionary, with his rapid acquisition of small Spanish banks, his joint venture with Bank of America (Bankinter), and the acquisition of Eléctrica de Viesgo in 1983, although he did not become proficient at the art of investing in industrial companies. Compared to his son, however, he is remembered in the history of Spanish finance as a relatively traditional banker.

The Current President: Emilio Botín III

If Emilio Botín II catapulted Santander to national prominence, his son turned it into the largest bank not just in Spain but in the Euro Zone, and into one of the world's largest. Through this remarkable growth, the family has managed to hold its position, even against the opposition of merger partners. Our interviews with family members, executives, competitors, regulators, scholars, analysts, and journalists, in Spain and abroad, clearly indicated that everyone continues to perceive the bank to be a family affair. The differences of opinion focused more on the beneficial or harmful effects of that character rather than on its accuracy. People also used a wide variety of terms to refer to the bank's family character, ranging from the admiring to the outright pejorative. A relatively neutral assessment by some interviewees was that Santander is a *presidencialista* bank.[2]

It is almost inevitable that a figure as successful as Emilio Botín III should elicit opinions ranging from staunch admiration to blistering criticism.[3] Virtually everyone agrees on one key fact that our research unambiguously established: people inside and outside the bank see him as the leading force in decision making, someone who sets both strategic direction and the overall tone. His own assessment is that the decision-making process at Santander is not a one-man show and that his key role is leadership by example. His defenders point out that he projects ambition, dedication, hard work, and shrewdness, coupled with humanity and financial disinterestedness. Within the international financial community he has managed to present himself effectively as someone who has single-mindedly pursued the growth of the bank not for his own personal gain but for the benefit of both shareholders and employees. (Of course, his interests are aligned with those of shareholders, given his small though not negligible equity stake.) His critics disagree with every one of these points.

Critics and supporters alike credit him with the considerable feat of turning Santander into a formidable global competitor. As Leslie Crawford, the Madrid correspondent of the *Financial Times* (22 February 2002) once put it, "Mr. Botín [III] ... differs from his forebears in the scope of his ambitions." His first few years as the top executive were strikingly similar to those of third-generation Thomas Buddenbrook in Thomas Mann's famous novel: "Once the reins had passed into Thomas Buddenbrook's hands, a fresher, more inventive, more enterprising spirit pervaded the firm. Now and then a little risk was taken. The firm's credit, which had been merely a theoretical luxury under the old regime, was put to work and made the most of" (Mann [1901] 1994, 261). According to *Euromoney* (July 2005), "Botín has become one of the greatest consolidators in the history of modern banking." Every strategic move has been a well-calculated leverage of the bank's existing resource base, with each successive acquisition facilitating the next one, though each represented a grasping of opportunity rather than a step in a detailed plan.

According to Santander's executives, everyone at the bank shares a "sensación de dueño" (a sense that there is an owner, someone in command), which has nothing to do with the equity stake the family holds but with the culture, the history, and the tradition of Santander as enshrined in the Botíns. Top executives—and many rank-and-file employees—report that he is in command, something many find reassuring. Santander employees point out that top management—and Emilio Botín III, in particular—has been very effective at accepting and taking responsibility for losses (especially in 2001 and 2002 in some Latin American countries). That, they argue, is leadership. Naturally, he has also taken credit for the successes, such as the growth in assets, revenues, profits, and shareholder value.

There are three key episodes that illustrate Emilio Botín III's influence at Santander: first, his bold seizure of the opportunity to acquire Banesto in 1994; second, his backstage maneuvering to regain control of the bank that resulted from the merger between Santander and BCH in 1999; and, third, his unanticipated and unprecedented acquisition of Abbey National Bank in 2004.

Euromoney (July 2005) recounts the first of these episodes:

Tales of the purchase of Banesto are now the stuff of leg-
end. The bank had run into trouble under the stewardship of its previous [president], Mario Conde. It had been
rescued by the Bank of Spain [in December 1993], which
put it up for auction in 1994. At a board meeting, the
price Santander should pay was discussed. After several
hours, Botín called an end to the meeting and, away from
prying eyes, wrote down the figure he thought would
secure Banesto, before sealing the envelope. Botín's bid
won, but he and the board were worried he might have
overpaid. They don't believe that now. "When we submitted the bid for Banesto we knew we could not afford to
lose the opportunity. So we bid high. But what was €100
to €200 million in relation to the long-term success of the
business?" Botín says.

Santander's bid of 762 pesetas per share easily beat Argentaria's 566 and BBV's 667. But the most revealing aspect of the auction
was an incident involving the bidding process itself rather than its
outcome. Emilio Botín III explains: "I had spent most of the after-
noon reviewing and initialing the 50-page offer document which
set out the bid terms, but when I got to the separate page where
I had to put in the price, well, I simply forgot to sign it." Central
Bank governor Luis Angel Rojo immediately called Botín, who
rushed to his office in order to sign the document.[4] Apparently, the
board had delegated the final decision entirely to Botín.

The second illustration of Botín's firm grip is the highly publicized drama that unfolded between the announcement of the merger
between Santander and BCH on 15 January 1999 and the managerial
changes at the merged entity (SCH) more than three years later, on
14 February 2002, which consolidated the power of the Botíns. The
merger was a stunning event—Spain and Europe's largest banking
consolidation to date. Moreover, the two banks could not be more
different in terms of history, corporate culture, and managerial style.
BCH's president was José María Amusátegui—a seasoned manager
with a long pedigree in the state-owned holding company INI as well
as at Banco Hispano Americano. The CEO was Angel Corcóstegui,
a much younger, Wharton-educated executive (PhD and MBA) who

had worked for Banco de Vizcaya before leaving for Banco Central after he and his former colleagues lost the postmerger battle at BBV.

The merger agreement called for the co-presidency of Amusátegui and Botín, with Corcóstegui firmly established as the CEO and apparent successor after his two more senior partners retired in 2002 and 2007, respectively. Unlike the top executive team, the twenty-seven-seat board of directors tilted in Santander's favor: it consisted of thirteen directors from Santander, twelve from BCH, and two independent, outside directors. The board's ten-person executive committee consisted of five people from Santander (Emilio Botín III, his brother Jaime Botín, his daughter Ana Patricia Botín, Rafael Alonso Botín, and Matías Rodríguez Inciarte), and five from BCH (José María Amusátegui, Ángel Corcóstegui, Antonio Escámez, Santiago Foncillas, and Fernando de Asúa).

What disrupted this reasonably clear state of affairs was the publication five weeks later of a lengthy and lavishly illustrated article in the Sunday magazine of Spain's largest newspaper, *El País Semanal* (circulation: 826,000). The magazine featured a photo of Ana Patricia Botín on its cover; the front-page caption simply read: "Spain's Most Powerful Woman" (Rodríguez and Rivera 1999). At the time, Ana Patricia Botín, was responsible for wholesale banking at SCH, as well as a member of the executive committee and of the board of directors. The article glossed her life and highlighted her professional accomplishments in a fairly evenhanded way, presenting her as "la princesa heredera" or the princess-heiress of the new, merged SCH. But the bombshell came toward the end of the otherwise innocuous article, in a rather ill-intentioned comment that the magazine attributed to a top executive of a rival bank: "And Corcóstegui [the CEO of SCH] ... is just a professional executive; brilliant, to be sure, but merely an executive, and he will not do any better than that. *Time will surely confirm this*" (Rodríguez and Rivera 1999, 32; emphasis added). The suggestion that Ana Patricia Botín and not the new CEO of the bank, Corcóstegui, would eventually become president, that is, the top executive, outraged the executives on the BCH side. On Monday, 22 February 1999, within twenty-four hours of the publication of the article, Emilio Botín III had no choice but to accept his daughter's resignation from all executive positions, although she continued to serve on the board of directors, a key detail to keep in mind for future developments. People we interviewed for this book described the move as a "tactical retreat."

Tactical or not, this event must have been very difficult for both father and daughter. The printed press almost unanimously announced the end of the Botín era—the only exception was the economic daily *Expansión* (24 February 1999): "The market sees the resignation as a loss to the new bank given her important role in the organization." Some media even commented that the resignation was "a decision that don Emilio el viejo [the elder, i.e., Emilio Botín II]—her grandfather—could not have imagined" (El Mundo, 28 February 1999). It is important to note that El País disclosed the day after the resignation was announced that preparations for the article that triggered the controversy had begun in October 1998, well before news of the merger had broken. The newspaper also pointed out that Ana Patricia Botín had declined to be interviewed for it.[5]

Reports of the demise of the Botín family's rule at Santander, however, proved premature. Over the following months, Santander executives quietly improved their positions at SCH. On 15 August 2001, about six months ahead of schedule, Amusátegui resigned. On 14 February 2002, Corcóstegui stepped down from his position as CEO. Amusátegui received a severance pay package worth €43 million; Corcóstegui's golden parachute was worth €140 million. Although the SCH board had approved the severance payments, it subsequently caused Emilio Botín some legal troubles that were eventually resolved in 2006. The *Financial Times* (22 February 2002) reported on the unfolding events: "After last week's boardroom reshuffle and the resignation of Angel Corcóstegui, SCH's respected chief executive, Spain's top bank has reverted to being a family-run affair." Alfredo Sáenz, Corcóstegui's former senior colleague at Banco Vizcaya and at the time president of Banesto, took Corcóstegui's place, while Ana Patricia Botín replaced Sáenz as head of Banesto. *El País* (14 February 2002) reported:

> The power crisis at SCH began with the removal of Luis Abril, Communications Director, last June. By that time, the clash between Amusátegui and Botín had become open warfare. In July, the former, after threatening legal action, sought to get the government and the Banco de España involved. He failed and resigned his co-presidency on 15 August. This was followed by the departure of four board directors named by BCH last January, and, finally, Corcóstegui's resignation.

Amusátegui had asked the powerful minister of the economy, Rodrigo Rato, who was on very good terms with Emilio Botín, to compel Santander to honor the merger agreements.[6] Rato, however, held the view that the dispute was a matter internal to the bank that the board of directors should resolve. It is also important to note that the struggle began with the removal of the communications director, an indication of how important public relations became during the protracted crisis.

But the board was becoming even more tilted in favor of Botín. In October 2001 Santiago Foncillas, president of the construction firm Dragados and one of the BCH-nominated directors, left the board upon his seventy-second birthday, in the wake of a heated dispute over the Botín-supported merger of Dragados with another construction firm, Sacyr. By early 2002 Botín had managed to persuade other BCH directors to leave the board, including such prominent entrepreneurs and executives as Felipe Benjumea (president of construction firm Abengoa), Gonzalo Hinojosa (president of clothing firm Cortefiel), Pedro Ballvé (president of food-processing firm Campofrío), and the representative of Commerzbank (*ABC*, 10 February 2002; *El País*, 3 February 2002). Furthermore, although Corcóstegui was the CEO, Botín reserved for himself decisions over auditing, personnel, and international operations (Gómez Escorial 2004).

During 1999 and 2000 Botín and his premerger Santander managers (including Matías Rodríguez Inciarte and Francisco Luzón, whom he had recruited after being forced to step down as president of Argentaria) undertook a series of important moves. These included the acquisition of the Champalimaud banking group in Portugal, the support offered to the Royal Bank of Scotland in its takeover of NatWest, the acquisitions of Serfin in Mexico and Banespa in Brazil, and the agreement with Vodafone over Spanish mobile operator Airtel. Slowly but surely, Botín was regaining the initiative, aided by the bickering among some former BCH managers (several of whom were at odds with Amusátegui), his influence over the board of directors, and his outside allies in Portugal and the United Kingdom. Meanwhile, Corcóstegui's prestige suffered during 2001 because of the slow pace of the integration following the merger and because of his support for the costly and ultimately ill-fated acquisition in 2000 of 75 percent of Patagon for $529 million, an Internet banking portal based in Argentina but with a presence throughout Latin America.[7] Emilio Botín III thus emerged from Europe's largest banking merger as the victor, installing his most trusted collaborators—Alfredo Sáenz, Matías Rodríguez Inciarte, Francisco Luzón, and Ana Patricia Botín—in key executive and board positions.

Several of our interviewees pointed out that another factor accounting for the outcome is the different goals of the three key players. Among several other similar accounts, the former communications director Luis Abril explained in an interview years after his dismissal that "[Emilio] Botín wanted all the power in the merged bank, a huge Santander. By contrast, Amusátegui longed for a golden retirement. And Angel [Corcóstegui], what did Angel want? Ah, that is an enigma!" (García de la Granja 2005, 195). It seems to be the case that Corcóstegui positioned himself for a while as the successor to the two co-presidents upon their retirement—as the press reported—but realized sometime in 2000 or 2001 that his chances were actually rather slim. Thus, Botín ultimately won because he was the only key actor deeply committed to gaining control of the merged bank, and he enjoyed a majority on the board. We would further argue that the Botíns' long-standing identification with the bank also played a key role in the outcome.

The end result of the BCH and Santander merger is not unprecedented in the history of modern banking. The 1972 combination of the Wallenberg family's Stockholms Enskilda Bank with Skandinaviska Banken to form Skandinaviska Enskilda Banken had resulted in a similar postmerger battle, except that it occurred in the midst of the transition from the third to the fourth family generations and involved disagreement between the two key brothers, Marc and Peter, over the merits of the merger. Marc committed suicide in 1971, and the press declared the end of the "Wallenberg era." Indeed, the family lost control over the bank and its associated industrial holdings until the mid-1980s. By the 1990s, however, Peter Wallenberg had reorganized the family's holding companies and foundations, reasserted control, and resolved the internal family feud by appointing his deceased brother's son as well as his own son to key executive and board positions (Lindgren 2007).

The examples of the acquisition of Banesto and the merger with BCH demonstrate not only Emilio Botín III's grip but also his patience to wait for the right moment and his decisiveness when it comes to making his move. As Eduard Ballarín, a professor at IESE

Business School and a former vice president for strategy at Banco de Vizcaya, put it: "Mr. Botín [III] always does the opposite of what he says. Look at Santander historically. Its pattern has always been to move boldly when the competition is in a difficult situation and cannot react" (*The Banker*, May 2002).

A third, revealing example of this pattern of action is the acquisition of Abbey National Bank in 2004. Some eight months before the announcement of the takeover, Botín published a lengthy article in the *Financial Times* (Botín 2004) speaking his mind about future strategy:

> I am very skeptical about the merits of [a] strategy
> [of cross-border mergers in Europe]. It will be some time
> before Europe is sufficiently integrated and the many
> barriers—regulatory, fiscal and cultural—that impede
> the functioning of the single market are overcome. Many
> would still regard as unacceptable the takeover of a
> large local bank by a foreign institution. Even without
> these barriers, a cross-border merger could create more
> problems than it would solve. The difficulties in merging
> different management styles and establishing a clear chain
> of command are obvious.... This is not to rule out the
> possibility of future European cross-border mergers. But, in
> current circumstances, I doubt they would create value for
> shareholders.

His recent experience during the BCH-Santander merger was obviously casting a long shadow over these thoughts. A few months later, after acquiring Abbey National Bank in July 2004, he further reflected: "If mergers are already complicated within one country, imagine the situation when two are involved" (*AFX UK Focus*, 20 July 2004). When a reporter asked if he had changed his mind about cross-border deals in the wake of the Abbey acquisition, he wryly noted:

> I still have the same opinion, and I said it three years ago,
> and I said it again last year, and I said it again this year
> in an article in the *Financial Times*. I think that mergers
> are always very complicated, mergers between equals.
> Mergers are one thing, and purchases or takeovers are
> another. They are very complicated, as we know from

the experiences that we've seen, when they're carried out in a specific country and, even more, when they're done between different countries—cross-border operations. I am not saying that this is not going to happen; I'm just saying that Santander is not going to carry them out, because in my opinion this does not create value for the shareholder, which is what the management of Santander is working for. An operation like the Abbey National one is different. It's a purchase. Santander is purchasing Abbey National. (*Dow Jones International News*, 26 July 2004)

Perhaps the *Wall Street Journal* (3 February 1999) best captured what friends and foes alike think of him: "Mr. Botín's ability to identify and then quickly seize an opportunity has always been the key to much of Santander's success." In a recent interview he explained: "Banesto taught us that when a unique opportunity arises you have to take it. That was the case with Abbey. It was the only opportunity to get into the U.K. banking market. Now everyone is looking to go cross-border, but we have at least a 12-month head start" (*Euromoney*, July 2005). This is perhaps the main advantage that Santander has enjoyed over its Spanish and European competitors: the decisiveness with which it has undertaken strategic moves in the midst of a rapidly changing banking market As one interviewee at Citibank pointed out, "at other banks every strategic decision, let alone an acquisition, has to make its way through several executive committees." Certainly not at Santander.

Corporate Governance at Santander

The fact that at Santander a family influences corporate governance is evident from the structure and composition of the board of directors. As of the end of 2006, the board consisted of eighteen members: Botín family members occupied three seats; current or former Santander executives, four; representatives of insurance companies Assicurazioni Generali and Mutua Madrileña Automovilista, with which the bank has an alliance, occupied two; independent outsiders, six; and an executive once associated with merger partner BCH, electrical utility Unión Fenosa, and Abbey National Bank occupied one each (see table 8.1). No shareholder owns more than the approximately 5.56 percent of the shares required to name a director. At the end of 2006, a 1 percent stake in Santander was worth €884 million or US$1,149 million in the market. Hence, the price of a seat on the board of Santander would amount to about US$6.4 billion. In February 2006, Emilio Botín III and his children (Ana Patricia, Emilio, and Francisco Javier) syndicated their shareholdings (0.71 percent of the total at the time). The Fundación Marcelino Botín, over which Emilio Botín III presides, owned 1.45 percent as of the end of 2006. As we noted earlier, the ratio of independent to family directors is 2:1, exactly the optimal to maximize shareholder wealth, as calculated by Anderson and Reeb (2004) using data on the Standard & Poor's 500.

Of the five mechanisms by which someone may exercise control in excess of ownership at a publicly listed company (multiple share classes, ownership pyramids, cross-holdings, alliances, and voting agreements), Emilio Botín III has used only cross-holdings, alliances, and voting agreements; all shares belong to the same class, and there are no ownership pyramids. The cross-holdings and alliances with Antonio de Sommer Champalimaud and with Royal Bank of Scotland are good examples. After 1999, when Santander acquired Totta & Açores and Crédito Predial Portugués from Champalimaud, Emilio Botín III was able to count on a faithful ally on the board Champalimaud, who owned 1.5 percent of Santander, passed away in 2004. The alliance and cross-shareholding with Royal Bank of Scotland (RBS) began in 1988 and lasted until 2004. Another important alliance has been with Assicurazioni Generali of Italy, which owns about 1.3 percent of Santander and has dispatched a director to the board since 1999. In turn, Ana Patricia Botín has been a board member of Generali since 2004. Lastly, Mutua Madrileña Automovilista, another insurer, owned 1.2 percent of the shares of Santander until late 2007, and had a representative on the board since 2004. Combined, the Botín family and its allies on the board own nearly 4 percent of the equity.

These alliances surely entail some implicit or explicit voting agreements. "Until his death in May [2004], Antonio de Sommer Champalimaud ... regularly delegated his vote to Botín. A similar arrangement continues with Antoine Bernheim, the chairman of Generali, the Italian insurer that holds a 1.07 percent stake in Santander" (*Sunday Telegraph*, 3 October 2004). Such agreements are quite widespread and certainly legal.

In the area of corporate governance, Emilio Botín III has recently demonstrated that he understands the importance of creating value for shareholders. Acknowledging the delicate issue of the potential clash of interests between managers and shareholders, and between controlling and minority shareholders, he has pointed out that "we have to be managers with the mentality of owners and, above all, as if we bore the responsibility of being owners" (*Financial Times*, 24 July 2004). At the 2002 annual shareholders' meeting, he announced a code of conduct and disclosed his compensation package (*New York Times*, 12 July 2002). This move was in part meant to dissipate criticisms about his heavy-handed resolution of the clash of cultures between BCH and Santander after the merger and about the return of Ana Patricia Botín as an executive.[8] But other factors played a role as well. First, foreign institutional investors—which together hold about two-thirds of Santander's shares—were at the time shocked by the corporate governance scandals in the United States and increased their scrutiny of prominent corporations around the world. Second, the troubles at Spanish rival BBVA, which lost half of its board members to a quickly escalating investigation into illegal offshore accounts, had turned the spotlight on Spanish financial institutions. Third, Mr. Botín himself was facing the increasingly likely prospect of lawsuits over two highly publicized matters. The earlier had to do with "loan assignments" (*cesiones de crédito*), a financial product that helped Santander's customers exploit a tax loophole, which enabled the bank to attract as much as €4,500 million in new deposits between 1987 and 1991. The second legal matter involved the mounting controversy over the multimillion severance payments for Amusátegui and Corcóstegui. In 2006 Botín was cleared of charges over the severance payments—largely because Santander made the payments with the approval of the board of directors and there was no evidence of harm to the shareholders—and the loan assignment case was dropped by the prosecutor.

The enhanced international visibility of the bank and the Botín family due to the Abbey acquisition in 2004 has increased the demands for transparency. The British press, in addition to airing criticisms about Santander's competence as a bank and the court cases against its president,[9] accused Emilio Botín III of nepotism in corporate governance as yet another reason against letting Santander take over Abbey and in favor of a counterbid by HBOS.[10]

Some of the media even attacked him, using quite pejorative terms to characterize his role at Santander. For instance, the press referred to him as "the 70-year-old predator" who was "seeking to enlarge his empire" (*Daily Mail Reporter*, 24 July 2004). In another example, even one of the most serious British newspapers wrote about Santander as a "benevolent dictatorship," in a veiled attempt to establish a baseless parallel between the Spanish bank and the Franco regime (*Daily Telegraph*, 24 October 2004). Some in the London financial community argued for more evenhanded reporting:

> "When looking at the current Santander situation, it is upsetting that the press is taking such a negative view," says María José Lockerbie, managing director at Fitch Ratings in London. "They have a point in that the Botín family exercises a lot of influence in the bank. But this has been the situation for years and shareholders, including international investors, don't seem to be unhappy with its performance. They know how Santander works and the shares have been quite stable. This bank is managed in a dynamic and aggressive way."[11]

Emilio Botín III complains about the accusations that corporate governance at Santander is not transparent. "Our bank compares with any international bank in terms of corporate governance. We have independent directors and proper boards. We also happen to have executives who own shares, which means they have a commitment to good management, and this goes for the family as well" (*The Banker*, May 2002). In 2005 Deminor, the independent international corporate governance rating consultancy, stated that Santander "is one of the leading corporate governance actors in Continental Europe and performs particularly well on its disclosure standards and in its board functioning." On a scale from 0 to 10, Deminor rated Santander 7.5 for its protection of shareholder rights and its commitment to generate shareholder value, and 8.0 in its information practices and the functioning of the board of directors. In an important paragraph of its twenty-seven-page report, Deminor noted:

> The Botín family is represented with around 2.17 percent of the share capital [in 2005] as one of the largest shareholders and holds 3 out of 18 board seats. Despite the small stake, the family could potentially exercise a strong influence on

the Bank's operations via tacit agreements between itself and other shareholders and board members due to the respect and connections it wields as a successful banking dynasty. However, there is no indication that long-term interests of stakeholders should deviate from that of shareholders.[12]

The extent to which Santander is a family bank—in terms of strategic decision making—is no secret to present shareholders, bondholders, employees, and competitors alike. For this reason, it is hard to criticize the family for lack of transparency. Besides, shareholders and bondholders always have the option of selling, although employees are more constrained. Some bankers and equity analysts observed in interviews that the presence of a highly motivated family at the helm of the bank should be reassuring to shareholders because its members are owners as well as managers and directors. Thus, many see the family character of the bank as providing a set of strong incentives for maximizing shareholder returns, an argument consistent with stewardship theory (Davis et al. 1997). As noted earlier, some interviewees also pointed out that in a turbulent and ever changing banking environment, having a president who is resolute and decisive when it comes to grabbing opportunities for growth can be a competitive advantage, though that is a characteristic of the individual, not of family ownership per se.

Regarding employees, Santander does not seem to be any different from its big Spanish or European counterparts. There are no signs that the bank either behaves in a paternalistic way toward its employees or is especially benevolent or generous when it comes to labor relations. Banking unions have a presence among Santander's labor force, as they do at its competitors. The bank's family character has not become an issue in labor negotiations or conflicts. Collective bargaining in Spain takes place for the banking sector as a whole in negotiations between the Spanish Banks' Association, on the one hand, and the communist and socialist labor unions, on the other. The collective agreement regulates almost every aspect of the employment relationship (e.g., hiring and firing procedures, pay scales by occupational category, job mobility, work schedules, holidays, pension payments) and includes a profit-sharing clause that ensures that employees as well as shareholders benefit from profit increases. The Spanish banking sector has not witnessed a major strike in years (Sagardoy Bengoechea 2006). In foreign countries Santander has not experienced any significant labor conflicts either. Moreover, in Brazil it has agreed that "any restructuring or change would be undertaken in a negotiated way with the unions" (Guillén 2005, chap. 9), although the unions there criticized some of its job-cutting measures.[13] In sum, as far as shareholders, bondholders, and employees are concerned, Santander's family-led character does not seem to be a negative. Quite the contrary, some interpret its peculiar tradition as a plus. Even when it comes to the most delicate issue at family firms—succession—there has been relatively little controversy, a surprising fact given the stakes.

The Issue of Succession

As we mentioned at the beginning of this chapter, a central aspect related to family influence over corporations is the intention to transfer such influence from one generation to the next. With the current president rapidly approaching what many would consider a reasonable retirement age, it seems pertinent to ask whether the fourth generation is likely to retain the family's influence. Virtually everyone interviewed for this book assumed that Ana Patricia Botín will likely succeed her father.[14] The press has written about "la línea sucesoria" (line of succession), a "banking dynasty," the "Botín dynasty," and a "patriarchal practice."[15]

Still, corporate stakeholders, analysts, journalists, and the public in general will surely demand some sort of an explanation as to why the fourth generation should continue to run the bank. In order to analyze this issue, one must consider the different ways in which business leaders can secure legitimacy for their rule—that is, justify their authority. Table 8.2 summarizes the three classic bases of authority: *personal authority* (including charismatic), which is the way in which founders or empire builders justify their claim to be the leaders; *traditional authority*, or the way in which heirs assert their claims; and *legal-rational authority*, or the way in which professional managers establish their legitimacy (Bendix [1956] 2001, xxv–xxviii; Weber 1978, 215–48).

The three types of authority differ substantively from each other. In order to establish their authority, founders of companies, or the "empire builders" who grow them, rely on the ideas of personal

TABLE 8.2
The Three Types of Authority in the Firm

Type of Authority	Agent	Staff	Legitimation	Limitations
Personal, including charismatic	Successful entrepreneur (founder or empire builder)	Confidants, personal retainers, disciples, inner circle	Personal gifts, talent, exemplary character, success; business legend; divine inspiration	Employees and customers demand proof of gifts and continued success
Traditional	Heir of founder or empire builder	Collaborators of founding entrepreneur or empire builder	Custom or family tradition	Need to show capacity to honor the tradition
Legal-rational	Professional manager	Officials or bureaucrats, other professional managers	Technical competence, formal knowledge, success in other managerial positions, ability to maximize owners' wealth	Failure in the market, antibureaucratic or antitechnocratic reactions

Sources: Weber (1978, 215–48) and Bendix ([1956] 2001, xxv–xxviii).

gifts, talent, exemplary character, demonstrated success, or even divine inspiration. They surround themselves with confidants, personal retainers, and disciples, with an inner circle of unconditional supporters and collaborators who further solidify the founder's grip on the company. The most important limit to their authority is that employees and customers demand proof of personal gifts and continued success.

By contrast, heirs of founders or empire builders face a different task altogether. Their main challenge is to honor the family tradition. As the fictional Thomas Buddenbrook put it to his sister Antonie, "What we should do, damn it, is to sit ourselves down and accomplish something, just as our forebears did" (Mann [1901] 1994, 259). Heirs face a particularly difficult task for a number of reasons.

First, they must appear to be modest and hardworking. Thomas Buddenbrook made this point to his wayward brother Christian: "You will impress [the employees] more by behaving as an equal and energetically doing your duty, than by making use of your prerogatives and taking liberties" (Mann [1901] 1994, 260). Second, heirs need to ensure that the collaborators of the founder or empire builder do not undermine their plans and commands. Third, heirs must create the perception that they embody the family tradition:

> Thomas Buddenbrooks's prestige was of a different sort. He was not just one man—people honored in him the unique and unforgettable contributions of his father, his grandfather, and great-grandfather; quite apart from his own success in commercial and public affairs, he was the representative of a century of civic excellence. The most important factor, to be sure, was the easy, refined, and irresistibly charming way he had of embodying that history and turning it to his own account. (Mann [1901] 1994, 402)

Lastly, heirs must learn to navigate the all-too-frequent feuds within the family, such as the one noted in the case of the Wallenberg family during the early 1970s. As Johann Buddenbrook put it,

> Father—we sat here so cheerful this evening, it was such a lovely celebration, we were so happy and proud of our accomplishments, of having achieved something, of having brought our firm and our family to new heights, to a full measure of recognition and respect. But this acrimony with my brother, your eldest son, Father—let us not have a hidden crack that runs through the edifice we have built with God's gracious help. A family has to be united, to hold together, Father; otherwise, evil will come knocking at the door. (Mann [1901] 1994, 44)

The third classic way of justifying one's authority in the firm is totally different from personal and traditional rule. Professional managers build the legitimacy of their authority on the basis of their technical competence, academic qualifications, formal knowledge, or success in other managerial positions (Kerr et al. [1960] 1964, 123–24). Failure in the marketplace, or antibureaucratic or antitechnocratic reactions from employees or customers can undermine their authority.

Ana Patricia Botín faces a complex, if manageable, situation. Her father, Emilio Botín III, is both an heir and an "empire builder." Thus, his authority is more of the personal, even charismatic kind, as some of the evidence in this chapter seems to indicate. It will be hard for her to match or surpass her father's record of accomplishment given that the denominator has grown so much. In order to be legitimate as an heiress, she needs to honor the family tradition and to work with the collaborators of her father, the empire builder, without alienating them, a nontrivial task to say the least.

As the family's stake is very small and the likelihood of building a new empire, or of significantly adding to the existing one, appears to be lower than in the past, she will find it relatively hard to obtain traditional legitimacy for her claims to succession. However, Ana Patricia Botín can claim to be a professional banker, someone with a distinguished record of accomplishment at several banks in various countries, and across businesses, from investment banking to asset management, and from wholesale to retail banking. She has herself indicated that establishing her technical qualifications for the job and her demonstrated experience is perhaps the best way for her to lay a claim to the presidency: "What annoys me is the presumption that I am not qualified for the job. I have spent 20 years in banking. I built Santander's Latin American network from scratch. Before the merger [with BCH in 1999], I was running Santander's corporate treasury, private banking and asset management divisions, and I was managing 50,000 people in Latin America" (*Financial Times*, 24 March 2002). Naturally, there is a serious limitation to this strategy. As Gloria Alonso, the CFO of Acciona (a large family-owned construction and energy company), has put it, "her surname has been both an advantage and a handicap.... Being a Botín also means that she will never get full credit for her work."[16]

Our argument is that Ana Patricia Botín will be more successful if she seeks to justify her authority by reference to her technical competence, formal knowledge, and success in other managerial positions, including her years at J.P. Morgan, Banco Santander de Negocios, Banco Santander, and Banesto. She has founded Suala (a private equity fund) and Razona (an Internet banking consultancy) and two foundations, Empresa y Crecimiento (a venture

TABLE 8.3
Recent Awards, Prizes, and Distinctions Earned by Ana Patricia Botín

Year	Award, Prize, or Distinction	Institution
2006	#1 European Businesswoman of the Year	*Financial Times*
2005	#1 European Businesswoman of the Year	*Financial Times*
2005	#8 Most Powerful Businesswoman outside the United States	*Fortune*
2005	#99 Most Powerful Women	*Forbes*
2005	A.T. Kearney Prize for Best Manager in the Financial Sector	A.T. Kearney
2005	#33 Most Influential People in Spain	*Actualidad Económica*
2004	#2 European Businesswoman of the Year	*Financial Times*
2004	One of the 25 Most Influential Business People	CNN
2004	#6 Most Powerful Businesswoman outside the United States	*Fortune*
2003	#20 Most Powerful Businesswoman outside the United States	*Fortune*

Source: Factiva.

capital fund for Latin America) and Conocimiento y Desarrollo (a business-university partnership in Spain). She has lived—studying or working—in several European and Latin American countries as well as in the United States. She speaks several languages. The press has identified her on several occasions as one of the most influential businesspeople in the world (table 8.3). Her immediate challenge is to excel as president of Banesto, to demonstrate that she can run a major bank all by herself (Márquez Dorsch and Barbat Hernández 2005).

The latest figures show that under Ana Patricia's leadership, Banesto has consolidated itself as one of the country's five largest banks. Her biggest accomplishment is the "Banespyme" program, which has helped the bank attract some 16,000 new customers among small and medium enterprises, lured by a sophisticated information

TABLE 8.4
Stock Analysts' Recommendations concerning Banesto Shares

		Strong buy	Buy	Hold	Underperform	Sell	Total	Net
2006	End	5	0	3	3	1	12	1
	Beginning	6	2	1	3	0	12	5
2005	End	1	3	5	3	1	13	0
	Beginning	1	5	4	2	1	13	3
2004	End	2	4	6	3	0	15	3
	Beginning	2	3	8	2	0	15	3
2003	End	2	5	3	1	0	11	6
	Beginning	2	6	2	1	0	11	7
2002	End	0	0	0	0	0	0	0
	Beginning	0	0	0	0	0	0	0
2001	End	0	0	0	0	0	0	0
	Beginning	0	0	0	0	0	0	0
2000	End	0	0	0	0	1	1	−1
	Beginning	0	0	0	0	1	1	−1
1999	End	0	0	0	2	0	2	−2
	Beginning	0	0	2	0	0	2	0
1998	End	1	1	4	1	3	10	−2
	Beginning	1	2	3	1	3	10	−1
1997	End	0	0	6	6	2	14	−8
	Beginning	0	0	6	6	2	14	−8
1996	End	4	1	0	5	3	13	−3
	Beginning	1	1	5	2	4	13	−4
1995	End	0	0	5	4	4	13	−8
	Beginning	0	0	6	4	3	13	−7
1994	End	1	0	1	3	4	9	−6
	Beginning	0	0	1	3	5	9	−8
1993	End	2	0	11	1	5	19	−4
	Beginning	3	0	10	1	5	19	−3
Total		34	33	92	57	48	264	

Source: I/B/E/S (Institutional Brokers Estimates System).
Note: The NET column was calculated subtracting the sum of "underperform" and "sell" from the sum of "strong buy" and "buy."

technology platform. Stock analysts have responded favorably to the changes at Banesto since 2003, increasing their coverage and issuing more positive recommendations (see table 8.4). In addition, she has managed to improve the bank's efficiency and productivity rates above those of the average for the Spanish banking sector. A former executive at the bank explained:

> The image of Ana Patricia and that of Banesto are merging with each other, which is very good for the bank. Until a few years ago, Banesto was perceived as a rural, anti-quated, obsolete and inefficient bank; now it is perceived as modern. The fact that the president is a young woman has undoubtedly contributed to the success, especially in a moment that Spanish society expects and values change. (quoted in *Dinero* 952, March 2006, p. 14)

Ana Patricia Botín has the potential of prolonging Santander's impressive two-decade period of outstanding performance. As president of Santander, she would face many challenges, including not only the legitimacy issues just analyzed but also the fact that she is a woman. Banking is still a boys' club everywhere around the world. It is simply admirable that she has made it so far, even over-coming a painful, three-year "exile" between 1999 and 2002. She is not only hardworking and ambitious but also cosmopolitan, smart, and persistent, as anyone who has conversed with her can testify. Some interviewees pointed out that she combines the intelligence of her grandfather and the intuition of her father. According to many, she has the "right stuff"—to use Tom Wolfe's (1979) terminology—to be the top executive of one of the world's ten largest banks, and perhaps to turn it into one of the five largest.

For many outsiders, however, the issue is not so much whether Ana Patricia is qualified for the job, but rather whether she is *the most* qualified among the executives who could potentially become president. Observers point out that, among the bank's executives, CEO Alfredo Sáenz, is a superb candidate, a veteran of several merg-ers, and a seasoned executive who knows commercial banking in and out. However, given that he is only eight years younger than Emilio Botín III, he would be a transition president rather than one who could lead the bank to a new level of competitiveness and prominence. Some observers think that Matías Rodríguez Inciarte is another potential candidate, but he has never run a bank by himself, although he has actively participated in most of Santander's key decisions over the past two decades and has counterbalanced the president's impulsive decision making with his good judgment and prudence. Another, even less likely possibility, would be Francisco Luzón, the former president of Argentaria. Although one might conceive that an outsider could become president of Santander, most observers believe this is highly improbable.

If one restricts the choice set to the four well-qualified individuals we have just mentioned (see table 8.5), our prediction is that Ana Patricia Botín will become the next president of Santander. First, she is younger than the three other inside candidates and thus her appointment as president could represent a new and potentially exciting chapter in the history of Santander, as opposed to a transition regime. Second, she has achieved more public visibility, in spite of the fact that she has continued to avoid daily contact with the press and that she was not active in the banking sector for three years (1999–2002). While 334 articles in the *Financial Times*, the *Wall Street Journal*, and the *Wall Street Journal Europe* prior to the end of 2005 have mentioned Emilio Botín III, 84 have mentioned Ana Patricia Botín, 77 Francisco Luzón, 76 Alfredo Sáenz, and just 7 Matías Rodríguez Inciarte (see figure 8.1). Third, Sáenz, Inciarte, and Luzón share with Ana Patricia the fact that they all owe their position at Santander to Emilio Botín III. Lastly, our evidence indicates that a majority of observers, analysts, and even the market at large expect her to become the next president of Santander.

It is also important to mention that Santander has started to prepare the ground for the transition by replacing some top managers with Ana Patricia's close collaborators. For instance, in the summer of 2006 two young executives recruited by her to join Santander a few years ago have been appointed to top positions at Abbey and Banesto (*El País*, 16 July 2006). This move is yet another demonstration of how skillful the family has become at running the bank. Rather than waiting for the succession to take place before key managerial changes are made, they are ensuring that if Ana Patricia becomes president she will have the foundation of a team of trusted executives in place, people who belong to her same generation.

From the point of view of who is in control and who influences the most important strategic decisions, Santander has been a

TABLE 8.5

Key Executives of Santander and Their Origins in Other Spanish Banks
or Institutions

Name and Education	Professional Origin	Santander Positions
Emilio Botín-Sanz de Sautuola y García de los Ríos (b. 1934) Lawyer and economist, Universidad Comercial de Deusto	Banco Santander (1958–present)	Director General (1967–86) Member of the board of directors (1960–present) President (1986–99) Co-president, SCH (1999–2001) President, SCH (2001–present)
Ana Patricia Botín-Sanz de Sautuola y O'Shea (b. 1960) Economist, Bryn Mawr College	J.P. Morgan (1981–88)	Banco Santander (1988–91) Board member (1989–present) Director general, Banco Santander de Negocios (1991–94) CEO, Banco Santander de Negocios (1994–99). President, Banesto (2002–present)
Alfredo Sáenz (b. 1942) Lawyer and economist, Universidad Comercial de Deusto	Tubacex and other steel firms (1965–82) Banco de Vizcaya (1982–88). CEO, BBV (1988–93)	President, Banesto (1993–2002) CEO, SCH (2002–present)
Matías Rodríguez Inciarte (b. 1948) Economist, Universidad Complutense de Madrid	Trade attaché, Spanish Embassy in Chile (1973–77) Technical secretary-general, Ministry of Economy and Finance (1977–78) State secretary for relations with the EEC (1978–80) Secretary-general for economic affairs (1980–81) Minister of the presidency (1981–82)	Banco Santander (1984–present) Member of the board of directors (1984–present) Subdirector general, Banco Santander (1986–94) Second or third vice president, Banco Santander and SCH (1994–present)

(continued)

TABLE 8.5 *(continued)*

Name and Education	Professional Origin	Santander Positions
Francisco Luzón (b. 1948) Economist, Universidad Comercial de Deusto	Banco de Vizcaya (1972–88) President, Banco Exterior de España (1988–91) President, Argentaria (1991–96)	Banco Santander (1996–present) Director general for Latin America (1996–present)
José María Amusátegui (b. 1932) Lawyer, Universidad Complutense de Madrid	Abogado del Estado (Corps of State Attorneys) Altos Hornos de Vizcaya (1967–70) Vice president, Instituto Nacional de Industria (1970–74) President, Intelsa (1975–80). Vice-president, Instituto Nacional de Hidrocarburos (1981–85) Vice-president, Telefónica (1985–91) Vice-President and CEO, Banco Hispano Americano (1985–91) President, Banco Hispano Americano (1991) Co-president, BCH (1991–92) President, BCH (1992–99)	Co-president, SCH (1999–2001)
Angel Corcóstegui (b. 1951) Civil engineer, Universidad de Cantabria PhD and MBA, The Wharton School.	Chase Manhattan Bank Banco de Vizcaya BBV CEO, BCH (1994–99)	CEO, SCH (1999–2002)

Sources: Factiva; *Who's Who in Spain;* www.gruposantander.com.

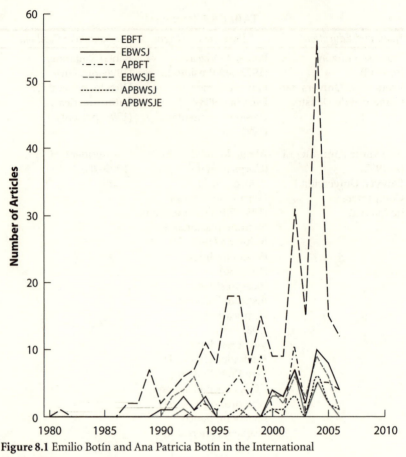

Figure 8.1 Emilio Botín and Ana Patricia Botín in the International
Financial Press, 1980–2006

Source: Factiva.

Notes: EBFT (Emilio Botín in the *Financial Times*); EBWSJ (Emilio Botín in the *Wall Street Journal);* EBWSJE (Emilio Botín in the *Wall Street Journal Europe*); APBFT (Ana Patricia Botín in the *Financial Times*); APBWSJ (Ana Patricia Botín in the *Wall Street Journal);* APBWSJE (Ana Patricia Botín in the *Wall Street Journal Europe*).

family bank since half a century ago. During this time it has grown to become one of the largest and best-performing banks in the world. In the next chapter, we analyze whether its managerial style, corporate governance, and succession practices have affected its growth prospects and performance.

9

The Future of a Global Group

> Banking is a difficult business, rooted in prudence and patience, in which one cannot lower one's guard.[1]

—Emilio Botín III, in *El País,* 26 April 1994

Santander's remarkable trajectory is open-ended. It is hard to assess with accuracy how much the bank can continue growing and delivering good returns, whether it will successfully weather changes in the regulatory and competitive environment, and for how long members of the Botín family will continue to exert a decisive influence over governance and strategic decision making. In this concluding chapter, we look toward the future based on the trends of the past, while keeping an eye on possible contingencies and discontinuities. We begin by assessing Santander's performance in terms of growth, efficiency, shareholder returns, and the quality and impact of key strategic decisions. Based on that analysis, we evaluate the extent to which the bank's present corporate governance arrangements are sustainable into the future. A deterioration in financial performance in general, and stockholder returns in particular, could potentially affect the stability of the present ownership and control structure at the bank. We end with an analysis of the lessons to be drawn from Santander's trajectory as an emerging global bank.

Santander's Phenomenal Growth and Its Efficiency

If growth were the sole indicator by which to measure performance, then the management of Santander over the past two decades has been an unmitigated success. Since 1985 it has climbed from 7th to 1st place in Spain, from being a negligible player to being ranked number one in both Latin America and the Euro Zone, and from 152nd to 10th in the world. Market capitalization has grown from approximately US$3 billion to US$115 billion, and the customer base from 750,000 to 66 million. No other major bank in the world has grown so quickly over a comparable period of time, except for HBOS, the former Bank of Scotland (see table 4.2).

As we have argued in previous chapters, several considerations motivated the bank's management to pursue growth. One motive was the increasing importance of scale in the midst of the globalization of financial markets. Another was the competitive threat posed by the much larger European rivals in the wake of Spain's entry into the European Community in 1986. Rivalry with the other large Spanish banks, also affected by the same competitive forces, was a third factor. A fourth motivation was the family's desire to turn Santander into a nationally and internationally prominent bank, even at the risk of losing control. Emilio Botín III's own preference for growth appears to be present at each of the main strategic decisions of the past two decades. These factors and motivations played a role independent of each other. Combined, they provided a strong, almost irresistible thrust for growth.

Santander also stands out as a relatively efficient bank when one compares it to its international peers of similar size. In 2005 only two banks among the world's ten largest—HSBC and Bank of America—had a lower cost-to-income ratio than Santander's, which stood at 53 percent. Citibank and the Royal Bank of Scotland had worse efficiency ratios. Within Spain, BBVA had a lower ratio of 48 percent, and Popular, which is one of the world's most efficient banks, had a stunning 39 percent. Some of the large European rivals had ratios in excess of 60 (e.g., Barclays, ING) or even 70 percent (e.g., Deutsche). Santander's efficiency has been boosted by its information technology investments, personnel training efforts, and stable framework for collective bargaining and employee relations.

Santander's Shareholder Returns

While Santander's rate of growth over the past two decades has been truly outstanding, its financial performance, although solid, has not been as stellar. The bank has consistently delivered profits every year in an amount equivalent to between 10 and 20 percent of the book value of equity (return on equity). In 2005 Santander reported profits in the amount of US$7.7 billion, and a stunning US$10.3 billion in 2006. However, profitability does not accurately capture whether Santander's managers have furthered the interests of shareholders, who care about returns, not profits.

Returns to shareholders are also important to strategy. First, Santander's future expansion plans depend on whether it can attract and retain equity investors. As the bank's CEO, Alfredo Sáenz, remarked in an interview, Santander does not have enough cash to continue making large acquisitions, and income from the disposal of nonfinancial investments no longer suffices. Second, and most important for the purposes of this book, control of the bank is vulnerable to shareholder dissatisfaction, given that the Botín family and the board of directors together hold less than 5 percent of the outstanding shares. If shareholder returns were to deteriorate significantly, outsiders with a credibly better idea as to how to improve management of the bank could launch a takeover by offering Santander's 2.34 million individual shareholders a better deal for their investment. Still, as Alfredo Sáenz noted, a prospective acquirer would need to offer Santander's small shareholders a premium of some 50 to 60 percent given that the bank is growing at some 20 percent per annum, and its profits at an even higher rate.

We use total annual shareholder returns as the key indicator. We calculate these as the increase in the market value of the shares plus any amount paid out as dividends and any other payments such as reductions in the nominal value of shares or stock repurchases that took place during the year. We then reduce the sum by any payments for capital increases and any conversions of convertible bonds. Lastly, we express the difference as a percentage of market capitalization at the beginning of the year.

Tables 9.1 and 9.2 display the annual total shareholder returns for Santander and other banks since 1986, and the geometric

TABLE 9.1A

Total Shareholder Returns in Dollar Terms (in percentages) for the Major Global Banks and Spanish Domestic Banks, Ranked in Terms of Market Capitalization as of 2006 (1986–1996)

	1986	1987	1988	1989	1990	1991	1992	1993	1994	1995	1996
Citigroup	-2.0	10.2	-1.7	32.6	-18.6	74.7	25.0	62.9	-15.4	97.7	46.3
Bank of America		-16.7	64.3	74.1	-48.3	85.0	30.6	-1.4	-4.4	59.8	44.4
HSBC	52.3	-4.6	2.0	34.7	-24.9	101.1	62.0	114.0	-25.3	45.1	45.9
JP Morgan Chase & Co.	-1.7	-45.5	59.0	4.3	-62.4	105.0	88.1	7.4	-6.5	68.8	56.9
Mitsubishi UFJ	63.4	87.2	35.4	-12.6	-30.6	35.5	-10.0	28.7	3.3	-3.6	-17.1
UBS	51.7	-31.1	-6.3	56.2	-23.4	29.4	9.3	87.6	-9.9	22.3	-21.1
Royal Bank of Scotland	17.7	60.5	-0.7	41.6	-2.9	4.0	12.0	121.7	-4.9	53.7	10.7
Wells Fargo	22.5	6.6	36.0	45.5	-3.4	81.9	21.5	15.9	-1.2	46.0	35.6
Santander			**19.4**	**-11.4**	**-6.7**	**-11.1**	**-5.4**	**27.9**	**1.2**	**36.6**	**31.9**
BNP Paribas									-3.6	0.2	-12.0
ING							20.4	67.6	3.6	47.9	38.9

Wachovia	15.1	-16.5	18.1	-2.8	-20.5	104.9	50.4	-2.1	4.3	39.9	37.5
Mizuho Financial Group	52.1	95.4	20.5	-14.5	-29.8	34.7	-30.3	19.0	19.4	4.9	-26.5
BBVA				3.6	-26.5	14.3	-23.4	13.5	16.7	51.0	54.3
Deutsche Bank	13.0	-40.4	32.9	58.1	-17.3	13.1	-7.3	30.7	-7.0	5.2	0.7
Crédit Agricole											
ABN AMRO						41.8	22.9	38.6	-0.7	38.3	48.4
Banco Popular Español			22.2	9.4	20.9	17.9	-8.4	24.5	10.5	61.0	9.7
Banesto			3.7	6.9	-27.8	-0.8	-36.8	-11.6	-37.3	-1.5	11.6

Source: Datastream International.

Notes: Data for Mitsubishi UFJ in the years 2001 and prior are the returns of Bank of Tokyo-Mitsubishi. Data for Mizuho Financial Group in the years 2000 and prior are the returns of Dai-Ichi Kangyo Bank.

TABLE 9.1B

Total Shareholder Returns in Dollar Terms (in percentages) for the Major Global Banks and Spanish Domestic Banks, Ranked in Terms of Market Capitalization as of 2006 (1997–2006)

	1997	1998	1999	2000	2001	2002	2003	2004	2005	2006	1991– 2006	2003– 2006
Citigroup	79.7	–6.8	70.1	23.5	0.0	–23.9	41.6	2.7	4.6	19.6	26.4	16.1
Bank of America	27.3	1.3	–14.0	–4.5	42.7	14.5	20.1	21.5	2.4	20.7	19.1	15.9
HSBC	18.3	4.7	73.6	8.5	–18.0	–2.5	51.0	12.9	–2.2	19.1	26.1	18.7
JP Morgan Chase & Co.	25.5	32.8	11.7	–10.0	–17.4	–30.7	60.3	10.0	5.7	25.6	21.6	23.7
Mitsubishi UFJ	–25.0	–24.6	35.0	–28.1	–13.9	–18.2	44.4	30.8	34.1	–7.9	1.0	23.6
UBS	68.6	8.7	–10.9	27.0	–7.2	–1.1	45.2	25.9	16.7	31.2	17.0	29.3
Royal Bank of Scotland	36.8	29.7	13.8	45.5	5.5	1.0	27.7	18.1	–7.2	35.0	22.2	17.2
Wells Fargo	82.1	5.0	3.3	40.7	–20.2	10.3	29.5	9.0	4.5	16.8	21.0	14.5
Santander	**60.4**	**22.8**	**14.5**	**–3.2**	**–19.9**	**–15.4**	**78.7**	**8.0**	**9.3**	**46.2**	**14.7**	**32.5**

BNP Paribas	42.7	58.0	14.5	-1.7	5.3	-6.0	60.7	20.0	15.4	41.1	15.8	33.1
ING	20.2	47.8	0.9	35.2	-34.1	-31.1	46.2	36.7	20.1	33.1	19.8	33.7
Wachovia	42.2	22.1	-43.5	-9.8	16.1	19.5	31.8	16.8	4.3	12.0	17.6	15.8
Mizuho Financial Group	-58.7	-9.4	76.5	-23.7	-66.2	-54.2	218.2	68.6	59.3	-9.6	-2.9	66.7
BBVA	83.1	46.7	-8.3	6.7	-15.2	-20.4	49.0	32.4	3.4	39.1	17.7	29.8
Deutsche Bank	54.2	-15.7	49.9	0.5	-14.1	-33.6	84.6	9.3	12.0	42.4	10.4	33.9
Crédit Agricole					-1.5	67.3	34.2	5.8	38.2	26.5	34.6
ABN AMRO	23.5	10.9	21.5	-5.1	-25.9	6.6	51.6	19.8	3.6	29.8	18.4	25.0
Banco Popular Español	46.4	10.3	-12.0	10.0	-3.2	28.1	50.6	13.9	-5.0	53.1	17.2	25.7
Banesto	27.4	34.1	19.7	-14.7	-8.5	-33.5	67.6	22.8	7.2	52.4	2.0	35.4

Source: Datastream International.
Notes: Data for Mitsubishi UFJ in the years 2001 and prior are the returns of Bank of Tokyo-Mitsubishi. Data for Mizuho Financial Group in the years 2000 and prior are the returns of Dai-Ichi Kangyo Bank.

TABLE 9.2A

Total Shareholder Returns in Local Currency Terms (in percentages) for the Major Global Banks and Spanish Domestic Banks, Ranked in Terms of Market Capitalization as of 2006 (1986–1996)

	1986	1987	1988	1989	1990	1991	1992	1993	1994	1995	1996
Citigroup	−2.0	10.2	−1.7	32.6	−18.6	74.7	25.0	62.9	−15.4	97.7	46.3
Bank of America		−16.7	64.3	74.1	−48.3	85.0	30.6	−1.4	−4.4	59.8	44.4
HSBC	52.0	−4.8	2.5	34.7	−24.9	100.6	61.4	113.5	−25.2	45.0	46.0
JP Morgan Chase & Co.	−1.7	−45.5	59.0	4.3	−62.4	105.0	88.1	7.4	−6.5	68.8	56.9
Mitsubishi UFJ	29.3	43.6	39.3	0.5	−34.5	24.9	−10.1	15.0	−7.6	−0.4	−6.8
UBS	18.7	−45.5	10.4	60.4	−36.7	37.5	18.2	90.2	−20.6	7.5	−7.9
Royal Bank of Scotland	14.8	26.6	3.1	58.8	−18.9	7.2	38.4	126.8	−10.1	54.8	0.5
Wells Fargo	22.5	6.6	36.0	45.5	−3.4	81.9	21.5	15.9	−1.2	46.0	35.6
Santander			**25.8**	**−14.5**	**−18.6**	**−9.8**	**12.4**	**59.3**	**−6.8**	**25.9**	**41.4**

BNP Paribas									-12.9	-8.2	-6.5
ING							28.2	78.8	-7.4	36.6	49.9
Wachovia	15.1	-16.5	18.1	-2.8	-20.5	104.9	50.4	-2.1	4.3	39.9	37.5
Mizuho Financial Group	20.1	49.9	24.0	-1.6	-33.8	24.1	-30.4	6.4	6.7	8.5	-17.4
BBVA				-0.1	-35.9	15.9	-9.0	41.3	7.5	39.2	65.5
Deutsche Bank	-11.1	-51.2	49.5	50.8	-26.9	14.8	-1.0	40.1	-17.0	-2.8	8.4
Crédit Agricole											
ABN AMRO						43.7	30.8	48.0	-11.3	27.8	60.1
Banco Popular Español			28.7	5.5	5.4	19.6	8.9	55.0	1.7	48.4	17.6
Banesto			9.3	3.1	-37.1	0.7	-24.9	10.1	-42.2	-9.2	19.6

Source: Datastream International.
Notes: Data for Mitsubishi UFJ in the years 2001 and prior are the returns of Bank of Tokyo-Mitsubishi. Data for Mizuho Financial Group in the years 2000 and prior are the returns of Dai-Ichi Kangyo Bank.

TABLE 9.2B

Total Shareholder Returns in Local Currency Terms (in percentages) for the Major Global Banks and Spanish Domestic Banks, Ranked in Terms of Market Capitalization as of 2006 (1997–2006)

	1997	1998	1999	2000	2001	2002	2003	2004	2005	2006	1991–2006	2003–2006
Citigroup	79.7	–6.8	70.1	23.5	0.0	–23.9	41.6	2.7	4.6	19.6	26.4	16.1
Bank of America	27.3	1.3	–14.0	–4.5	42.7	14.5	20.1	21.5	2.4	20.7	19.1	15.9
HSBC	18.5	4.7	74.2	8.9	–18.0	–2.5	50.3	13.0	–2.4	19.4	26.1	18.6
JP Morgan Chase & Co.	25.5	32.8	11.7	–10.0	–17.4	–30.7	60.3	10.0	5.7	25.6	21.6	23.7
Mitsubishi UFJ	–16.0	–34.6	22.3	–19.7	–1.3	–26.1	30.7	25.1	55.2	–7.6	0.2	23.7
UBS	83.1	2.4	3.9	28.6	–5.0	–17.6	29.9	15.7	35.3	21.5	16.7	25.4
Royal Bank of Scotland	42.3	28.3	17.4	57.0	8.3	–8.7	14.8	10.1	3.8	18.4	22.1	11.7
Wells Fargo	82.1	5.0	3.3	40.7	–20.2	10.3	29.5	9.0	4.5	16.8	21.0	14.5
Santander	88.0	14.2	34.1	3.3	–15.5	–28.2	48.6	0.3	26.0	30.8	16.7	25.2
BNP Paribas	65.1	46.7	34.1	4.9	11.1	–20.2	33.7	11.4	32.9	26.2	11.4	25.7

ING	40.9	36.9	18.2	44.3	-30.5	-41.5	21.6	26.9	38.3	19.1	18.3	26.3
Wachovia	42.2	22.1	-43.5	-9.8	16.1	19.5	31.8	16.8	4.3	12.0	17.6	15.8
Mizuho Financial Group	-53.6	-21.5	60.3	-14.9	-62.1	-57.9	192.7	59.9	82.6	-8.8	-3.7	67.1
BBVA	114.6	36.4	7.5	13.9	-10.6	-32.4	23.9	22.8	19.1	24.4	19.8	22.6
Deutsche Bank	79.9	-21.9	75.6	7.3	-9.5	-43.7	53.5	1.4	29.0	27.4	10.3	26.5
Crédit Agricole						-16.4	39.2	24.5	21.9	23.6	5.0	27.1
ABN AMRO	44.7	2.6	42.3	1.3	-21.8	-9.6	26.1	11.2	19.3	16.1	18.4	18.1
Banco Popular Español	71.6	2.5	3.0	17.4	2.0	8.7	25.3	5.7	9.4	36.9	19.3	18.7
Banesto	49.3	24.7	40.2	-8.9	-3.6	-43.5	39.4	13.9	23.5	36.3	3.8	27.9

Source: Datastream International.

Notes: Data for Mitsubishi UFJ in the years 2001 and prior are the returns of Bank of Tokyo-Mitsubishi. Data for Mizuho Financial Group in the years 2000 and prior are the returns of Dai-Ichi Kangyo Bank.

means for the 1991–2006 and 2003–6 periods. No matter whether one expresses the returns in dollars or in local currency, Santander trails most of its international and domestic competitors. This essentially means that investors could have done better had they invested in the stock of other banks, including BBVA. Thus, Santander's current power balance is indeed vulnerable. However, one may attribute most of the gap in shareholder returns to the Latin American crisis (2001–2) and the acquisition of Abbey in 2004. In fact, during 2006 Santander ranked at the top of its peer group in terms of shareholder returns, possibly a sign that its acquisition strategy is paying off. As CEO Alfredo Sáenz explained in an interview, Santander is keenly aware that acquisitions in developed markets need to show results within three years and within one or two years in emerging economies, for shareholders to continue to trust management.

Another useful comparison is to observe if investing in Santander shares was worth the risk of any equity investment relative to a risk-free investment such as government bonds. According to Fernández and Carabias (2006), the ten-year Spanish government bond paid an average of 7.0 percent between 1992 and 2005, and most stock analysts applied an average risk premium of between 3.5 and 4.5 percent. As a result, shareholders would expect at least an 11.5 percent return during that period. Santander actually offered a return of 17.9 percent. This performance was higher than for the blue-chip Ibex-35 index, which yielded 13.6 percent over the same period (excluding Santander's contribution), and the Madrid Stock Exchange general index, which returned 14.9 percent (Fernández and Carabias 2006).

Finally, there is the issue of whether Santander should let shareholders diversify their holdings themselves rather than engage itself in acquisitions in various parts of the world. This potential criticism is based on the notion that managers should let their shareholders make the decision as to where they would like to invest their money. Although intuitively appealing, the argument suffers from several flaws. First, bank managers may have better information than shareholders about which banks to acquire to create an optimal portfolio of bank holdings around the world. Alfredo Sáenz articulated a second, more important problem with the point of view that shareholders, not companies, should diversify: "When you make an acquisition, you are not purchasing a bank; you are acquiring a collection of banking businesses." Hence, good acquisitions bring with them the potential for synergies that can end up creating value for shareholders. Good banks are those that manage to realize the gains from such opportunities.

The Reaction to Key Decisions and Events

In addition to profitability and returns, it is important to examine reactions to a company's strategic decisions. We use four indicators: abnormal stock market returns to a series of key decisions and events; the recommendations of equity analysts at the world's most influential investment banks; the diversification gains from the decision to expand internationally; and visibility in the international financial press.

Abnormal Stock Market Returns

Abnormal stock market returns are a widely used indicator of the market's reaction to important events. One note of caution is necessary. The methodology we employ in calculating abnormal returns is subject to one limitation: it is impossible to totally isolate the effect of the event of interest on stock prices from the many confounding factors internal and external to the company that may have also played a role during the same time period.

    With this caveat in mind, our analysis yields some interesting results. Table 9.3 displays the abnormal stock returns to a series of key events using a five-day, a three-day, and a one-day window in order to assess how robust the results are.[2] The only event that produced consistent and relatively large positive returns was the announcement of the merger with BCH in 1999. At the other extreme, the event that yielded the most negative abnormal returns was the Banco de España's announcement that Santander had won the bid for Banesto. The launching of the *supercuenta* back in 1989 yielded negative results, mainly because the market feared that Santander's margins would suffer, although its deposit market share increased. The Argentine default of late 2001

TABLE 9.3

Abnormal Stock Market Returns to Santander Stock Price in Response to Key Events (in percentages)

Date of Announcement	Event	One Day	Event Window Three Days	Five Days
12 Sept. 1989	Launch of *supercuenta*	-2.4	-1.6	-3.2
25 Apr. 1994	Santander wins Banesto bid.	-10.7	-4.0	-6.6
15 Jan. 1999	Merger with BCH	6.5	8.5	11.1
22 Feb. 1999	Ana Patricia Botín resigns her executive positions.	-1.2	2.7	5.4
15 Aug. 2001	José María Amusátegui resigns as co-president.	0.4	0.0	1.3
23 Dec. 2001	Argentina defaults on its foreign debt.	-2.8	-4.9	-3.3
05 Jan. 2002	Argentina ende peso-dollar convertibility.	0.0	2.6	2.4
13 Feb. 2002	Sáenz replaces Corcóstegui as CEO. Ana Patricia Botín becomes president of Banesto.	-0.3	-1.2	-1.0
26 Jul. 2004	Acquisition of Abbey National Bank	-2.6	-4.9	-3.0
24 Oct. 2005	Acquisition of stake in Sovereign Bancorp	-2.5	-1.7	0.4

Source: Wharton Research Data Services.

Note: We estimated abnormal stock market returns by taking into account the actual change in Santander's stock price during a time window of one, three, or five days on and after the event date. We then compared the observed returns to expected returns that we derived by using Sharpe's model, which we calibrated on Santander's stock price and the market index during the 180-day period from 200 days to 21 days before each event took place.

also drew a strongly negative reaction from the market, but the end to peso-dollar convertibility two weeks later had a somewhat positive effect on Santander's share price. The announcement of the Abbey acquisition in 2004 elicited a negative reaction as well. Finally, the purchase of a nearly 20 percent stake in Sovereign Bank in 2005 drew a mildly negative reaction. Acquisitions typically tend to depress the value of the stock of the acquirer. For example, half of UBS's cross-border acquisitions have resulted in negative abnormal returns (Walter 2004, 196).

The events related to managerial appointments elicited a mixed market reaction. The resignation of Ana Patricia Botín from her various executive positions at the bank in 1999 generated a strong positive reaction from the market using the five-day and the three-day windows, but a mildly negative one using the one-day window. One interpretation is that the market initially disapproved of her departure, but that in the next few days it reassured itself.[3] Amusátegui's resignation as co-president in 2001 elicited a small positive reaction, perhaps because it helped resolve the uneasy situation in which two co-presidents shared power. Corcóstegui's departure as CEO in 2002—announced the same day that Sáenz was replacing him and Ana Patricia Botín became president of Banesto—generated very small negative reactions. Overall, the abnormal returns indicate that the market has been either mildly concerned about or indifferent to changes at Santander, whether in strategy or in management, with the notable exception of the merger with BCH, which it received with enthusiasm.

The Recommendations of Equity Analysts

Table 9.4 displays the recommendations of equity analysts. The data are based on 668 recommendations made by analysts at investment banks between 1993 and 2006. Overall, analysts recommend "strong buy" or "buy" more often than "underperform" or "sell." Only a handful of sell recommendations were issued during this period. The analysts responded to important events as one would expected. For instance, the merger with Central Hispano in 1999 was hailed by improving recommendations, whereas the Argentine crisis in 2001 and 2002 and the acquisition of Abbey in 2004 resulted in a drop in the net balance of recommendations. In summary, equity analysts

TABLE 9.4

Stock Analysts' Recommendations concerning Santander Shares

		Strong buy	Buy	Hold	Under-perform	Sell	Total	Net
2006	End	2	7	4	1	1	15	7
	Beginning	1	7	5	1	1	15	6
2005	End	7	10	10	1	0	28	16
	Beginning	4	14	6	3	1	28	14
2004	End	4	4	18	6	1	33	1
	Beginning	2	7	16	6	2	33	1
2003	End	5	11	16	1	0	33	15
	Beginning	4	12	11	5	1	33	10
2002	End	4	5	18	6	0	33	3
	Beginning	4	9	16	4	0	33	9
2001	End	5	9	14	6	0	34	8
	Beginning	6	5	16	7	0	34	4
2000	End	7	5	8	1	0	21	11
	Beginning	5	7	7	2	0	21	10
1999	End	9	11	7	2	0	29	18
	Beginning	9	10	8	2	0	29	17
1998	End	4	4	7	2	1	18	5
	Beginning	6	5	6	1	0	18	10
1997	End	4	2	10	0	1	17	5
	Beginning	4	3	6	2	2	17	3
1996	End	6	5	6	1	1	19	9
	Beginning	6	4	8	1	0	19	9
1995	End	4	3	9	1	1	18	5
	Beginning	5	1	9	1	2	18	3
1994	End	8	1	12	0	0	21	9
	Beginning	11	3	5	0	2	21	12
1993	End	7	3	5	0	0	15	10
	Beginning	8	3	4	0	0	15	11
Total		151	170	267	63	17	668	241

Source: I/B/E/S (Institutional Brokers Estimates System).

Note: The NET column was calculated subtracting the sum of "underperform" and "sell" from the sum of "strong buy" and "buy."

have generally approved of key strategic decisions and managerial changes at Santander, although the market itself has punished Santander share prices in the wake of some major acquisitions and managerial changes.

Geographical Diversification and Profitability

Santander has pursued international expansion aggressively, first into emerging economies and more recently in Europe. Using data on sixty-two banks—including Santander—headquartered in eight rich countries during the 1995–2004 period, researchers at the Banco de España and the International Monetary Fund concluded that returns on assets increased as banks expanded abroad, especially into emerging economies. They also found that excessive concentration of assets in one region (e.g., Latin America or Europe) reduced the gains from international expansion (García-Herrero and Vázquez 2006).

Santander scored considerably higher than most other banks in the sample used for this study in terms of the percentages of assets located in different geographical areas outside the home country. The average in the sample was 7 percent in other rich countries and 2 percent in emerging economies, compared to about a third in each category for Santander. It is clear that the strongly negative returns the bank suffered in 2001 and 2002 were to a very large extent due to the bank's overexposure to Latin America, a problem that also afflicted other Spanish multinationals (Guillén 2005). The Abbey acquisition in 2004 and the continued growth of its consumer finance operations on the Continent have helped Santander rebalance its geographical presence.

Santander's Image in the International Financial Press

The international financial press has generally devoted an increasing attention to Santander over the past two decades. Back in the 1980s, the *Financial Times*, the *Wall Street Journal*, and the *Wall Street Journal Europe* rarely published an article mentioning Santander, even in passing (see figure 9.1). Interest in the bank started to pick up after Spain's entry into the European Community in 1986. Coverage increased markedly during the 1990s as Santander bought Banesto, merged with Banco Central Hispano, and expanded throughout

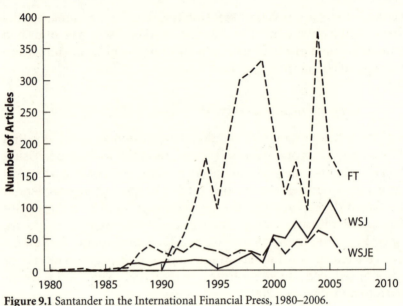

Figure 9.1 Santander in the International Financial Press, 1980–2006.
Source: Factiva.
Notes: FT *(Financial Times)*; WSJ *(Wall Street Journal)*; WSJE *(Wall Street Journal Europe)*.

Latin America. Interest waned when events in that region took a turn for the worse in 2001–2, and then experienced a sudden increase with the Abbey acquisition, which made the bank truly internationally prominent, at least to journalists based in the United States, Europe, and the United Kingdom.

Aside from the frequency of coverage, the international financial and business media have shifted their views of Spanish companies in general, and Santander in particular, several times since these firms started to make headlines around the world for their foreign expansion. One can identify four distinct phases: the initial surprise and disbelief (until 1996 or 1997), growing understanding and adulation (1997–2000), severe warnings about Latin American exposure (2001–2), and realization that Santander is a globally competitive bank (2003 onward).

Until the mid-1990s international financial and business journalists assessed Santander's ascendancy with a mixture of surprise and disbelief. This was particularly evident in the case of the Latin American acquisitions. At best, the media would point out the diversification opportunities from international growth.

But news stories would stop short of referring to Santander as the up-and-coming global competitor it was soon to become, mainly because of its presumed weak or dubious technological, marketing, and managerial capabilities, a perception based on prejudice or ignorance rather than facts.[4]

During the early 1990s journalists used terms such as "Eldorado," "colonization," "invasion," and, most famously, "new conquistadors" (or even "acquistadors") to convey the perception of a primitive but determined, daring, and audacious cadre of Spanish firms—including Santander—taking over a number of Latin American companies that nobody else wanted to buy. Interviews with current or former Madrid correspondents of the international print media indicated that editors' dismissive attitudes meant many of the initial stories about the Spanish firms and managers did not even get into print. Still, both the correspondents and the editors in London and New York played a role in creating a distorted image that grossly underestimated Santander and other Spanish firms at the beginning of what would be a decade-long effort to consolidate a foreign presence that eventually turned several of them into serious European and global contenders.

Santander's relentless foreign expansion through the late 1990s, with no apparent pitfalls or spectacular mistakes, helped it overcome the initially negative image. For instance, *Fortune* magazine (3 April 2000) included two Santander executives—Emilio Botín III and Angel Corcóstegui—among a celebrity-packed list of seventeen names of what it called "the new European business elite," noting not only the bank's Latin American successes but also its new, higher profile within Europe. While the problems of integrating foreign and domestic acquisitions were duly noted, the media recognized the inescapable need for Spanish firms to look for growth abroad and their largely successful process of internationalization (*Economist*, 23 January 1999; *Wall Street Journal Europe*, 4 May 1999).

Many other glowing news stories followed. Particularly adulatory was *Business Week's* cover story on "Spain's Surge" (European edition, 22 May 2000). Interestingly, when Citibank acquired Mexico's largest bank, Banamex, the media pointed out that the move simply enabled the American financial group to match Santander's and BBVA's earlier forays into Mexico as well as other Latin American countries. Implicitly, they were portraying Citibank as a follower rather than a leader (*Wall Street Journal*, 18 May 2001; *Wall Street Journal Europe*, 22 February 2001).

Turmoil in emerging markets, starting with the Brazilian devaluation of 1999 and intensifying with the Argentine economic crisis and default in early 2002, provoked a major shift in the media's assessment of Spanish companies, including Santander. Some of the coverage of the effects of the Latin American crisis was plainly hostile: "After years of boasting about their expanding empire in Latin America, Spain's biggest companies are now suffering because of it" (*Economist*, 5 January 2002). But most of the news stories were evenhanded, reporting with admirable objectivity. They first issued warnings about the dire consequences of crises and defaults in Latin America for companies, such as Santander, with significant exposure to the region (*Financial Times*, 16 October 2001, 22 December 2001; *Wall Street Journal*, 20 July 2001). Later they reported about falling earnings and stock prices as a result of the Argentine collapse. Madrid's Ibex-35 blue-chip stock index and Santander's own share price fell by about 30 percent during 2002. (At the time, Santander was obtaining 52 percent of its profits in Latin America.) The media routinely admonished Santander and other large Spanish companies for concentrating too much of their investments in such a volatile region.[5] In a representative piece, the *Wall Street Journal Europe* (18 June 2001) pointed out in a front-page article that "in the worst-case scenario, a financial meltdown in Argentina would shake investor confidence in Spain and cast doubt on its companies' strategies for the region."

Interestingly, in 2003, after the worst of the crisis in Argentina and elsewhere in Latin America had passed, seeing that Spanish firms were staying the course (while some of those from other countries had exited) and making appropriate provisions and write-offs, the press started to see the situation in a rather different light:

> While Europe's economy continues in the dumps, Spain's largest companies are getting some welcome relief from an unexpected place: Latin America, one of last year's biggest economic basket cases.... So far this year, the Madrid Stock Exchange has been one of the best performing markets in Europe—a feat that many analysts attribute in part to the changing fortunes of Brazil. (*Wall Street Journal*, 2 June 2003, and *Wall Street Journal Europe*, 2 June 2003)

Santander's stock price surged by 43.6 percent during 2003, twice as fast as the 20.6 percent average for Euro Zone banks that year, as reflected in the Dow Jones Euro Stoxx indexes.

Thus, by mid-2003 the international print media had changed their coverage once again, now praising Santander and other Spanish firms for weathering the storm in Latin America successfully and for managing to turn themselves into European and even global players in their own right (e.g., *Wall Street Journal*, 16 September 2003; *Financial Times*, 22 January 2004). The announcement of the acquisition of Abbey in July of 2004 resulted in a barrage of openly critical news stories in the British domestic press and, to a lesser extent, in the *Financial Times* and the *Wall Street Journal*. However, after the competition authorities in Britain, the European Union, and the United States had approved the deal, the press even started to speculate about the newly established "global" bank's future acquisitions (e.g., *Financial Times*, 2 September 2004). And after HBOS abandoned plans for a counterbid in mid September, both the *Financial Times* and the *Wall Street Journal* started to praise the wisdom of Santander and its president, although they continued to point out the many difficulties of turning Abbey around. By mid-2005, however, the international financial press started to report on Santander's progress in terms of implanting its information technology (IT) platform and restructuring the bank, although the *Financial Times* continued to be skeptical regarding Abbey's ability to retain customers. In July 2005 Euromoney selected Santander as the best global bank, labeling it "one of the most remarkable stories in modern banking," and the *Financial Times* chose Ana Patricia Botín as European Businesswoman of the Year in October 2005 and again in 2006. Santander had once and for all become a prominent global player in banking, a contender to be reckoned with, a reference point for analysis and benchmarking, and an example to emulate.

The Lessons from Santander's Experience

Above all, Santander illustrates that commercial banking is currently a business with great international potential. For many years, observers viewed retail or commercial banking as a quintessentially domestic business. Now Citibank, HSBC, and Santander are building their strategies around the transfer of managerial skills across national boundaries in this famously fragmented industry. Moreover, Santander has shown that even a relatively small bank with little international experience based in a comparatively backward country can use retail banking to lift itself into the upper reaches of the rankings. In many ways, Santander's success is a textbook example of the implementation of a technologically based product differentiation strategy coupled with a keen eye for seizing opportunities for international growth.

Another important way in which Santander offers novel insights into managerial problems has to do with the exercise of decision-making influence in excess of ownership. Members of the Botín family continue to exert considerable influence over the bank's governance and strategic decision making thanks to a skillful use of alliances and voting agreements. The present balance, however, is vulnerable to fluctuations in financial performance, given that the board controls less than 5 percent of the equity, and there are 2.3 million individual shareholders. Thus, to a much greater extent than in the past, future growth and expansion will be subject to the usual constraint of keeping shareholders happy.

Our analysis in previous chapters established that the stability and decision-making style promoted by the presence of Botín family members on the board of directors and the management team facilitated Santander's domestic and international growth. Santander's family-led character seemed to bring about at least three advantages during this process of growth. First, while other domestic and foreign banks were enmeshed in difficult postmerger integration battles, Santander—except for three years in the wake of its merger with BCH—benefited from the decisive and unquestioned leadership of a top executive with a clear goal in mind, surrounded by a cadre of close collaborators who implemented strategic decisions in an expeditious and professional manner. Second, Santander's decisive decision making enabled the bank to seize acquisition opportunities and to accomplish the integration of the targets in record time. Third, the Botín family has undoubtedly projected an image of being in control, both inside and outside the bank, which has so far eliminated the threat of a possible takeover, thus giving the top managers breathing room to make decisions, even risky ones.

It seems obvious that family leadership has also brought some disadvantages. Some observers, inside Spain and outside, perceive Santander as a "traditional" bank and have often assailed its corporate governance practices—even though these practices comply with standard criteria of transparency. If Ana Patricia Botín takes the helm—prepared as she is for the job—she will receive more scrutiny than the average chief executive both because she is a woman and because she is a Botín. It is difficult to measure the effect on executives' motivation if they feel that reaching the top position depends on ascriptive characteristics rather than meritocratic considerations. All in all, though, Santander's performance seems to indicate that the balance of the pros and cons of the influence of members of a family over governance and decision making is positive.

The case of Santander does illustrate that family leadership over corporate governance and strategic decision making can deliver excellent growth and performance results. It certainly has become a textbook example of how a family can exert influence well in excess of ownership. Emilio Botín III will surely enter managerial history not just as an outstanding banker but also as someone who thoroughly understood the intricacies of corporate governance in an age in which financial markets exert enormous pressure on the publicly listed business corporation.

Looking toward the Future

Santander has gone through several important transformations. It started as a provincial bank and did not become a national one until a century after its founding. It then experimented with industrial holdings but without losing its character as a commercial bank. International expansion in Latin America and Europe turned the bank into a global competitor. Given management's revealed preference for growth, the most intriguing question for the future is whether Santander will engage in further acquisitions. During our field work we came across rumors and reasoned analyses as to the possibility that Santander might target the likes of Commerzbank, ABN AMRO, or Wells Fargo. We also heard arguments against such possibilities. Our most important conclusion in this regard is that one cannot underestimate Santander in light of the bold moves it has made in the recent past. Also, its present size and performance make it a formidable and capable acquirer. Furthermore, the bank has demonstrated a rare ability to turn underperforming acquired banks around. True, it has had trouble in some Latin American countries such as Bolivia and Peru and, most notably, Argentina. But the overall record in terms of post-acquisition performance is quite distinguished, especially in the cases of large banks, such as Serfin in Mexico, Banespa in Brazil, and Abbey in the United Kingdom.

In Continental Europe, Santander stands to benefit from increasing market integration. Moreover, the existing political constraints on cross-border acquisitions may be receding. Santander has over the years learned about various European markets through its alliances and shareholdings in the United Kingdom (Royal Bank of Scotland), France (Société Générale), Italy (San Paolo IMI), and Germany (Commerzbank). In addition, Santander has operated in consumer finance in as many as ten different Southern, Central, and Eastern European countries for ten to twenty years. Our prediction is that Santander will become the largest bank in the Euro Zone and in Eastern Europe not just in market capitalization but also in operational terms. It all depends on whether suitable acquisition targets becomes available. In 2007, Santander joined forces with Royal Bank of Scotland and Fortis to acquire ABN AMRO for about $US 100 billion. With this deal, Santander significantly strengthens its presence in Brazil.

There is much speculation in financial and journalistic circles as to what Santander plans for the U.S. market, especially after allying itself with Bank of America in Mexico; taking a nearly 20 percent stake in Sovereign, which it has recently increased to almost 25 percent; and entering the automobile finance business. Santander's strategy seems to be one of gaining experience in the U.S. market, just as it did in the United Kingdom with the Royal Bank of Scotland alliance. But a major acquisition is certainly plausible.

If Santander is to become a truly global bank, it must establish a presence in Asia. Top executives have been traveling to China and elsewhere in the region on a regular basis. Though earlier initiatives in Japan, the Philippines, and elsewhere proved disappointing, Santander, BBVA, and Sabadell (a much smaller bank) have established representative offices in China. Other large Spanish multinationals are establishing a presence, as in the case of Telefónica's 10 percent stake in Netcom, China's second-largest fixed-line telecommunications operator. Several of Santander's competitors—Citibank, Bank of America, BBVA, HSBC, and Royal

Bank of Scotland—have taken 5 to 10 percent stakes in some of China's largest banks, while ING, ABN-AMRO, Allianz, and Fortis have established alliances. Some analysts and scholars argue that Spanish banks and companies have an important bargaining chip in their possession when it comes to entering China: their presence in Latin America. The Chinese government and the country's major energy and mining companies have a keen interest in growing their presence in that region of the world, which is rich in natural resources (Blázquez-Lidoy et al. 2005). Because Spanish firms are running much of the basic energy and financial infrastructure, they have come to be seen as natural partners. "Triangulation" among China, Spain, and Latin America has become a popular topic, and speculation about the increasing ties between large Spanish and Chinese companies is mounting. We do not see this as the only, or even the most likely, path for Santander's likely foray into this part of the world. The bank has more often than not gone against the prevailing trend or been a trendsetter. Given the paucity of attractive acquisition targets in markets such as China or India, Santander will probably use minority shareholdings or consumer finance as ways to establish a platform from which bolder moves could be launched in the future. The key constraint has been the difficulty of finding executives that know the region and that also enjoy top management's confidence.

Our interviewees also speculated as to whether Santander should abandon its focus on retail or commercial banking in favor of the corporate segment and "higher" forms of finance such as investment banking. The recent experiences of Deutsche Bank or Dresdner Bank in investment banking should give some pause to those urging Santander to move up the ladder (Smith and Walter 2003; Walter 2004, 154–68). There is plenty of room for growth in retail and commercial banking. There is still scope to improve performance by increasing efficiency, both by reducing costs and by enhancing revenue through increased cross-selling of products via IT platforms such as Partenón, especially in the banks it has acquired.

Developing a capability in investment banking depends on building both expertise and a customer base. One can buy expertise, but it is difficult to own it as the individuals involved are notoriously footloose. Building a solid, relationship-based customer base takes time, as the best clients are those who have grown to need investment banking services. Furthermore, one can make a good case that the organizational cultures of commercial banking and investment banking do not sit well together. Although Santander has made efforts in building an investment bank since the mid-1980s, notable success has eluded it in a way that it has not in retail and commercial banking.

Another tantalizing possibility for the future is that one or two Spanish construction groups might acquire a stake in Santander and dispatch directors to the board. For almost three years, non-profit automobile insurer Mutua Madrileña owned just over one percent of Santander shares and dispatched a director to the board. Mutua Madrileña also used to own 3 percent of ACS and continues to own 5 percent of Sacyr, two of the largest construction and services groups in the country. ACS has recently become a major shareholder of Iberdrola and Sacyr of Repsol-YPF, both Fortune Global 500 companies. Santander has provided credit facilities for both Sacyr and Acciona, another large construction firm, which recently became Endesa's largest shareholder, also a Global 500 firm. Thus, it appears that Santander is becoming deeply involved in the cross-shareholdings linking some of Spain's largest multinational companies, a move that could help preserve the status quo at the bank as well as boost its investment banking business.

————

Santander stands as a useful case study to illustrate that, under conditions of rapid regulatory and competitive change, family influence may prove to be more enabling than constraining, especially when there is a need to combine intuition in decision making with swift and systematic implementation. It also represents a reminder—based on a sample of only one longitudinal observation, to be sure—that family ownership, control, and/or strategic decision making are not necessarily at odds with professional management, meritocracy, shareholder orientation, labor relations based on collective bargaining at the industry level, and other similar attributes of what some consider characteristics of the "modern" business corporation. As for Santander's continued success into the future, it will largely depend not only on balancing the demands of corporate growth and shareholder returns but also on strengthening its intangible assets in the areas of technology and marketing to deliver better financial services at lower cost. Some would say the easy part has been done. Getting from 152nd to 10th place pales in comparison with becoming, or at least approaching, number one in the world. The competition can only get tougher as one gets nearer to the top.

Appendix

A Chronology of Banco Santander

		Grupo Santander		
Year	Economic and Political Context	Domestic Events	International Expansion	Management and Corporate Governance
1857	Banco de Bilbao founded	Banco de Santander is founded.		
1859	First foreign investments in railways			
1868	Peseta adopted as national currency			
1869	Figuerola's free trade reform			
1873	First Spanish Republic (short lived)			
1874		Banco de Santander refuses to join the recently created Banco de España, which monopolizes the issue of currency. It turns itself into a credit society the following year.		
1875	Crowning of Alfonso XII			
1876	End of the Carlist Civil War			
1878	Banco de España given monopoly of note issuance	Banco de Santander establishes a "caja de ahorros" or savings bank.		

1879	Spanish Socialist Workers' Party (PSOE) founded	
1885	Regency of María Cristina	
1891	Adoption of protectionist tariff regime	
1895		Rafael Botín y Aguirre becomes managing director, a position he holds until his death in 1903.
1898	Spanish-American War, leading to loss of Cuba, Puerto Rico, and the Philippines	
1900	Banco Hispano-Americano founded	
1901	Banco de Vizcaya founded	
1902	Banco Español de Crédito (Banesto) founded	Emilio Botín I joins the board of directors.
1903		Emilio Botín II is born (1903–93).
1904	Steeper tariff regime adopted	José María Gómez de la Torre y Botín becomes managing director, a position he occupies until 1923.

(continued)

| | Grupo Santander | | |
Year	Economic and Political Context	Domestic Events	International Expansion	Management and Corporate Governance
1909				Emilio Botín I becomes president of Banco de Santander for the first time, a rotating position which he occupies again in 1911, 1913, 1917, 1919, and 1920–23.
1918	Banco Urquijo founded			
1919	Banco Central founded			
1920				The position of president becomes fixed. Emilio Botín I occupies it until his death in 1923.
1921	Banking Law consolidating self-regulating cartel of six banks (Hispano Americano, Bilbao, Urquijo, Central, Vizcaya, and Banesto)			
1923	Primo de Rivera, dictator			Emilio Botín I dies. Saturnino Briz Larín becomes president until 1949.

1925	First branch outside of home region of Cantabria opens in Osorno, Palencia.	
1926	National Corporatist Organization created	
1930		Emilio Botín II joins board of directors.
1931	Second Spanish Republic	
1934	Revolution in northern region of Asturias repressed by General Franco	Emilio Botín II becomes director general (i.e., managing director), but leaves board. Emilio Botín III is born.
1936	Start of Civil War	Emilio Botín II leaves Spain until Franco's troops enter the city of Santander in August 1937.
1938	Franco, head of rebel government	
1939	End of Civil War	
1940	Restrictive Banking Law passed	

(continued)

| | | Grupo Santander | | |
Year	Economic and Political Context	Domestic Events	International Expansion	Management and Corporate Governance
1941	Instituto Nacional de Industria created			
1942	Banco Central and Banco Internacional de Industria y Comercio merger	Santander acquires Banco de Ávila, Banco Riva Herrero, and Banco de Torrelavega.		
1944	Bretton Woods agreements	"Las Jarillas" Pact between Banco Hispano Americano and Banco Urquijo is adopted.		
1946	Nationalization of Banco de España and reinstatement of self-regulating banking cartel	Acquisition of Banco Mercantil de Santander signals beginning of domestic expansion.		Emilio Botín II joins the board and continues as managing director. Marcelino Botín joins board of directors.
1947			Santander establishes its first presence abroad through an agreement with the Trust Company of Cuba.	
1948	Exclusion of Spain from Marshall Plan			

1950		A Latin American Department is created.	Emilio Botín II becomes president and CEO.
1951		Santander opens a representative office in Havana.	
1952	Santander acquires Banca Hijos de Vázquez López, Huelva.		
1953	Santander acquires Banco Agrario de Baleares. Spanish-American Friendship and Cooperation Treaty		
1955		Santander opens a representative office in London.	
1956	Santander acquires Banco Soler y Torra, in Barcelona.	Santander opens a representative office in Mexico City.	Marcelino Botín is named vice president.
1957		Santander opens a representative office in Caracas and takes a minority equity stake in Banco Intercontinental do Brasil.	

(continued)

| | Grupo Santander | | | |
Year	Economic and Political Context	Domestic Events	International Expansion	Management and Corporate Governance
1958	Spanish membership in IMF and World Bank	Santander acquires Banco Majó Hermanos and Banco Alfonso Mon Pascual.		Emilio Botín III joins Banco de Santander.
1959	Introduction of liberal economic reforms			
1960				Emilio Botín III and his brother Jaime Botín join the board. Ana Patricia Botín is born.
1963			Banco de Santander acquires Banco El Hogar Argentino and renames it Banco de Santander-Argentina.	
1964	First Development Plan			The Fundación Marcelino Botín is created.
1965		Santander founds Banco Intercontinental Español (Bankinter), together with Bank of America.		
1966	BankAmericard and Master Charge credit cards			

Year			
1967		Santander acquires Banco de Fomento de Gerona and Banco Cid, in Galicia.	Emilio Botín III is named a director general (among several).
1968	Second Development Plan	Santander acquires Banco Jaúdenes Bárcena, Vigo, and Banco de Mataró.	
1969		Santander acquires Banco Industrial de Cataluña	
1970	Preferential agreement with EEC	Santander acquires Banco Continental, in Madrid.	
1971	Seven Big Banks' Club created		
1973			Marcelino Botín dies. Emilio Botín III becomes second vice president.
1975	After death of Franco, monarchy of Juan Carlos I		
1976	Adolfo Suárez appointed premier by king		Santander acquires First National Bank of Puerto Rico and Banco Condal Dominicano.

(continued)

		Grupo Santander		
Year	Economic and Political Context	Domestic Events	International Expansion	Management and Corporate Governance
1977	Legalization of Communist Party; first democratic elections; banking crisis in Spain; fiscal reform, personal income tax		Santander opens a branch in New York.	Emilio Botín III becomes CEO of Banco de Santander, with his father continuing as president.
1978	Spanish Constitution	Santander acquires the majority of the capital of Banca Jover and Banco Comercial Español.	Santander acquires Banco Crédito y Ahorro Ponceño with its 13 branches in Puerto Rico and 1 branch in New York.	
1981	Failed coup d'état Leopoldo Calvo-Sotelo premier; partial deregulation of interest rates			Ana Patricia Botín joins J.P. Morgan.
1982	Socialist Party leader Felipe González, premier; Latin American debt crisis	Santander launches telex and telephone banking services.	Santander acquires Banco Español de Chile and Banco del Litoral Asociados in Uruguay.	
1983	Nationalization of Rumasa, including several banks			
1984		Santander acquires Banco Comercial de Cataluña and Banco de Murcia.		Matías Rodríguez Inciarte leaves politics and joins Banco de Santander.

1985	Liberalization of branching		Banco de Santander is traded on the London Stock Exchange.	
1986	Spain and Portugal in EEC; transition period for banking as part of accession treaty	Santander adopts its present logo.	Santander acquires Banco Osorno y La Unión in Chile.	Emilio Botín III and Jaime Botín become presidents of Banco de Santander and Bankinter, respectively, after their father steps down.
1987	Removal of interest rate ceilings	Banco de Santander changes its name to Banco Santander. Bank of America reduces its stake in Bankinter. Santander starts to offer *cesiones de crédito* (loan assignments) to customers, taking in €4,500 million in deposits over five years.	Santander acquires Bankhaus Centrale Credit (CC Bank) in Germany. Banco Santander is traded on the New York Stock Exchange.	
1988	Liberalization of Spanish stock markets; Bilbao–Vizcaya merger forming BBV		Santander signs alliance with cross-shareholding with Royal Bank of Scotland and acquires former Belgian subsidiary of France's Credit du Nord (CC–Banque Belgique).	Ana Patricia Botín joins Banco Santander after working for J.P. Morgan. Rodrigo Echenique named CEO of Santander.

(continued)

| | | Grupo Santander | | |
| | | | | |
Year	Economic and Political Context	Domestic Events	International Expansion	Management and Corporate Governance
1989	Failed Banesto–Banco Central merger; deregulation of savings banks	*Supercuenta*, a high-interest checking account, is launched. Banesto, BBV, and Hispano Americano respond in kind five months later. Santander adopts red as the corporate color.	Santander acquires assets of Bayamon Federal Savings Bank in Puerto Rico from the FDIC and changes the name to Santander National Bank.	Emilio Botín II leaves Santander board of directors. Ana Patricia Botín and her brother Emilio Botín IV join board.
1990		BBV launches the Libretón, a lottery-linked savings account. Santander responds in 1993.	Santander acquires Banco de Comércio e Indústria in Portugal. Banco Santander acquires substantially all the assets of Caguas Central Federal Savings Bank (CCFS) from the Resolution Trust Corporation. The acquisition makes Santander the second-largest bank in Puerto Rico.	

Year				
1991	Banco Central and Banco Hispano-Americano merger forming BCH; merger of state-owned banks forming Argentaria	Santander sells its Banco Jover and Banco Comercial Español subsidiaries to Crédit Lyonnais. Santander launches an investment fund. BBV responds in kind three months later.	Santander purchases minority stake in First Fidelity Bancorporation.	Ana Patricia Botín named a director general of Banco Santander de Negocios.
1992	Seville Expo and Barcelona Olympic Games; European currency crisis affects peseta	Santander sells its Banco Murcia subsidiary to Caja de Ahorros de Valencia, Castellón y Alicante.		Emilio Botín IV joins Bankers Trust.
1993	European Single Market; rise in Spanish foreign direct investment abroad; Bank of Spain intervention in Banesto	Santander launches the *superhipoteca*, a low-interest mortgage. A few days later BBV and Central Hispano follow suit.		Emilio Botín II dies.
1994	Banco de España granted institutional autonomy; Mexican currency crisis	Airtel (including Santander) obtains mobile phone license, beating a consortium led by BBV. Santander acquires Banesto. Santander reduces its stake in Bankinter. Santander launches a personal credit card, and BBV responds in kind within the month.	Banco Santander opens a subsidiary in Mexico. Santander merges Santander National Bank and Banco Santander Puerto Rico.	Matías Rodríguez Inciarte named second vice president of Santander. Angel Corcóstegui named CEO of BCH. Ana Patricia Botín named CEO of Banco Santander de Negocios and joins board of Santander. Rodrigo Echenique steps down as CEO of Santander.

(*continued*)

| | Grupo Santander | | |
Year	Economic and Political Context	Domestic Events	International Expansion	Management and Corporate Governance
1995			Santander acquires Banco Interandino & Intervalores and Banco Mercantil in Perú.	
1996	Conservative Party leader José María Aznar, premier		Santander acquires Banco de Venezuela and Banco Central Hispano-Puerto Rico.	
1997			Santander acquires Banco Río de la Plata in Argentina, Banco Comecial Antioqueño in Colombia, Grupo Financiero InverMéxico, and Banco Noroeste and Banco Geral do Comercio in Brazil and sells stake in First Union.	Emilio Botin II chosen as most influential Latin American banker by *Latin Trade*.

Year			
1998	Santander acquires 200 hectares of land in Boadilla del Monte, 20 km West of Madrid for €210 million, with a view to building its world headquarters.		Emilio Botín IV leaves his executive position at Santander and sets up a hedge fund.
1999	Euro traded for the first time in currency markets, replacing national currencies (including the peseta); Argentaria-BBV merger forming BBVA	Santander-BCH merger creates SCH. Santander helps Royal Bank of Scotland acquire NatWest.	Santander agrees with Grupo Champalimaud to acquire Totta & Açores and Crédito Predial Português.	Emilio Botín III and José María Amusátegui become joint presidents of SCH, while Angel Corcóstegui is named CEO. A month later Ana Patricia Botín leaves her executive positions at the bank.
2000		Santander acquires Banespa (Banco do Estado de São Paulo) and Banco Meridional in Brazil, Banco Serfín in Mexico, and Patagón in Argentina.	
2001	The unified brand, "Santander Central Hispano," in red, is created. Banesto is kept as separate brand.	Santander acquires AKB-Bank in Germany.	Emilio Botín III becomes sole president of BSCH after Amusátegui retires.

(conti–

	Grupo Santander		
Year	Economic and Political Context	Domestic Events	International Expansion	Management and Corporate Governance
2002	Euro coins and notes in circulation; Argentina's debt default and currency devaluation		Santander sells a 24.9% stake in Grupo Financiero Santander Serfin to Bank of America for $1.6 billion.	Alfredo Sáenz replaces Corcóstegui as CEO of SCH. Ana Patricia Botín becomes president of Banesto. Jaime Botín steps down as president of Bankinter and becomes first vice president of Santander.
2003	U.S. invasion of Iraq with support of Premier José María Aznar		Santander forms alliance with Bank of America for the Mexican market, acquires PTF in Poland, and creates Santander Consumer, the consumer finance division in Europe. SCH acquires 12.74% stake in Banco Santander Portugal from the Royal Bank of Scotland, increasing its overall stake to 98%.	

| 2004 | Terrorist bombings in Madrid; Socialist Party leader José Luis Rodríguez Zapatero, premier | Court proceedings begin over the loan assignments (*cesiones de crédito*) case in which Emilio Botín III and other executives are accused of helping bank customers evade up to €48 million in taxes. Santander's Ciudad Financiera, its new corporate campus in Boadilla del Monte, is inaugurated. | Santander acquires Abbey National Bank in the UK and ELCON Finans in Norway and signs a commercial agreement with Bank of China. Santander Consumer Finance signs an agreement to acquire Polskie Towarzystwo Finansowe and an agreement with SNS REAAL to acquire the group's vehicle finance company Abfin. | Emilio Botín III resigns his seat on Bankinter's board of directors, which he occupied since its founding in 1965. Javier Botín O'Shea replaces Jaime Botín on the board of Santander. Ana Patricia Botín is chosen by CNN and *Time* as one of the 25 Global Business Influentials. Antonio de Sommer Champalimaud, owner of 1.5% of Santander and a board member, dies. |
| 2005 | | | Santander is chosen as best global bank by *Euromoney,* purchases largest minority stake in Sovereign Bancorp, and sells stake in Royal Bank of Scotland and Banco Santa Cruz in Bolivia. | *Financial Times* chooses Ana Patricia Botín European Businesswoman of the Year. Her brother, Emilio Botín IV, leaves Santander's board of directors. Elías Masaveu, owner of 0.2% of Santander and board |

(*continued*)

| | | Grupo Santander | | |
| | | | | |
Year	Economic and Political Context	Domestic Events	International Expansion	Management and Corporate Governance
				member, dies. Emilio Botín III, Amusátegui, and Corcóstegui found not guilty in a trial over the severance package of the latter two executives.
2006		Santander provides credit facilities to Sacyr and Acciona, which they use to purchase stakes in Repsol-YPF and Endesa, respectively.	Santander reports profits of US$10.3 billion.	Charges related to the loan assignments are dropped.
2007	Trouble in Spanish real-estate market		Santander joins Royal Bank of Scotland and Fortis in a bid for ABN AMRO.	Santander celebrates its 150th anniversary.

Note: Emilio Botín I stands for Emilio Botín López. Emilio Botín II stands for Emilio Botín-Sanz de Sautuola y López. Emilio Botín III stands for Emilio Botín-Sanz de Sautuola y García de los Ríos. Emilio Botín IV stands for Emilio Botín-Sanz de Sautuola y O'Shea.

Chapter 1: Family-Led Banks in the Global Economy

1. Archaeologists have identified records of banking activity, especially foreign exchange trading and lending, dating to at least four millennia ago. The New Testament mentions the story of Jesus Christ driving the money changers from the Temple in Jerusalem. The world's oldest bank, Banca Monte dei Paschi di Siena, traces its origins to 1472, that is, just after the fall of Constantinople but before the Spanish discovery of the New World.

2. There is some disagreement concerning the exact wording of these quotations. We have obtained them from various sources on the Internet and offer them here merely for the purpose of illustration.

Chapter 2: A Family Bank's Origins

1. "El que da primero, da dos veces."

2. "No hay privilegio de familia, ni de herencia, que no sea arrasado por la ley implacable del mercado libre."

3. Santander's president remained in the city until the arrival of Franco's troops. He and two other board members were imprisoned for a few days by the Republican government. Emilio Botín II, the director general at the time, exiled himself in London and Basle between December 1936 and August 1937 (Martín Aceña 2007, 115–31).

4. This section relies heavily on Hoyo Aparicio (1993; 2000) and Hernández Andreu (2000).

5. In his speech at the 1968 annual shareholders' meeting, Emilio Botín II railed against the campaign waged at the time by "the press and some young economists" in favor of the nationalization of the banks. He had in mind the Madrid daily *Pueblo*, which was directed by a socially conscious Francoist named Emilio Romero. The young economists he was referring to included the author of the book, *The Power of Banks in Spain* (Muñoz 1967), and his mentor, University Professor Juan Velarde Fuertes, a noted economist (see Tortella and García Ruiz 2003).

Chapter 4: Survival of the Biggest?

1. Quoted in García Ruiz and Tortella (1994, 425).

2. In 1989 the government permitted Deutsche Bank to acquire 100 percent of Banco Comercial Transatlántico, which it had helped found in 1950

and of which it already owned 39 percent, in the first foreign takeover of a Spanish bank. (The year also represented the 100th anniversary of Deutsche Bank's first entry into Spain.) In 1994, Deutsche Bank acquired Banco de Madrid. It is now the second largest foreign bank in Spain after Barclays Bank.

3. *Economist*, 19 December 1987; Reuters News, 11 December 1987.

4. *New York Times*, 7 December 1987.

5. Reuters News, 11 December 1987.

Chapter 5: The New World

1. "Para alianzas, para compras, para cualquier tipo de operación futura, la empresa española que tenga una gran presencia en Latinoamérica tiene unas cartas de negociación superiores a las que no tienen inversiones fuera." *Diario de Sesiones del Senado: Comisión de Asuntos Iberoamericanos* 141 (7 June 2001): 16–17.

2. Confidential interview.

3. Local merchants established Banco Español de la Isla de Cuba, which traced its origins to the Caja Real de Descuentos (est. 1854). In 1856 this became the Banco Español de La Habana; the bank failed in 1926. In 1851 Antonio de Urbiztondo y Eguia, then governor-general in the Philippines, encouraged the formation of the first bank there, El Banco Español Filipino de Isabel II. In 1889 the bank changed its name to El Banco Español Filipino, and in 1912 the name changed again to Bank of the Philippine Islands (Banco de las Islas Filipinas); it is the only one of the three banks still functioning today. In 1936 Banco Popular de Puerto Rico absorbed Banco Español de Puerto Rico, which had been established in 1888.

4. Representative offices perform liaison activities for the parent bank but cannot make loans or take deposits because they do not keep their own books.

5. The Trust Company of Cuba, which U.S. and Cuban investors had established in 1905, was a Cuban bank that merged in 1952 with Banco del Comercio. The owners of the bank, the Falla family, were of Spanish origin.

6. A subsidiary or an affiliate—which is minority owned—can fail while the parent bank remains solvent or vice versa.

7. Like a representative office, a branch is part of the parent bank and cannot fail unless the parent fails, and does fail when the parent fails. The branch benefits in its dealings from the entire capital base of the bank. Banks normally use foreign branches for wholesale and corporate banking as well as treasury management but not for retail banking activities (Heinkel and Levi 1992).

8. Barry Newman, "Spain Seeks Commercial, Political Gains through Stronger Ties," *Wall Street Journal*, 3 May 1983, p. 36.

9. In the previous twelve months Royal Bank of Canada and Bank of America had also sold their Dominican subsidiaries to local banks.

10. In 2006 HSBC bought Grupo Financiero del Istmo, giving it 42 branches in Panama and another 178 branches spread out over Costa Rica, Honduras, Colombia, El Salvador, and Nicaragua.

11. Banco Interandino was the former branch of Bank of America. Its executives had bought the bank for a pittance when Bank of America decided to withdraw from Peru during the tenure of the Alan Garcia regime, which was hostile to foreign investors.

12. Banco de Caracas has a subsidiary in the Netherlands Antilles that Santander now wishes to dispose off.

13. Santander sold Banesto Banco Shaw in Argentina to Banamex, which combined it with its subsidiary Banco del Sud. When Citibank acquired Banamex, it sold Banco BanSud to Argentina's Banco Macro. Santander also sold Banesto Chile, the former Banco del Pacifico, which Banesto had acquired in 1991, to Banco Hipotecario y de Fomento (BHIF), which BBVA later acquired.

14. John Tagliabue, "Spanish FDI in LA: With Capital in Hand, Spain Revisits Its Empire," *New York Times*, 29 June 2003. sec. 3, p. 4, col. 1.

15. *Expansión*, 22 January 2002.

16. The interviewee emphasized the word "Mexican."

17. "Trimming Off Unprofitable Latin American Business and Expanding Further ...," *The Banker*, 1 May 2002.

18. Clive Horwood, "The Masters of Retail Banking," *Euromoney*, 1 July 2005.

19. Actually, Santander submitted a joint bid together with Banco Popular de Puerto Rico. Popular took over the thirty-six branches (representing about two-thirds of the deposits) that were not located close to its existing branches. Santander took the branches that were competing with existing Popular branches.

20. Both these acquirers were Puerto Rican banks.

21. Royal Bank of Canada had first entered Puerto Rico with a branch in 1907. Then in 1978 it had bought Banco de San Juan and its fourteen branches, which it combined with the six it already owned. Despite its long tenure in Puerto Rico and the Caribbean, in 1985 the bank had decided to exit the region, selling this and other operations.

22. An Edge Act corporation is a federally chartered U.S. corporation that may only engage in international banking or other financial transactions related to international business, particularly those involved in financing and stimulating foreign trade. A bank may create an Edge Act subsidiary to offer international banking services across state borders. Until recently, U.S. banks could not legally establish a branch across state lines and so used Edges as a partial substitute.

23. The purchaser was Coral Gables–based Commercebank, whose customer base consists of Venezuelan expatriates living in the United States. In 2005 Commercebank bought some deposits from Banco Sabadell's Miami branch.

24. Santander received US$1.6 billion, an amount a little higher than it had paid to acquire the whole bank back in 2000, for a capital gain of about US$700 million. At the same time, the gains from the sale enabled Santander to increase its core capital ratio to 5.5 percent.

Chapter 6: Alliances and Their Limits

1. The thirteen members are AIB Group of Ireland, Banco Santander of Spain, Banco Espirito Santo of Portugal, BHF of Germany, Credit Commercial de France, ING of the Netherlands, Instituto Bancario San Paolo di Torino of Italy, Kredietbank of Belgium, Merita Bank of Finland, National Bank of Greece, Nordbanken of Sweden, the Royal Bank of Scotland, and Unibank of Denmark. William & Glynn's Bank, which RBS subsumed, was one of the five founding banks.

2. In 1990 Crédit Lyonnais had bought another Santander subsidiary, Banco Comercial Español, which had about 100 branches around Madrid. Crédit Lyonnais's purchase of two banks in Spain essentially finished its alliance with Banco Hispano Americano. At the time, Crédit Lyonnais was in the throes of an aggressive international expansion, but when it ran into financial difficulties, it had to sell its foreign acquisitions as a condition of qualifying for a state bail-out. Among many other disposals, it sold Banco Jover and now Crédit Lyonnais España to Caja Madrid and Caja Duero (Tschoegl 2003).

3. T. Burns and S. Iskander, "SG Forms Spanish Alliance," *Financial Times*, 1 February 2000.

4. Ian McConnell, "No Spanish Fly in Royal Ointment," *Herald*, 18 February 2000.

5. *Euromoney*, 1 July 2005.

6. "BSCH Not to Raise Stake in Commerzbank," *Retail Banker International*, 31 October 2000.

7. "Botin Sees No Advantages from Cross Border Mergers," *Reuters News*, 31 January 2000.

8. Ibid.

Chapter 7: Back to Europe

1. "Una vez culminada su expansión por Latinoamérica y cerrada la salida del First Union, el Santander 'afronta,' en palabras de su presidente, 'los desafíos y las oportunidades que va a suponer la Unión Económica y Monetaria Europea. En este posicionamiento estratégico frente al euro es fundamental el reforzamiento de los recursos propios del grupo.'"

2. Lloyds had been operating in Portugal since 1863, when Bank of London and South America established a branch in Lisbon. The Crédit Lyonnais unit, Crédit Franco Portugues, had been operating in Lisbon since 1892.

3. Banco Chemical was the bank that Manufacturers Hanover had set up in 1984 when it became the first foreign bank allowed to enter Portugal since the revolution of 1975.

4. Santander now has four official languages: Spanish, English, Portuguese, and Brazilian Portuguese.

5. Arnold had been ousted as CEO of UBS after reportedly having fallen out with UBS's chairman, Marcel Ospel.

6. This paragraph draws heavily on the account in Horwood (2005).

7. Interview with Alfredo Sáenz, 3 and 4 October 2006.

8. *Financial Times*, 15 October 2004, p. 21.

Chapter 8: Managerial Style, Governance, Succession

1. For a review of the arguments and counterarguments, see Galve Górriz and Salas Fumás (2003).

2. *Actualidad Económica*, 27 November 1995; *El País*, 16 January 1999.

3. Perhaps the most outspoken critic is Rafael Pérez Escolar, a former director of Banesto prior to its takeover by the Banco de España who was subsequently convicted of fraud (sentenced to a ten-year prison term), who caused Emilio Botín some serious legal problems between 2001 and 2005 over the severance payments for Amusátegui and Corcóstegui. His *Memorias* (2005) are filled with unsubstantiated criticisms of the Banco de España and of Emilio Botín. Some journalists have also criticized Mr. Botín, using a mixture of sensationalism and conspiracy theory (Almirón 2003; Novoa 2003). By the end of 2005, all charges against Botín had been dropped.

4. *Euromoney*, January 1995; see also *El País*, 3 February 2002.

5. *El País*, 23 February 1999. Luis Abril, communications director of SCH, however, recounts a different story, in which Ana Patricia Botín actively collaborated with *El País Semanal* on the article but asked not to be on the cover, a request that was ignored. See García de la Granja (2005, 187–88).

6. Botín was a staunch defender of Premier Aznar's economic policies, even before Aznar's election, something that annoyed sitting premier Felipe González (*El País*, 30 January 1996; see also *Expansión*, 27 July 2001.

7. See *El Mundo*, 10 March 2000; *Retail Banker International*, 27 June 2001; *La Vanguardia*, 27 June 2001; *El País*, 27 June 2001; *Business Week*, 4 March 2002.

8. See *Wall Street Journal*, 18 February 2002; *Financial Times*, 22 February 2002; *Wall Street Journal Europe*, 22 March 2002. Some specialized publications reacted quite strongly to the return of family rule to Santander. *The Banker* editorialized: "For the good of SCH, *The Banker* calls for Ms. Ana Patricia Botín to stand down. This is not a reflection of her qualifications. Her only crime is her surname, but in today's world [i.e., after Enron and WorldCom], nepotism, and its threat to proper corporate governance, is unacceptable" (*The Banker*, 1 May

2002). But see the more cogenial article in the same publication 1 September 2005.

9. On 1 August 2004, see *Sunday Telegraph, Sunday Times, Sunday Herald, Express on Sunday, Daily Mail*, the *Observer, and EIU-Business Europe*. See also *Mirror*, 4 August 2004; *Independent on Sunday*, 5 August 2004; the *Herald*, 7 August 2004; *Daily Mail*, 8 August 2004; *Scotland on Sunday* and the *Observer*, 15 August 2004; the *Times*, 24 August 2004; the *Independent*, the *Herald* and *Guardian*, 26 August 2004; and the *Daily Telegraph*, 8 September 2004.

10. See *Independent on Sunday*, 25 July 2004; *Express on Sunday*, 1 August 2004; the *Guardian*, 16 August 2004; *Daily Telegraph*, 12 August 2004; *Financial Times*, 14 August 2004; *Sunday Telegraph*, 15 and 22 August 2004, 3 October 2004; *Sunday Times*, 19 September 2004. The *Times* (27 July 2004) was perhaps the most caustic: "They are at Santander Central Hispano perhaps not up with the most recent developments in post-Higgsian corporate governance as carried out in London. Emilio Botín, the bank's chairman, was asked about the weekend departure of his brother Jaime from the board. 'It's OK because my son (Javier) has replaced him.'"

11. *Euromoney*, September 2004. See also *Corporate Counsel*, 1 September 2005.

12. Deminor Rating, *Corporate Governance Rating and Investor Report: Banco Santander Central Hispano SA* (7 April 2006), p. 2.

13. See the official journals of the Spanish Communist labor union CCOO: *Gaceta Sindical* (digital edition) 129 (19 April 2001): 3, www.ccoo.es, and of the Socialist labor union UGT, *Unión* 174 (1998): 19.

14. Among Ana Patricia's siblings, only Emilio Botín IV and Javier Botín have a banking background. Emilio worked for Bankers Trust and then for Santander until 1998; he had become a director of Santander in 1990. He later set up a hedge fund.

15. See *El País*, 14 February 2002; *Wall Street Journal*, 8 November 2004; *Knight Ridder Tribune Business News*, 17 February 2002; *Financial Times*, 22 February 2002; *BBC*, 6 October 2004.

16. *Financial Times*, 25 March 2002; see also the *Economist*, 6 April 2002. The frustration that these challenges surely generate is captured by the following quote attributed to her by the *Wall Street Journal* (10 May 2004) in an interaction she had with a German journalist who asked about her father's commitment to make Banesto the most profitable bank in Spain: "Did I ask you whether your father is a good journalist?"

Chapter 9: The Future of a Global Group

1. "La banca es un negocio difícil, hecho de prudencia y paciencia, en el que no se puede nunca bajar la guardia."

2. We examined whether any other announcements took place in a five-day interval around the event date as shown in table 8.2. We searched

newspapers and news sources for events such as acquisitions, alliances, dividend payouts, financial performance announcements, important contracts signed with the government, or the launching of new products of services, all of which could also affect stock prices. We only found a potentially confounding event in the case of the announcement of the Sovereign partial acquisition, which was followed two days later by an announcement of quarterly financial results. Thus, in this case the one-day window seems more appropriate than the other two windows.

3. *Expansión*, 24 February 1999.

4. For examples of coverage during this early period, see *Economist*, 30 April 1994, 14 December 1996; *Financial Times*, 30 June 1995, 20 October 1998; *Wall Street Journal*, 23 May 1996; *Wall Street Journal Europe*, 24 May 1996.

5. See *Economist*, 5 January 2002; *Financial Times*, 1 February, 3 September, 8 October, 31 October, and 18 November 2002; *Wall Street Journal*, 23 July, 14 August, and 29 September 2002.

BIBLIOGRAPHY

Archives and Libraries
Banco de España, Library, Madrid.
Biblioteca Nacional, Madrid.
Comisión Económica para América Latina (CEPAL), Buenos Aires.
Comisión Nacional del Mercado de Valores, Library, Madrid.
Fundación Fondo para la Investigación Económica y Social, Library, Madrid.
Instituto Nacional de Industria, Library and Archives, Madrid.
Ministerio de Economía y Hacienda, Biblioteca, Madrid.
New York Public Library, New York City.

Interviews

Argentina
Juan Miguel Arranz, Vice President, Santander Investment, Buenos Aires, 7 May 1998
Rodolfo A. Corvi, Assistant General Manager, BBV Banco Francés, Buenos Aires, 7 May 1998
Carlos M. Fedrigotti, President, Citibank Argentina, Buenos Aires, 8 May 1998
Fernando Fragueiro, Dean, Instituto de Altos Estudios Empresariales, Buenos Aires, 4 October 1998
Ricardo Augusto Gallo, Vice President, Banco de Boston, Buenos Aires, 22 March 1995
Julio J. Gómez, President, Asociación de Bancos de la República Argentina, Buenos Aires, 8 May 1998
Alejandro Henke, Deputy Director, Superintendency of Financial Institutions, Banco Central de la República Argentina, 7 May 1998
Enrique Ruete, CEO, Banco Roberts, Buenos Aires, 22 March 1995
Gloria Sorensen, Staff Economist, BBV Banco Francés, Buenos Aires, 7 May 1998

Brazil

Angelim Curiel, Director for Latin America, Citigroup, São Paulo, 9 February, 2006

Jean Philippe Leroy, Managing Director, Bradesco, São Paulo, 10 February, 2006

Gabriel Jaramillo, President, Santander Banespa, São Paulo, 9 February 2006

José Paiva Ferreira, Executive Vice President, Santander Banespa, São Paulo, 10 February 2006

Walter Piacsek, Manager, Banco Safra, São Paulo, 10 February 2006

Caio C. O. Ribeiro, Manager, Santander Banespa, São Paulo, 10 February 2006

Sérgio Ribeiro da Costa Werlang, Executive Director, Banco Itaú, São Paulo, 9 February 2006

Luiz Simione, Manager, Santander Banespa, São Paulo, 10 February 2006

Veronica Valente Dantas, Partner, Opportunity, Rio de Janeiro, 6 February 2006

Chile

Claudio Chamorro, Research Director, Superintendencia de Bancos e Instituciones Financieras, Santiago, 6 May 1998

Guillermo LeFort, Banco Central de Chile, Santiago, 4 May 1998

Francisco León, Citibank, Santiago, 5 May 1998

Ernesto Livacic, Superintendencia de Bancos e Instituciones Financieras, Santiago, 4 May 1998

Raimundo Monje, Chief Financial Officer, Banco Santander, Santiago, 5 May 1998

Arturo Tagle, Adjunct to the President, Banco de Chile, Santiago, 6 May 1998

Mexico

Alejandro Díaz de León Carrillo, Deputy Director, Financial Sector Analysis, Bank of Mexico, Mexico, DF, 13 May 1998

Carlos García Fernández, Director General of Foreign Investment, Secretaría de Comercio y Finanzas, México, DF, 13 May 1988

Javier Gavito Mohar, Vice President, Comisión Nacional Bancaria y de Valores, Mexico, DF, 13 May 1998

Gabriel Kuri, Grupo Santander Mexicano, Mexico, DF, 14 May 1998

Miguel Navas Moreno, Director, BBV, Mexico, DF, 14 May 1998

Gerardo Vargas Ateca, Operations Director, Fondo Bancario de Protección al Ahorro, México, DF, 15 May 1998

Spain

Luis Abril, former Director of Communications, Santander Central Hispano, Madrid, 9 March 2006

Víctor Barallat, Director of Strategy and Investor Relations, Banco Santander, Madrid, 25 June 1998

Ana Patricia Botín, President, Banesto, Madrid, 30 November 2004

Ángel Corcóstegui, CEO and Vice President, Banco Central Hispano, Madrid, 17 June 1998

Fernando Delage, Director of the Training Center, Casa Asia, Madrid, 28 April 2006

Fernando González Urbaneja, President, Asociaciación de la Prensa, Madrid, 3 February 2006

Keith Grant, former Communications Manager at Abbey National Bank and at Banco Santander, Madrid, 6 March 2006

Francisco Martín, General Director, Banco Santander, Cambridge, Mass., 27 April 1994

Miguel Angel Noceda, Director of the Economy Section, *El País*, Madrid, 8 March 2006

Carmen Posadas, writer, Madrid, 7 March 2006

Jaime Requeijo, Vice President, Banco Zaragozano, 14 June 1995

Juan Rodríguez Inciarte, General Director, Banco Santander, Cambridge, Mass., 27 April 1994

Alfredo Sáenz, CEO, Banco Santander, Madrid, 4 October 2006

United Kingdom

Paul Beckett, *Wall Street Journal*, London, 26 April 2006

Fiona Maharg Bravo, journalist, breakingviews.com, London, 26 April 2006

Francisco Gómez Roldán, President, Santander Abbey, London, 25 April 2006

Kato Mukuru, Stock Research Analyst, Citigroup, London, 25 April 2006

Michael Verdin, journalist, breakingviews.com, London, 26 April 2006

Secondary Sources

Almirón, Núria. 2003. *Juicio al poder: El pulso de la justicia con el BSCH*. Madrid: Temas de Hoy.

Alvarez Junco, José. 2001. *Mater dolorosa: La idea de España en el siglo XIX*. Madrid: Taurus.

Alvarez Llano, Roberto, and José Miguel Andreu García. 1986. *Una historia de la banca privada en España*. 2 vols. Madrid: Orbis.

Amsden, A. H. 1989. *Asia's Next Giant: South Korea and Late Industrialization*. New York: Oxford University Press.

Anderson, R. C., and D. M. Reeb. 2003. "Founding Family Ownership and Firm Performance: Evidence from the S&P 500." *Journal of Finance* 59: 1301–29.

———. 2004. "Board Composition: Balancing Family Influence in S&P 500 Firms." *Administrative Science Quarterly* 49 (2): 209–37.

Bartelsman, E. J., and M. Doms. 2000. "Understanding Productivity: Lessons from Longitudinal Microdata." *Journal of Economic Literature* 38 (3) (September): 569–94.

Benedict, B. 1968. "Family Firms and Economic Development." *Southwestern Journal of Anthropology* 24 (1) (Spring): 1–19.

Bendix, Reinhard. [1956] 2001. *Work and Authority in Industry*. New Brunswick, N.J.: Transaction.

Ben-Porath, Y. 1980. "The F-Connection: Families, Friends, and Firms and the Organization of Exchange." *Population and Development Review* 6 (1) (March): 1–30.

Berger, Allen N., R. DeYoung, H. Genay, and G. Udell. 2000. "Globalization of Financial Institutions: Evidence from Cross-Border Banking Performance." *Brookings-Wharton Papers on Financial Services*, vol. 3, 23–125.

Berges, Angel. 2003. "Bancos y cajas: Estrategias divergentes." In *1987–2003: Integración económica y financiera de España*, edited by AFI, pp. 321–43. Madrid: Analistas Financieros Internacionales (AFI).

Berglof, E. 1988. "Capital Structure as a Mechanism of Control: A Comparison of Financial Systems." In *The Firm as a Nexus of Treaties*, edited by M. Aoki, B. Gustafsson, and O. Williamson, pp. 237–62. Newbury Park, Calif.: Sage.

Blázquez-Lidoy, Jorgue, Javier Rodríguez, and Javier Santiso. 2005. "Angel or Devil? Chinese Trade Impact on Latin American Emerging Markets." Working paper. Madrid: BBVA Research Department.

Bocigas Solar, Olga. 2001. *El Banco de Santander: Motor del marketing entre los grandes bancos españoles*. Madrid: Universidad Pontificia de Comillas.

Bodnar, Gordon M., Charles Tang, and Joseph Weintrop. 2003. "The Value of Corporate International Diversification." Working paper. SAIS, Johns Hopkins University.

Boldt-Christmas, M., S. F. Jacobsen, and A. E. Tschoegl. 2001. "The International Expansion of Norwegian Banks." *Business History* 43 (3): 79–104.

Botín, Emilio. 2004. "The Most Profitable Course for Europe's Banks." *Financial Times*, 22 January, p. 17.

Buch, C., and G. Delong. 2003. Determinants of Cross-Border Bank Mergers. In *Foreign Direct Investment in the Real and Financial Sector of Industrial Countries*, edited by H. Herrmann and R. Lipsey, pp. 323–48. Frankfurt: Springer Verlag.

Burkart, M., F. Panunzi, and A. Shleifer. 2003. "Family Firms." *Journal of Finance* 58 (5): 2167–2201.

Cameron, Rondo, ed. 1972. *Banking and Economic Development: Some Lessons of History* New York: Oxford University Press.

Cameron, Rondo, Olga Crisp, Hugh T. Patrick, and Richard Tilly, eds. 1967. *Banking in the Early Stages of Industrialization*. New York: Oxford University Press.

Capgemini. 2006. *World Retail Banking Report, 2006*. Paris: Capgemini.

Cardim de Carvalho, F. J. 2000. "New Competitive Strategies of Foreign Banks in Large Emerging Economies: The Case of Brazil." *BNL Quarterly Review* 213: 135–69.

———. 2002. "The Recent Expansion of Foreign Banks in Brazil: The First Results." *Latin American Business Review* 3 (4): 93–119.

Cardone-Riportella, C., and L. Cazoria-Papas. 2001. "The Internationalisation Process of Spanish Banks: A Tale of Two Times." *International Journal of Bank Marketing* 19 (2): 52–67.

Cardoso, Fernando Henrique, and Enzo Faletto. [1973] 1979. *Dependency and Development in Latin America*. Berkeley: University of California Press.

Casanova, Lourdes. 2002. "Lazos de familia: La inversión española en América Latina." *Foreign Affairs en Español* (Web edition, Summer issue). www.foreignaffairs-esp.org.

Casilda Béjar, Ramón. 1997. *La banca española: Análisis y evolución*. Madrid: Pirámide.

Chandler, Alfred D. 1990. *Scale and Scope*. Cambridge, Mass.: Harvard University Press.

Choi, S.-R., D. Park, and A. E. Tschoegl. 1996. "Banks and the World's Major Banking Centers, 1990." *Weltwirtschaftliches Archiv* 123 (4): 774–93.

———. 2003. "Banks and the World's Major Banking Centers, 2000." *Weltwirtschaftliches Archiv* 139 (3): 550–68.

Choi, S.-R., A. E. Tschoegl, and C.-W. Yu. 1986. "Banks and the World's Major Financial Centers, 1970–1980." *Weltwirtschaftliches Archiv* 122 (1): 48–64.

Church, Roy. 1993. "The Family Firm in Industrial Capitalism: International Perspectives on Hypotheses and History." *Business History* 35 (4) (October): 17–43.

Claessens, S., A. Demirgüç-Kunt, and H. Huizinga. 2001. "How Does Foreign Entry Affect Domestic Banking Markets?" *Journal of Banking and Finance* 25: 891–911.

Claessens, S., and M. Jansen, eds. 2000. *The Internationalization of Financial Services: Issues and Lessons for Developing Countries*. Boston: Kluwer Academic Press.

Colli, Andrea, and Mary B. Rose. 2003. "Family Firms in Comparative Perspective." In *Business History around the World*, edited by Franco Amatori and Geoffrey Jones, pp. 339–52. Cambridge: Cambridge University Press.

Cuervo, Alvaro. 1988. *La crisis bancaria en España, 1977–1985* Barcelona: Ariel.

Davis, James H., F. David Schoorman, and L. Donaldson. 1997. "Toward a Stewardship Theory of Management." *Academy of Management Review* 22 (1): 20–47.

de Gregorio, J., and P. Guidotti. 1995. "Financial Development and Economic Growth." *World Development* 23 (3): 433–48.

de Paula, L. F. R. 2002. "Expansion Strategies of European Banks to Brazil and Their Impacts on the Brazilian Banking Sector." *Latin American Business Review* 3 (4): 59–91.

Deeg, Richard E. 1999. *Finance Capitalism Unveiled: Banks and the German Political Economy*. Ann Arbor: University of Michigan Press.

Demirgüç-Kunt, A., and H. Huizinga. 1999. "Determinants of commercial bank interest margins and profitability: Some international evidence." *World Bank Economic Review* 13 (2): 379–408.

Denis, D. J., D. K. Denis, and K. Yost. 2002. "Global Diversification, Industrial Diversification, and Firm Value." *Journal of Finance* 57 (5): 1951–79.

Dietsch, M., and A. Lozano Vivas. 1996. "How the Environment Determines the Efficiency of Banks: A Comparison between French and Spanish Banking." Wharton Financial Institutions Center Working Paper No. 97-29.

Dopico, L. G., and J. A. Wilcox. 2002. "Openness, Profit Opportunities and Foreign Banking." *Journal of Financial Markets, Institutions, and Money* 12 (4–5): 299–320.

Doukas, J. A., and O. B. Kan. 2006. "Does Global Diversification Destroy Firm Value?" *Journal of International Business Studies* 37: 352–71.

Doz, Y. L. 1996. "The Evolution of Cooperation in Strategic Alliances: Initial Conditions or Learning Processes?" *Strategic Management Journal* 17: 55–83.

Dufey, G., and B. Yeung. 1993. "The impact of EC 92 on European banking." *Journal of Financial Management* 2 (3–4): 11–31.

Echenique Gordillo, Rodrigo, and Joan-David Grimà Térre. 2001. "Rentabilizar las inversiones industriales: Estrategia del Santander Central Hispano." *Economía Industrial* 341: 79–82.

Eisenmann, Thomas, R., G. Parker, and M. van Alstyne. 2006. "Strategies for Two-Sided Markets." *Harvard Business Review* 84 (10): 92–101.

Engwall, L, and M. Wallenstäl. 1988. "Tit for Tat in Small Steps: The Internationalization of Swedish Banks." *Scandinavian Journal of Management* 4: 1147–55.

Evans, Peter. 1979. *Dependent Development*. Princeton, N.J.: Princeton University Press.

Fernández, Pablo, and José María Carabias. 2006. "Creación de valor para los accionistas del Banco Santander." Working paper. Madrid: IESE.

Fields, Karl J. 1995. *Enterprise and the State in Korea and Taiwan*. Ithaca, N.Y.: Cornell University Press.

Flowers, E. B. 1976. "Oligopolistic Reactions in European and Canadian Direct Investment in the United States." *Journal of International Business Studies* 7: 43–55.

Frank, André G. 1967. *Capitalism and Underdevelopment in Latin America*. New York: Monthly Review Press.

Fry, Maxwell J. 1995. *Money, Interest, and Banking in Economic Development*. Baltimore: Johns Hopkins University Press.

Galve Górriz, Carmen, and Vicente Salas Fumás. 2003. *La empresa familar en España: Fundamentos económicos y resultados* Madrid: Fundación BBVA.

García de la Granja, Pilar. 2005. "Luis Abril: El Comunicador." In *!Me equivoqué! Los grandes empresarios españoles nos cuentan sus mayores fracasos*, pp. 181–202. Barcelona: Planeta.

García-Herrero, Alica, and Francisco Vázquez. 2006. "International Diversification Gains and Home Bias in Banking." Working paper. Bank of Spain and International Monetary Fund.

García López, and José Ramón. 1994. "El sistema bancario español del siglo XIX." In *Lecturas de Historia Empresarial*, edited by Juan Hernández Andreu and José Luis García Ruiz, pp. 377–400. Madrid: Civitas.

García Ruiz, José Luis, and Gabriel Tortella. 1994. "Trayectorias divergentes, paralelas y convergentes: La historia del Banco Hispano Americano y del Banco Central, 1901–1965." In *Lecturas de Historia Empresarial*, edited by Juan Hernández Andreu and José Luis García Ruiz, pp. 401–27. Madrid: Civitas.

Gerschenkron, Alexander. 1962. *Economic Backwardness in Historical Perspective*. Cambridge, Mass.: Harvard University Press.

Goldstein, M., and P. Turner. 1996. "Banking Crises in Emerging Economies: Origins and Policy Options." BIS Economic Papers No. 46.

Gómez Escorial, Angel. 2004. *Los secretos de las fusiones*. Madrid: Cuadernos de Historia.

Gomez-Mejia, Luis R., Martin Larraza-Kintana, and Marianna Makri. 2003. "The Determinants of Executive Compensation in Family-Controlled Public Corporations." *Academy of Management Journal* 46 (2): 226–37.

González Urbaneja, Fernando. 1993. *Banca y poder*. Madrid: Espasa Hoy.

Grosse, R., and L. G. Goldberg. 1996. "The Boom and Bust of Latin American Lending, 1970–1992." *Journal of Economics and Business* 48, 285–98.

Grubel, G. H. 1977. "A Theory of Multinational Banking." *Banca Nazionale del Lavoro Quarterly Review* 123: 349–63.

Guillén, Mauro F. 2000. "Corporate Governance and Globalization: Is There Convergence across Countries?" *Advances in Comparative International Management* 13: 175–204.

———. 2001. *The Limits of Convergence: Globalization and Organizational Change in Argentina, South Korea, and Spain*. Princeton, N.J.: Princeton University Press.

———. 2005. *The Rise of Spanish Multinationals: European Business in the Global Economy*. Cambridge: Cambridge University Press.

Guillén, M., and A. E. Tschoegl. 2000. "The Internationalization of Retail Banking: The Case of the Spanish Banks in Latin America." *Transnational Corporations* 9 (3): 63–97.

———. 2002. "Banking on Gambling: Banks and Lottery-Linked Deposit Accounts." *Journal of Financial Services Research* 21 (3): 219–231.

Haggard, S., and C. H. Lee. 1993. "The Political Dimension of Finance in Economic Development." In *The Politics of Finance in Developing Countries*, edited by Stephan Haggard et al., pp. 3–20. Ithaca, N.Y.: Cornell University Press.

Haggard, S., and S. Maxfield. 1993. "Political Explanations of Financial Policy in Developing Countries." In *The Politics of Finance in Developing Countries*, edited by Stephan Haggard et al., pp. 293–325 Ithaca, N.Y.: Cornell University Press.

Heinkel, R. L., and M. D. Levi. 1992. "The Structure of International Banking." *Journal of International Money and Finance* 16: 251–72.

Hennart, J.-F. 1988. "A Transactions Costs Theory of Equity Joint Ventures." *Strategic Management Review* 9: 361–74.

Hernández Andreu, Juan. 2000. "Don Emilio Botín-Sanz de Sautuola y López: El banquero y la economía española." Unpublished manuscript.

Horwood, Clive. 2005. "The Masters of Retail Banking." *Euromoney*, July, pp. 52–55.

Hoyo Aparicio, Andrés. 1993. *Todo mudó de repente: El horizonte económico de la burguesía mercantil en Santander, 1820–1874* Santander: Universidad de Cantabria.

———. 2000. "Emilio Botín-Sanz de Sautuola y López (1903–1993)." In *Los 100 empresarios españoles del siglo XX*, edited by Eugenio Torres, pp. 398–402. Madrid: LID Editorial Empresarial.

Hymer, Stephen H. [1960] 1976. The International Operation of National Firms: A Study of Direct Investment Cambridge, Mass.: MIT Press.

Jacobsen, S. F., and A. E. Tschoegl. 1999. "The Norwegian Banks in the Nordic Consortia: A Case of International Strategic Alliances in Banking." *Industrial and Corporate Change* 8 (1): 137–65.

Jado Canales, Angel. 1957. "Fundación del Banco de Santander en el año 1857." In *Aportación al estudio de la historia económica de la Montaña*, pp. 613–47. Santander: Banco de Santander.

Johanson, J., and J. E. Vahlne. 1977. "The Internationalization Process of the Firm: A Model of Knowledge Development and Increasing Foreign Market Commitments." *Journal of International Business Studies* 9: 23–43.

Jones, Geoffrey. 1993. British Multinational Banking, 1830–1990. Oxford: Clarendon Press.

Jones, Geoffrey, and Mary B. Rose. 1993. "Family Capitalism." *Business History* 35 (4): 1–16.

Kerr, Clark, John T. Dunlop, Frederick Harbison, and Charles A. Myers. [1960] 1964. *Industrialism and Industrial Man* New York: Oxford University Press.

Kindleberger, Charles P. 1969. American Business Abroad. New Haven, Conn.: Yale University Press.

King, R., and R. Levine. 1993. "Finance and Growth: Schumpeter Might Be Right." *Quarterly Journal of Economics* 108 (3): 717–37.

Knickerbocker, Frederick. 1973. *Oligopolistic Reaction and Multinational Enterprise.* Boston: Division of Research, Harvard Business School.

Koford, K., and A. E. Tschoegl. 2005. "Foreign Banks in Bulgaria, 1875–2002." In *Capital Formation, Governance and Banking*, edited by E. Klein, pp. 179–206. Hauppauge, N.Y.: Nova Science.

Kogut, B. 1988. "Joint Ventures: Theoretical and Empirical Perspectives." *Strategic Management Journal* 9: 319–22.

La Porta, Rafael, Florencio Lopez-De-Silanes, and Andrei Shleifer. 2002. "Government Ownership of Banks." *Journal of Finance* 57 (1): 265–302.

Landes, D. S. 1951. "French Business and Businessmen in Social and Cultural Analysis." In *Modern France*, edited by E. Mead Earl, pp. 334–53. Princeton, N.J.: Princeton University Press.

———. 1993. "Bleichröders and Rothschilds: The Problem of Continuity in the Family Firm." *Family Business Review* 6 (1): 85–101.

———. 2006. *Dynasties: Fortunes and Misfortunes of the World's Greatest Family Businesses*. New York: Penguin Group.

Lazonick, William. 1991. *Business Organization and the Myth of the Market Economy*. Cambridge, Mass.: Harvard University Press.

Lewis, W. A. 1978. *The Evolution of the International Order*. Princeton, N.J.: Princeton University Press.

Lindgren, H. 2007. "Succession Strategies in a Large Family Business Group: The Case of the Swedish Wallenberg Family." Working paper. Stockholm: Stockholm School of Economics.

Linz, J. J. 1973. "Early State Building and Late Peripheral Nationalisms against the State: The Case of Spain." In *Building States and Nations*, vol. 2: *Analyses by Region*, edited by S. N. Eisenstadt and Stein Rokkan, pp. 32–116. Beverly Hills, Calif.: Sage.

Lopez-de-Silanes, F., and G. Zamarripa. 1995. "Deregulation and Privatization of Commercial Banking." *Revista de Análisis Económico* 10 (2): 113–64.

Loriaux, M. 1991. *France after Hegemony: International Change and Financial Reform*. Ithaca, N.Y.: Cornell University Press.

———. 1997a. "The End of Credit Activism in Interventionist States." In *Capital Ungoverned: Liberalizing Finance in Interventionist States*, edited by Michael Loriaux, pp. 1–16. Ithaca, N.Y.: Cornell University Press.

———, ed. 1997b. *Capital Ungoverned: Liberalizing Finance in Interventionist States*. Ithaca, N.Y.: Cornell University Press.

Maddison, A. 2001. *The World Economy: A Millennial Perspective*. Paris: OECD.

Mann, T. [1901] 1994. *Buddenbrooks: The Decline of a Family*. New York: Vintage International.

Marois, B., and T. Abdessemed. 1996. "Cross-Border Alliances in the French Banking Sector." *International Studies of Management and Organization* 26 (2): 38–58.

Márquez Dorsch, M., and J. Barbat Hernández. 2005. *Retratos de liderazgo*. Madrid: McGraw-Hill.

Martín Aceña, Pablo. 2007. *Banco Santander: 150 años de historia, 1857–2007*. Madrid: Banco Santander.

Martín Aceña, Pablo, and Francisco Comín. 1991. *INI: 50 años de industrialización en España*. Madrid: Espasa-Calpe.

Maudos, Joaquín, José Manuel Pastor, and Javier Quesada. 1997. "Technical Progress in Spanish Banking, 1985–1994." In *The Recent Evolution of Financial Systems*, edited by Jack Revell, pp. 214–45. London: Macmillan.

Mody, A. 1993. "Learning through Alliances." *Journal of Economic Behavior and Organization* 20: 151–70.

Montoya Melgar, Alfredo. 1975. *Ideología y lenguaje en las primeras leyes laborales de España*. Madrid: Civitas.

Mosley, L. 2006. "New Currency, New Constraints? The Euro and Government-Financial Market Relations." In *The Year of the Euro: The Cultural, Social, and Political Import of Europe's Common Currency*, edited by R. M. Fishman and A. M. Messina, pp. 186–211. Notre Dame, Ind.: Notre Dame University Press.

Muñoz, Juan. 1967. *El poder de la banca en España*. Madrid: ZYX.

Muñoz, Juan, Santiago Roldán, and Angel Serrano. 1978. *La internacionalización del capital en España, 1959–1977*. Madrid: Edicusa.

Nadal, J. 1975. *El fracaso de la revolución industrial en España, 1814–1913*. Barcelona: Ariel.

Nakamura, M., J. M. Shaver, and B. Yeung. 1996. "An Empirical Investigation of Joint Venture Dynamics: Evidence from U.S.-Japan Joint Ventures." *International Journal of Industrial Organization* 14: 521–41.

Novoa, Josep Manuel. 2003. *El botín de Botín*. Madrid: Foca.

O'Sullivan, M. 2000. *Contests for Corporate Control: Corporate Governance and Economic Performance in the United States and Germany*. New York: Oxford University Press.

OECD. 1995. "Financial Markets and Corporate Governance." *Financial Market Trends* 62: 13–35.

———. 1998. *Corporate Governance: Improving Competitiveness and Access to Capital in Global Markets*. Paris: Organization of Economic Cooperation and Development.

Pablo Torrente, Joaquín de. 2003. *45 Años de Economía en Libertad: 1958–2003*. Madrid: Actualidad Económica.

Papp, I. 2005. "Do Banking Crises Attract Foreign Banks?" *Journal of Emerging Markets* 10 (1): 42–50.

Pastor, J. M., S. A. Pérez, and J. Quesada. 2000. "The Opening of the Spanish Banking System: 1985–98." In *The Internationalization of Financial Services: Issues and Lessons for Developing Countries*, edited by S. Claessens and M. Jansen Boston: Kluwer Academic Press.

Pérez, Sofía. 1997. *Banking on Privilege: The Politics of Spanish Financial Reform*. Ithaca, N.Y.: Cornell University Press.

Pérez Escolar, Rafael. 2005. *Memorias*. Madrid: Foca.

Perotti, E. 1992. "Cross-Ownership as a Hostage Exchange to Support Collaboration." *Managerial and Decision Economics* 13: 45–54.

Porter, Michael E. 1980. *Competitive Strategy*. New York: Free Press.

Rivases, Jesús. 1988. *Los banqueros del PSOE*. Barcelona: Ediciones B.

Rodríguez, J. M. 1989. "The Crisis in Spanish Private Banks: An Empirical Analysis." *Rivista Internatinale di Scienze Economiche e Commerciali* 36 (10–11): 1033–55.

Rodríguez, Jesús, and Jorge Rivera. 1999. "La banquera de hierro." *El País Semanal* 1169 (21 February): 20–33.

Roe, M. J. 1993. "Some Differences in Corporate Structure in Germany, Japan, and the United States." *Yale Law Journal* 102: 1927–2003.

Roldán, Santiago, José Luis García Delgado, and Juan Muñoz. 1973. *La consolidación del capitalismo en España*. 2 vols. Madrid: Confederación Española de Cajas de Ahorro.

Ross, D. M. 1998. "European Banking Clubs in the 1960s." *Business and Economic History* 27: 353–66.

———. 2002. "Clubs and Consortia: European Banking Groups as Strategic Alliances." In *European Banks and the American Challenge*, edited by S. Battilossi and Y. Cassis, pp. 135–60. Oxford: Oxford University Press.

Rostow, W. W. 1960. *The Stages of Economic Growth: A Non-Communist Manifesto*. Cambridge: Cambridge University Press.

Sachs, J. 1993. *Poland's Jump to the Market Economy*. Cambridge, Mass.: MIT Press.

Sagardoy Bengoechea, Juan Antonio. 2006. *La evolución de las relaciones laborales en la empresa española, 1980–2005*. Madrid: Ediciones Cinca.

Schulz, H. 2005. "Foreign Banks in Mexico: New Conquistadors or Agents of Change?" University of Pennsylvania, unpublished manuscript.

Shleifer, A., and R. Vishny. 1986. "Large Shareholders and Corporate Control." *Journal of Political Economy* 94: 461–88.

Sjögren, H. 2006. "Family Capitalism within Big Business." *Scandinavian Economic History Review* 54 (2): 161–86.

Smith, R. C., and I. Walter. 2003. *Global Banking*. Oxford: Oxford University Press.

Snodgrass, D. R., and T. Biggs. 1996. *Industrialization and the Small Firm*. San Francisco, Calif.: International Center for Economic Growth.

Tamames, Ramón. 1977. *La oligarquía financiera en España*. Barcelona: Planeta.

———. 1986. *The Spanish Economy: An Introduction*. London: C. Hurst.

Tedde de Lorca, Pedro. 1974. "La banca privada española durante la Restauración, 1874–1914." In *La banca española en la Restauración*, vol. 1, edited by Gabriel Tortella, pp. 217–455. Madrid: Banco de España.

———. 1994. "La banca privada en España, 1830–1930." In *Introducción a la historia de la empresa*, edited by Gregorio Núñez and Luciano Segreto, pp. 176–89. Madrid: Abacus.

Tortella, G. 1994. *El desarrollo de la España contemporánea: Historia económica de los siglos XIX y XX*. Madrid: Alianza.

———. 1995. "The Hispanic American Connection in the Banco Hispano Americano of Madrid." In *Wirstchaft, Gesellschaft, Unternehmen: Festschrift fur Hans Pohl zum 60 Geburstag*, edited by W. Feldenkirchen, R. Schönert-Röhlk, and Günther Schulz, pp. 1179–85. *Vierteljahrschrift fur Sozial- und Wirtschaftsgeschichte*, Beiheft Nr. 120b. Stuttgart: Franz Steiner Verlag.

———. 2001. "Bank Mergers and Consolidation in Spanish History." In *A Century of Banking Consolidation in Europe*, edited by Manfred Pohl, Teresa Tortella, and Herman van der Wee, pp. 18–49. Aldershot: Ashgate-European Association of Banking History.

Tortella, G., and José Luis García Ruiz. 2003. "Banca y política durante el primer Franquismo." In *Los empresarios de Franco*, edited by Glicerio Sánchez Recio and Julio Tascón Fernández, pp. 67–99. Barcelona: Crítica.

Tortella, G., and Jordi Palafox. 1984. "Banking and Industry in Spain, 1918–1936." *Journal of European Economic History* 13 (2) (Fall): 81–111.

Tourani Rad, A., and L. Van Beek. 1999. "Market Valuation of European Bank Mergers." *European Management Journal* 15 (5): 532–40.

Tschoegl, A. E. 1987. "International Retail Banking as a Strategy: An Assessment." *Journal of International Business Studies* 19 (2): 67–88.

———. 2000. "Foreign Banks, International Banking Centers and Geography." *Financial Markets, Instruments and Institutions* 9 (1): 1–32.

———. 2002a. "FDI and Internationalization: Evidence from US Subsidiaries of Foreign Banks." *Journal of International Business Studies* 33 (4): 805–15.

———. 2002b. "The Internationalization of Singapore's Largest Banks." *Journal of Asian Business* 18 (1): 1–35.

———. 2003. Comment on "Determinants of Cross-Border Bank Mergers." In *Foreign Direct Investment in the Real and Financial Sector of Industrial Countries,* edited by H. Herrmann and R. Lipsey, pp. 349–63. Frankfurt: Deutsche Bundesbank.

———. 2004a. "'The World's Local Bank': HSBC's Expansion in the US, Canada and Mexico." *Latin American Business Review* 5 (4): 45–68.

———. 2004b. "Who Owns the Major US Subsidiaries of Foreign Banks? A Note." *Journal of International Financial Markets, Institutions and Money* 14 (3): 255–66.

———. 2005. "Financial Crises and the Presence of Foreign Banks." In *Systemic Financial Distress: Containment and Resolution,* edited by P. Honohan and L. Laeven, pp. 197–231. Cambridge: Cambridge University Press.

Tuñón de Lara, Manuel. 1984. "Progeso técnico y conciencia social, 1898–1936." In *España, 1898–1936: Estructuras y cambio,* edited by José Luis García Delgado, pp. 17–70. Madrid: Universidad Complutense.

Unal, H., and M. Navarro. 1999. "The Technical Process of Bank Privatization in Mexico." *Journal of Financial Services Research* 16 (1): 61–83.

UNCTAD (United Nations Conference on Trade and Development). 2003. *World Investment Report 2003: FDI Policies for Development* New York: United Nations.

———. 2004. *World Investment Report, 2004: The Shift towards Services.* New York: United Nations.

Villalonga, B., and R. Amit. 2006. "How Do Family Ownership, Management, and Control Affect Firm Value?" *Journal of Financial Economics* 80 (2): 385–417.

Walter, Ingo. 1988. *Global Competition in Financial Services.* Cambridge, Mass.: Harper and Row.

———. 1997. "Universal Banking: A Shareholder Value Perspective." *European Management Journal* 15 (4): 344–60.

———. 2004. *Mergers and Acquisitions in Banking and Finance.* Oxford: Oxford University Press.

Weber, Max. 1978. *Economy and Society.* Berkeley: University of California Press.

Weill, L. 2003. "Banking Efficiency in Transition Economies: The Role of Foreign Ownership." *Economics of Transition* 11 (3): 569–92.

Wolfe, T. 1979. *The Right Stuff*. New York: Farrar, Straus and Giroux.

Woo, Jung-En. 1991. *Race to the Swift: State and Finance in Korean Industrialization*. New York: Columbia University Press.

Yip, G. S. 1989. "Global Strategy … in a World of Nations?" *Sloan Management Review* 31 (1): 29–41.

Zysman, J. 1983. *Governments, Markets, and Growth: Financial Systems and the politics of Industrial Change*. Ithaca, N.Y.: Cornell University Press.